WRITING MATERNITY

WRITING MATERNITY

MEDICINE, ANXIETY, RHETORIC, AND GENRE

Dara Rossman Regaignon

THE OHIO STATE UNIVERSITY PRESS
COLUMBUS

Library of Congress Cataloging-in-Publication Data
Names: Regaignon, Dara Rossman, author.
Title: Writing maternity : medicine, anxiety, rhetoric, and genre / Dara Rossman Regaignon.
Description: Columbus : The Ohio State University Press, [2021] | Includes bibliographical
    references and index. | Summary: "Traces the rhetorical origins of maternal anxiety
    in Victorian literature—bringing concepts such as uptake and genre ecology into
    literary studies from rhetorical genre theory—by examining advice literature, British
    life writing, and novels by Charles Dickens, Charlotte Mary Yonge, Elizabeth Gaskell,
    Charlotte Brontë, and Anne Brontë"—Provided by publisher.
Identifiers: LCCN 2020047603 | ISBN 9780814214695 (cloth) | ISBN 081421469X (cloth) |
    ISBN 9780814281161 (ebook) | ISBN 0814281168 (ebook)
Subjects: LCSH: Motherhood in literature. | Anxiety in women. | Child rearing in literature.
    | English literature—19th century—History and criticism. | Children—Great Britain—
    Social conditions.
Classification: LCC HQ759 .R4564 2021 | DDC 306.874/30973—dc23
LC record available at https://lccn.loc.gov/2020047603

Cover design by Susan Zucker
Text design by Juliet Williams
Type set in Adobe Minion Pro

For Greg, Mari, and Anya:
always, and every day

CONTENTS

ILLUSTRATIONS

Historicizing Maternal Anxiety

How To Be A Mom in 2017: Make sure your children's academic, emotional, psychological, mental, spiritual, physical, nutritional, and social needs are met while being careful not to over stimulate, under stimulate, improperly medicate, helicopter, or neglect them in a screen-free, processed foods-free, GMO-free, negative energy-free, plastic-free, body positive, socially conscious, egalitarian but also authoritative, nurturing but fostering of independence, gentle but not overly permissive, pesticide-free two-story, multilingual home, preferably in a cul-de-sac with a backyard and 1.5 siblings spaced at least two years apart for proper development, also don't forget the coconut oil.

How To Be A Mom In Literally Every Generation Before Ours: Feed them sometimes.

(This is why we're crazy.)

—Bunmi Laditan, Publication Announcement for *Confessions of a Domestic Failure, Facebook,* 1 May 2017.

O N MAY 1, 2017, novelist and mommy-blogger Bunmi Laditan announced the imminent release of her latest novel, *Confessions of a Domestic Failure,* with a Facebook post that draws attention to one conviction of twenty-first-century middle-class motherhood: That it is newly trapped by a deluge of conflicting prescriptions. By this logic, mothering in 2017 requires more than it has any other moment in history. Specifically, it requires more—and more careful—attention not only to the nutritional parts of childrearing but also to its "academic, emotional, psychological, mental, spiritual, physical, nutritional, and social" aspects. This difference codes "being a mother" today as cultural pathology: "This is why we're crazy," Laditan explains parenthetically. *Crazy,* because apparently it can be taken as axiomatic that twenty-first-century mothers are not quite sane, the putatively inevitable result of the balancing act she describes.[1] The syntax enacts the state of mind Laditan ascribes to its contents: Her single sentence piles list upon list, with object following object in perpetual, breathless, anxious-making motion.

This post quickly went viral; within a few months, it was detached from Laditan's name, de-gendered, and had lost the explicit diagnosis. An image circulated on Twitter and Facebook, perhaps from a talk, of a White woman standing in front of a PowerPoint slide containing Laditan's text; in this version "mom" has become "parent," and the final parenthetical has been removed.[2] I think that it's important, though, that this paralyzing, crazy-making, internally contradictory list of prescriptions was first formulated by a mommy-blogger and around the question of being a mother. At least in the original formulation, mothers are responsible, mothers keep track, mothers navigate contradictory imperatives . . . quite simply, mothers *worry.* If that work is becoming less attached to the female gender, it's because fathers are starting to share in the neurotic labor of mothering, not because "being a mother" has become less neurotic. In other words, maternal concern is cultural rather than natural: The "craziness" of motherhood is induced by the deluge of *shoulds,* rather than inhering either in the biological transformations of pregnancy, childbirth, and lactation, or in the hormones released in bonding with an infant as its primary caregiver. This premise underwrites the historical contrast. By stripping down the complexities of raising children to the most basic biological necessity ("feed them") and then even making that seem optional ("sometimes"), Laditan posits a natural state of anxiety-free mothering before the contemporary flood of advice changed it. No previous generation, she suggests, has had it so bad, been so overwhelmed, made so crazy. Free from the burdens of satisfying every need a child might or might not have, pre-twenty-first-century mothers had all the agency as well as all the calm that contemporary mothers lack.

---

1. In Laditan's formulation, this involves not only finding the perfect midpoint between dangerous extremes—neither over- nor under-stimulating, helicoptering nor neglectful—but also controlling every aspect of the child's environment. The extent to which the mother's attention, energy, and identity are subsumed into this work is demonstrated by the inclusion of siblings, "spaced at least two years apart for proper development." Even a woman's reproductive choices facilitate the current and future physical and psychological health of her child(ren).

2. In his comments on the tweet in which he shares this image, Nick Quaranto quickly identifies Laditan as the original source of the content on the slide, although he does not seem to be able to identify the White woman in the image, who is apparently giving a presentation. (I have also not been able to identify her.) As far as I have been able to determine, she did not cite Laditan, who is a woman of color. Such appropriation of this expression of Laditan's rhetorical and professional maternity is particularly striking in the context of middle-class White families' appropriation of the bodily and emotional labor of nonwhite and poor women that I discuss in chapters 4 and 5.

Laditan's exaggerated historical contrast maps *now* onto *excess* and *then* onto *simplicity*: The familiarity of this nostalgic move can make it difficult to remember that prior to the discovery of analgesics like aspirin, ibuprofen, and acetaminophen, not to mention antibiotics and vaccines, parents spent considerable time and effort worrying about literal matters of life and death.[3] The nostalgia that forgets the challenges of raising children without vaccines, fever-reducers, and antibiotics also obscures the economic privilege on which modern ideals of childhood rely. In Laditan's post, we see this in the detailed description of the "home" in which 2017 mothering normatively takes place, a space clearly marked by a middle-class tradition that conflates emotional security with particular architectural features and geographic locations. The ideal home here is both a space apart—free from screens, processed foods, GMOs, and negative energy—and simply spacious: two stories, suburban cul-de-sac, backyard. The experiences of specifically middle-class mothering thus stand in for all maternal experience. Laditan's "we" (*This is why we're crazy*) pulls all her readers into the position of mothers with enough leisure, education, and wealth to know about and enact (or feel pressure to enact) these contradictory instructions.

In *Writing Maternity,* I demonstrate that none of this is new to the twenty-first century. Ours is no more the first generation to worry about childcare decisions than it is the first generation to worry about the psychological and social impacts of living at a moment of great technological change and global transformation.[4] But the contemporary resonance of representations such as

---

3. I can only speculate as to the changes the experience of COVID19 may (or may not) make to twenty-first-century maternal and parental experience, despite the fact that that virus is not a childhood illness. At this time, however, middle- and upper-middle-class White parents in Britain and the US (my primary geographic areas of focus) are not occupied with child mortality as a cultural *probability*. It's important to note, however, that an *expectation* of child life and health remains a condition of comparative luxury. The 2018 Unicef Child Mortality Report notes that while great strides have been made in lowering child mortality rates worldwide—they dropped 58% between 1990 and 2017—there are still significant regional and income-based disparities. The region with the highest child mortality rate is Sub-Saharan Africa, with 1 in 13 children dying before their fifth birthday. This rate is 14 times higher than the average ratio in high-income countries (6, 8). These data obscure the extent to which maternal and infant/child mortality are significantly higher in the US in low-income communities, particularly communities of color. This is not to condemn Laditan; as I hope is clear in the discussion above, I think that she brilliantly articulates a central emotional component of normative mothering in late postindustrialized capitalism.

4. Wolfgang Schivelbusch's *The Railway Journey* argues that perceptions of both time and space were significantly altered by the introduction of railway travel in the nineteenth century. On transformations in communications media and Victorian literature, see Menke; Worth. Fitzpatrick situates the vilification of television in postmodern fiction in a broader context of technophobia.

Laditan's is important, and suggests that anxiety is an inherent part of mothering—or perhaps parenting—in industrialized capitalism. This book is, in large part, an effort to understand how anxiety was written onto motherhood in the early nineteenth century—in other words, how that emotion came to be part of maternity's affective script.

ACKNOWLEDGMENTS

COMPLETED REVISIONS of *Writing Maternity* during the spring and summer of 2020, a season of pandemic and protest. These contexts leave traces on the book as well as my thinking about its process. I am grateful to the Huntington Library for a Fletcher Jones Foundation Fellowship, and to Princeton University, Pomona College, and New York University for the research funding that supported my work on this project, including research leaves from the latter two institutions. My offices and homes during the time I have worked on this book are located on unceded lands that are the ancient homes and traditional territories of the Lenni Lenape and Gabrieleño/Tongva peoples. The process of this book, then, is bound up in the legacies of slavery, colonization, and the exploitation of people of color that have benefitted White scholars such as myself for generations. This acknowledgement does little to redress that; I hope my day-to-day efforts do more.

To live in New York City during the COVID19 pandemic and the 2020 Black Lives Matter protests is to become acutely aware not just of my own racial and class privilege but also of the power and nature of community—even diffused or disembodied. My work as a scholar has been supported in a thousand ways invisible on these pages by administrative staff at NYU and Pomona, most importantly Chris Cappelluti, Lissette Florez, Jaysen Henderson-Greenbey, Christine Jensch, Nancy Jugan, Alyssa Léal, Stephanie Liu-Rojas, Joanna Mendoza, Mary Mezzano, and Patricia Okoh-Esene. Librarians have been indispensable allies: my thanks in particular to Gale Burrow at the Claremont University Consortium's Honnold-Mudd Library, Amanda Watson at NYU's Bobst Library, Joel Klein at the Huntingdon, and the staffs at the British Library and UCLA Clark Library Special Collections. Special thanks to my teachers—Judy Frank, Andy Parker, Karen Sánchez-Eppler, John Brereton, the late Gene Goodheart, Victor Luftig, Paul Morrison, Jenny Otsuki, Susan Staves, Ann Jurecic, Alfie Guy, and Kerry Walk—and to Pam Bromley and Jill Gladstein, who taught me not to be afraid to think quantitatively. Thanks, as well, to the Pomona College students who took Genre Theory in Spring 2013 and the NYU students I taught in Spring 2020. The latter listened, sympathized, and cheered as I chronicled the last months of writing and revision. My colleagues in the Pomona and NYU English departments, the Pomona College Writing Center and ID1 Program, and the NYU Expository Writing Program have challenged and inspired me to remain committed to this project and to make it better in every way. As a director of writing programs during most of the time I worked on *Writing Maternity*, I have benefitted from deans and department chairs who supported me as a scholar as well as an administrator, a clear-eyed generosity for which I am deeply grateful: my thanks to Gary Kates, Cecilia Conrad, Gabi Starr, Gene Jarrett, the late Toni Clark, Kevin Dettmar, Chris Cannon, Tom Augst, John Archer, and Liz McHenry.

I have benefitted enormously from writing alongside colleagues and friends: Anne Dwyer, Pardis Mahdavi, Erin Runions, and Tómas Summers Sandoval in Claremont; Jennifer Baker and Liz McHenry in New York; a memorable writing retreat with Dawn Dow; email check-ins with Kathleen Fitzpatrick. Kathleen, Jessica Enoch, Elaine Freedgood, Amanda Kotch, Julia Mickenberg, Sonya Posmentier, Catherine Robson, Colleen Rosenfeld, and Andrea Scott read parts of the manuscript and gave me vital feedback. Elaine, Sonya, and Lisa Gitelman—who generously read the whole thing—challenged me to "go bolder," for which I am forever grateful. My two anonymous readers from The Ohio State University Press saw the book this could be and advised me on how to move it in that direction; I am deeply indebted to them for their wisdom and generosity. Others expressed enthusiasm for the project at moments that they may have forgotten but I never will; my thanks to Risa Applegarth, Anis Bawarshi, Joe Bizup, Michelle Coghlan, Mary Jean Corbett, Dylan Dryer, Cheryl Glenn, David Gold, Perri Klass, Richard Miller, Deborah Denenholz Morse, John Plotz, Leah Price, Talia Schaffer, and Sally Shuttleworth. Kristen Elias Rowley, Rebecca Bostock, Tara Cyphers, and the staff at The Ohio State University Press were a dream to work with; everyone should have editors so smart, responsive, and caring. Kendra Millis created the index. Carrie A. A. Frye is another brilliant editor; she staged a writing and healing process for me over the course of 2018 that helped me remember how to be a writer, for which I cannot thank her enough.

Communities are personal as well as intellectual, and I've felt lucky in the many overlaps and intersections of my various worlds. My thanks to the following friends, family, colleagues, and institutions for the traces they've left on me and mine, and for care that continues to buoy us in difficult hours: Zivar Amrami, John Archer, Sue McWilliams Barndt, Will Barndt, Dan Birkholz, Rick Blackwood, Barbara Bloom, Perri Shaw Borish, Jana Brevick, The Brooklyn Latin School, Michelle Casteñeda, Catoctin Quaker Camp and the camping program of Baltimore Yearly Meeting, Paula Chakravartty, Claremont Monthly Meeting, Laurel Davis, Patrick Deer, Dawn Dow, Anne Dwyer, Russ Dyk, Oona Eisenstadt, Heath Elliott, Julie Elliott, David Evans, Kathleen Fitzpatrick, Juliet Fleming, Ani Fredman, Zach Fredman, Carrie Frye, Ryan Grace, Greenwich House, John Guillory, Nora Hanson, Sara Harbidge, Jo Hardin, Trudy Harpham, Stephanie Harves, Liz Hecht, John Heitkemper, International Montessori Preschools, Christine Jensch, Kevin Lahey, Debby Leonard, Harriet Lessy, Andrew Lohmann, Denice Martone, Paula McDowell, Matt McGuire, Tamara McGuire, Liz McHenry, Nell Menefee-Libey, Julia Mickenberg, Bill Morgan, Sahr MuhammedAlly, The New Shul, the building staff of NYU's Silver Towers, Oakmont Outdoor School, Veronica Ordoñez, Anne Pandey, Amit Pandey, Crystal Parikh, Keir Paterson, Teague Paterson, Yvonne Paterson, Olivier Pauluis, Elsa Pilichowski, Sonya Posmentier, PS3 The Charrette School, les Écoles Maternelle et Élémentaire Roland Vernaudon, Colleen Rosenfeld, Bob Rossman, Gretchen Rossman, Hahn Rossman, Milton Rossman, Jess Row, Erin Runions, Jeff Sacks, Sabrina Sarro, Laurie Schoelkopf, Shakespeare Youth Forum, Simon Baruch Intermediate School (MS104), Rob Smith, Stacie Slotnick, Ben Stewart, Deb Stull, Pacharee Sudhinaraset, Sycamore Elementary School, Simón Trujillo, Danièle Tzeutschler, David Tzeutschler, Ellen Tzeutschler, Hal Tzeutschler, Greg Vargo, Philippe Vasset, Jini Kim Watson, Becky Wilusz, Meg Worley, Amy Zhu, Leah Zimmerman, and: Leila, Chloe, Tassia, Asha, Eila, Pierce, Elektra, William, Ella, Elissa, Arlo, Noa, Lillian, Lucy, Ann, Lana, Asha, Tim, Buzz, Frannie, Mina, Mikayla, Annika, Asa, Violet, and Simon.

When I became friends with Greg Regaignon—then Greg Tzeutschler—30 years ago, I little suspected that he would be my life partner, or what a partner he would be. I am grateful beyond words to him for support, love, grounding, joy—and that we chose and continue to choose this particular miracle. And so my last thanks go to him and to our dearest ones, Mari and Anya Regaignon: for the laughter, the tears, the protests, the meals, the adventures, and perhaps most of all the rutabagas. I love you.

Chapter 5 expands on my article, "Infant Doping and Middle-Class Motherhood: Opium Warnings and Charlotte Yonge's *The Daisy Chain*," which appeared in *Other Mothers: Beyond the Maternal Ideal,* edited by Ellen Rosenman and Claudia Klaver, The Ohio State University Press, 2008, pp. 125–144. Chapters 1 and 2 draw from "Anxious Uptakes: Childrearing Advice Literature as a Rhetorical Genre," *College English,* vol. 78, no. 2, Nov. 2015, pp. 139–161. I am grateful to The Ohio State University Press and NCTE, respectively, for permission to reproduce that work here.

CHAPTER 1

The Rhetorical Origins of Maternal Anxiety

I N *THE PHYSICIAN'S VERDICT* by Belgian painter Émile-Carolus Leclerq (figure 1), the mother leans forward, her eyes focused on the elderly physician who sits calmly holding her hand. I imagine that the prognosis for the child in the cradle between them is grim: The baby's skin is nearly the same pallor as the white of the pillowcase, although their nose and eyes are swollen, dark, and likely painful. The mother is also pale, and while the girl standing by her side is the picture of health—rosy cheeks, sunlit blond curls—she, too, looks serious and concerned. There are no smiles of relief, suggesting a fever lately broken or a dangerous disease avoided. The baby centers the image, connecting family and physician while nearly disappearing into the cradle. Their illness—the prospect of their *death*—has already brokered an alliance that renders them nearly irrelevant. The bond between mother and medical man is exclusive: With clasped hands and locked eyes, the two of them could be alone in the room. While the little girl shares her mother's focus on the doctor, the nursemaid looks down—at the physical alliance that excludes her from personal involvement in the sick child's care.

This seems to be an upper-middle-class family. The mother's chair is upholstered in red velvet and her dress is silk taffeta. The carpet, the lamp and crystal on the sideboard, and the book carelessly left on the floor further testify to their wealth. The physician also appears wealthy: His top hat and walking stick in the background seem to be of good quality; the black

FIGURE 1. Émile-Carolus Leclerq, *The Physician's Verdict,* 1857.
Oil on canvas. Wellcome Library no. 45025i.

of his suit and the white of his shirt and cravat speak of a life of comparative
ease—and therefore the ability of the family to pay his (likely considerable)
fees. The shining white of his linen ties him to the scene—the child's bassinet,
the mother's collar, the nursemaid's cap, and the white reflections in the wine-
glasses above—while the black of his suit connects him most closely to the
baby, whose crib is similarly jet. The reds and pinks of the family unify them
with their room; he is just a visitor. (The nurse's blues and browns pull her into
the background, with the wallpaper.) The doctor sits back comfortably in his
chair, holding the hand the mother has stretched across the cradle. In profile,
he radiates both authority and calm. While the positions of the mother, nursemaid, and girl curve toward the cradle and the sick infant, he sits upright, legs
crossed. One hand is captured mid-gesture, emphasizing that our glimpse of
the scene is frozen at a moment when the expert answers the mother's anxious
question: Will my baby live?

•

In *Writing Maternity*, I argue that historically if not personally, maternal anxiety is a rhetorically catalyzed and perpetuated affect, a naturalized aspect of normative modern motherhood. Rather than marking the neurosis or failure of particular women, this emotion is precisely attached to the arrangement and control over temporal and spatial processes that is the managerial role in the neoliberal economy. Focusing the attention of those who identify as mothers on the future of the Child and the space of the domestic sphere, maternal anxiety is an essential, affective component of patriarchal capitalism, engineering its production and (re)production through genres and generations. The emotion, I contend, became an essential motivating component of the ideology of nurturing motherhood as that formation rose to dominance in newly industrialized Britain. Like that ideology, maternal anxiety inheres in and grounds the formations of the emergent middle class and its attendant systems of bourgeois individualism, patriarchal familiality, gendered separate spheres, and global capitalism.

Childrearing advice literature emerged as a distinct genre in the 1820s and '30s. This development reimagined the relationship between mothers and medical men (physicians, surgeons, apothecaries) and, in doing so, interpellated its maternal readers as ignorant, inexpert, and afraid. In confidently elevating emergent medical knowledge about childhood illness and well-baby care over the experiential wisdom of female caregivers, this genre not only contributed significantly to the development of pediatrics as a medical specialty but also participated in a sentimentalized idealization of motherhood that simultaneously elevated its symbolic importance and evacuated it of all but moral authority. Operating by rhetorically cultivating uncertainty and self-doubt in its addressees, the genre invokes an anxious reader—an anxious maternal subjectivity.

This invocation operates in stochastic concert with other early and mid-nineteenth-century genres concerned with the domestic sphere and familial reproduction. While the emergence of childrearing advice literature was central to the formation of maternal anxiety, that emotion could not have become dominant if advice literature were the only genre repetitively invoking a worrying mother. I therefore expand my focus to examine a schematic ecology of genres, tracing how the narrative patternings of memoir and domestic fiction extend, reinforce, precede, reiterate, and transform those of advice literature. Serial fiction, the multiplot novel, and fictional autobiography reveal the ways in which maternal anxiety is proleptic—experiencing future possibility in the present moment—and paraliptic—invoking alternatives by denying their relevance or force. Childrearing advice literature takes up these logics but also repatterns them through the forms of the prescription and warning. Narrating lived experience for public consumption, published memoir not only individualizes this felt sense of danger but also authenticates it, lending it the force of an affective-social fact.[1] Focusing on the three genres together allows us to see the contours and operations of this rhetorical emotion more clearly, mapping its temporal and spatial logics and ultimately its contribution to the felt experience of fragility that helped underwrite, justify, and maintain British colonial expansion.

I am using "anxiety" in ways that are both commonsensical and quite specific: to indicate generalized, low-level fear and to index the specific bodily and emotional relation(s) to time and space that theorists have located in that term. The emotion, in my usage, has two particularly important features. First—following a strain of psychoanalytic thinking influenced by Sigmund Freud—that it puts the body in a specific temporality in which future possibilities or dangers are experienced in the present moment and on the basis of previous experience or knowledge. In other words, part of the experience of anxiety is a kind of temporal overload in which past and future are compressed into the present. Second—following a philosophical trajectory partially indebted to Søren Kierkegaard—that anxiety inheres in the experience and movement of choice, the juxtaposition of and selection between multiple possibilities. These two frameworks intersect in important ways, as when the consideration of different prognoses for an ill child requires forecasting a range of future possible outcomes in order to make a treatment decision in the present moment, or when a narrative telos depends on the simultaneous progression of different plots. In addition, it is essential to my understanding that anxiety is relational, as Sara Ahmed has theorized emotions more broadly: It inheres neither in a particular individual (an anxious *person*) nor in particular objects (*that* makes me anxious) but in the movement of scene and situation itself. Furthermore, like Ahmed I am interested in "how social norms become affective over time" (195).

In considering the *rhetorical* origins of maternal anxiety, I am emphasizing the understanding of rhetoric as a form of symbolic action that has shaped the field for the last fifty years rather than the older notion, descended

---

1. I am drawing here on Massumi's concept of "affective facts," in which (for example) fear "is the anticipatory reality in the present of a threatening future," the "felt reality" (54). This insight extends and refines the notion of "social facts" as elaborated by Bazerman by considering the emotional or affective aspect: "Social facts are those things people believe to be true, and therefore bear on how they define a [rhetorical] situation" ("Speech Acts," 312).

from Aristotle, of rhetoric as a means of persuasion.[2] This more contemporary understanding of rhetoric takes seriously the relationships texts enact between writers and readers, the ways in which utterances draw their addressees into scenes and situations and provide them with roles, motives, and urgencies—horizons of possibility for ways of being, acting, and feeling. While none of these are total—no speech act fully constrains or dictates another, no matter how closely tied—one foundational insight of rhetorical studies is that discursive actions both catalyze and constrain the range of responsive possibilities. This is not to suggest, then, that the advent of a genre that positions mothers as anxious means that each individual mother within its sphere of discursive influence worries all the time. But it is to suggest that in the early nineteenth century in Britain, anxiety became one of the "natural" expressions of maternal love, part of motherhood's interpellative script. In arguing for the historicity of maternal anxiety—and of normative understandings of maternal love in the modern period as fundamentally shaped by anxiety—I doubt neither that mothers loved their children before the year 1800 nor that they worried about them. As Joanna Bailey contends: "Parental characteristics appear stable over time, usually rooted in love, provision, discipline, and instruction. Yet this is not evidence for lack of change. It simply means that words and images can mask different meanings and need to be carefully historicized" (2).[3] I also want to underscore the very real basis for (many of) those concerns as well as the very real class and racial differences that continue to shape the fears mother-identified individuals have for their children. My goal in *Writing Maternity* is to understand the peculiarly anxious form maternal love began to take in the rhetorical environment of early nineteenth-century Britain and British India, and to look at the way loving care and anxious concern were durably attached to one another at that time.

Anxiety

In philosophy and psychology, it's traditional to define *anxiety* in relation to *fear*, distinguishing the anticipatory but specific nature of the latter from the

---

2. In *Genre*, Anis Bawarshi and Mary Jo Reiff quote Kenneth Burke on the difference between "the 'old' rhetoric and the 'new'": "I would reduce it to this," writes Burke in "Rhetoric—Old and New," "The key term for the old rhetoric was '*persuasion*' and its stress was upon deliberate design. The key for the new rhetoric would be '*identification*' which can include a partially 'unconscious' factor in appeal" (qtd. in 61).

3. Emma Griffin, drawing on mostly early twentieth-century autobiographies of working-class childhoods, also seeks to understand maternal feeling during the Victorian period.

free-floating, objectless nature of the former. In his early writings, Sigmund Freud understood anxiety as symptomatic of and triggered by repression—in other words, catalyzed not simply by what lies ahead but also what lurks behind or below. In *Inhibitions, Symptoms, and Anxiety* (1926) and *The Problem of Anxiety* (1936), however, he revised his thinking and came to understand the emotion not as a response to the return of the repressed but as an engine for repression itself: "Anxiety is a reaction to a situation of danger. . . . Symptoms are created so as to avoid a *danger-situation* whose presence has been signalled by the generation of anxiety" (*Inhibitions* 57, italics in original). In this formation, we can see the anticipatory temporality of anxiety; triggered by the imminent occurrence of a recognizable danger-situation, the emotion initiates behaviors designed to avoid that particular future becoming the individual's present. This is refined in *The Problem of Anxiety*, where Freud emphasizes that anxiety "forewarn[s]" (73). It's essential that the danger-situation be perceived as such; Freud notes that anxiety is produced "whenever a state of that kind recurs" (*Inhibitions* 63, see also *Problem* 72): The danger-situation is structurally recurrent, a typified scene. Drawing on apperceptive stocks of knowledge—on memory—the emotion identifies and is triggered by its approach (*Inhibitions* 57–58; see also Salecl 29–30; LeDoux 1–9). In this paradigm, the anxious individual exists in a state of perpetual expectation and apprehension that draws on the residue of previous experience. Anxiety is thus both an anticipatory and a recollecting emotion: Drawing on the past, it forecasts a dangerous future. The individual, of course, experiences this emotion in the present moment; anxiety thus both enacts and collapses the temporality of modern selfhood.

The originary anxious-making scene for Freud is that of helplessness in the face of privation, specifically the absence of the mother: "The situation which the infant appraises as 'danger,'" he writes, is "one of not being gratified, or an *increase of tension arising from non-gratification of its needs*—a situation against which it stands powerless" (*Problem* 76).[4] Naming this an "economic situation" in order to emphasize its underlying structural component, Freud emphasizes that the specifics of danger change as an individual matures (*Problem* 76). Anxious-making recurrence is therefore rooted not in the specifics but in the structural experience: the recognition of one's own helplessness when anticipating non-gratification of needs. This relies, in turn, on the capacities to recognize recurrence and to forecast possibility, as well as understanding oneself as a choice-making agent, if a frustrated one. Sianne

---

4. Andrew Parker's analysis of Freud's work relative to questions of language in *The Theorist's Mother* is deeply illuminating along these lines. See 88–110.

Ngai emphasizes this last aspect of what she calls "ugly feelings," of which anxiety is one; she focuses on the "negative affects that read the predicaments posed by *a general state of obstructed agency* with respect to other human actors or the social as such" (3, emphasis added).

In apparent contrast, Søren Kierkegaard roots anxiety in the situation of possibility: Anxiety is the recognition that infinite options are possible. The emotion therefore propels self-conscious reflection. Kierkegaard's central figure for theorizing anxiety is the individual at a significant crossroads—Adam just before eating the forbidden apple, for example. While Kierkegaard's anxiety is a crippling, agonizing emotion, it is also the catalyst for self-conscious agency. "Anxiety can be compared with dizziness," he writes:

> He whose eye happens to look down into the yawning abyss becomes dizzy. . . . It is in this way that anxiety is the dizziness of freedom that emerges when spirit wants to posit the synthesis, and freedom now looks down into its own possibility and then grabs hold of finiteness to support itself. . . . In anxiety there is the selfish infinity of possibility. (75)

The "dizziness" Kierkegaard identifies in the moment of apprehending such possibility is then akin to the anxiety triggered for Freud by the need to avoid the danger-situation. Both rely on and perpetuate the conception of a continuous, developing, and reflective self that moves through time.[5] As Ngai emphasizes, this temporal understanding is represented spatially: as moving, as looking down, as existing in proximity or at a distance, as "something 'projected' onto others in the sense of an outward propulsion or displacement" (212). Her theory reads anxiety as less the effect of temporal or spatial distinction (now vs. someday, here vs. there) than as "a structural effect of spatialization in general" (212).[6] Ahmed similarly argues for a more iterative relationship than that suggested by Freud and Kierkegaard: Situations and objects may catalyze the emotion, but the movement of the emotion itself makes it adhere to situations and objects not previously associated with it. She writes, "In

---

5. Discussions of anxiety as a cultural phenomenon as well as a psychiatric diagnosis have proliferated since the end of World War II. Renata Salecl, building on Kierkegaard's identification of anxiety with choice and apprehension of possibility, connects contemporary anxiety both to increasing emphasis on ideologies of individual freedom and to the proliferation of consumer choice in hyper-capitalism (50–54).

6. Ngai's reading of works by Herman Melville, Alfred Hitchcock, and Martin Heidegger compellingly emphasizes anxiety's connection to a particular type of intellectual masculinity. My thinking about maternal managerialism in chapter 4 aligns with this in that I am connecting the middle-class mother's supervisory attention to that of the nineteenth-century professional man.

anxiety, one's thoughts often move quickly between different objects, a movement which works to intensify the sense of anxiety. One thinks of more and more 'things' to be anxious about" (66). In this process, these "'things'" are not themselves triggering; they *become* anxious-making as they are caught up in the rapid temporal movement of the emotion. Ahmed "suggest[s] that anxiety tends to generate its objects, and to stick them together. Anxiety is like Velcro: it picks up objects that are proximate to it" (80n2).

The concept of anxiety that I use in *Writing Maternity* thus draws on all of these formulations. First, anxiety is a structural emotion that emerges from and generates triggering danger-situations, including situations of spatialized choice; the evanescent particulars are less important than the process of typification. Second, anxiety has a distinctive temporality, in which forecasted possibilities as well as recollected experiences shape the present moment; it therefore enacts a relationship to time that projects hypothetical futures. Extending Ahmed's structural insight by drawing on rhetorical theory, I would argue that the circulation of objects involves the repetition of specific rhetorical situations—that is, of structural patterns involving particular subjects, objects, and communicative actions in exigent relation to one another. The structure and temporality of anxiety come together in the spatialized movement Ngai and Ahmed describe, the object-generating cycle of ever-more-rapidly projected and recognized choices and danger-situations. To return to maternal anxiety specifically, maternal subjects are both always worrying about a specific thing and will always have (find) something to worry about because *the rhetorical situation of motherhood is typified as anxious.*

Indeed, mothers seem to be a particularly attractive illustration of anxiety. Joseph LeDoux, for example, opens his comprehensive discussion of the current state of scientific understandings of anxiety with a description of his worrying, care-taking mother (1–2). The movement of anxiety that I describe aligns in many unsurprising ways with Sara Ruddick's influential work. Her practice-based definition of motherhood roots "maternal thinking" in the need to identify and implement "strategies of protection, nurturance, and training" that collapses future possibilities into the present moment (23). In identifying the variety of decisions a "reflective mother" makes, Ruddick's examples enact this movement rhetorically:

> If your older child, in her competitive zeal, pushes ahead of your younger, smaller child while climbing a high slide, do you inhibit her competitive pleasure or allow an aggressiveness you cannot appreciate? Should her younger brother learn to fight back? And if he doesn't, is he bowing too

easily to greater strength? Most urgently, whatever you do, is somebody going to get hurt? (23)

My interest here lies not only in the content of Ruddick's extended example, but also its motion—which, by piling choice upon choice and possibility upon possibility rhetorically attaches anxiety to the structural situation it describes. Indeed, Ahmed points out that care and anxiety are both gendered feminine. While her discussion emphasizes how this cultural affinity limits women's bodily agency (81n5), I want to draw out the identity. To worry, to be anxious, to be careful, to take care (and to take care of): These terms all rely not simply on the rapid projection of future possibilities in order to choose present action(s) but also on a generalized sense of looming or lurking danger. In other words, the directionality of caretaking is the directionality of anxiety. Mother love is formed in the movement of worry, the attentive projection forward and outward of danger-situations that only might (already) be occurring. Indeed, if "care" and "concern" are idiomatically inseparable, it's because each term collapses the distinction between nurture and the prevention of harm while their pairing seems to suggest that they can be separated, after all. Concentrated on a child figured as both precious and vulnerable, the anxious mother is overwhelmed not simply by too many choices and possibilities in the present but also by the future implications of each decision—including the very real possibility that her action will make no difference at all.

The Structure of Maternal Feeling

Motherhood has long fascinated scholars of nineteenth-century Britain at the same time that questions of maternal experience tend to slip out of view. Despite the iconographic importance of Victoria's spectacular fertility and the centrality of maternal rights to several legal reform efforts, the period's literature typically kills mothers off or otherwise elides them, as Carolyn Dever has discussed so trenchantly.[7] Natalie McKnight's *Suffering Mothers in Mid-Victorian Novels* and Sally Shuttleworth's "Demonic Mothers" both emphasize the cultural contradictions written into the role at this time, contradictions that seem to make maternal experience difficult to represent in literature, despite the outpouring of advice (see also Thaden). More recently the essays collected in Ellen Rosenman and Claudia Klaver's *Other Mothers* seek to fill

---

7. On Victoria's maternity, see Bobotis; Munich 187–210; Weltman.

this lacuna in literary scholarship in particular. But literary works that center characters' experience in that of motherhood are rare, and their exceptional status seems to make it difficult for scholars to use them to generalize about nineteenth-century literary motherhood rather than subsuming it into discussions of female sexuality, domesticity, women's rights, childhood and the family, or gender.[8] There is widespread historical consensus that the ideal of nurturing motherhood rose to dominance in nineteenth-century Britain; despite that consensus—but in tacit acknowledgement of the deflective aspect of that ideal—it seems that the representability of Victorian maternity has been an ongoing challenge both for nineteenth-century writers and for the scholars who work on them.

The ideal of maternal feeling as overwhelmingly tender and nurturing first emerged in the early eighteenth century. Its durable features include the notion that motherhood (rather than marriage) is the defining experience of a woman's life, and that maternal love is an all-engrossing, tender emotion that puts children ahead of self. Its practical manifestations are extended maternal breastfeeding, direct supervision of and daily care for children (including moral training and early education), and a more generalized centering of female attention in the domestic spaces of the home and toward the future of their progeny.[9] I find it useful to think of this formation as a structure of feeling as defined by Raymond Williams. A structure of feeling goes beyond the formal contours of ideology to encompass felt experience in relation to such systemic structures. Thinking nurturing motherhood as an ideology draws our attention to it as a symbolic system and therefore to the range of representations that work however unevenly to reinforce and normalize it. Thinking nurturing motherhood as a structure of feeling allows us to *also* consider

8. Some of the most famous Victorian texts that center on maternal experience include Elizabeth Barrett Browning's "The Runaway Slave at Pilgrim's Point" (1848) and *Aurora Leigh* (1856), Anne Brontë's *The Tenant of Wildfell Hall* (1848), Elizabeth Gaskell's *Ruth* (1853), and Ellen Wood's *East Lynne* (1861). There has been much excellent scholarship that has included important consideration of maternity even while it has not focused primarily on the experience or representation of mothers. On maternity and sexuality, see Matus; on childhood and the family, see Berry, Frost; on legal reforms, see Gruner, McDonagh, Poovey, *Uneven Developments*; on domesticity and motherhood, see Langland. Two recent historical studies are Marland and Reynolds.

9. On the historical origins of the cultural formation, see Bowers 28–29, 167–169; the essays collected in Greenfield and Barash also provide essential background for my study, as do Bailey; Davies; and Francus. What I term the ideology of nurturing motherhood sociologist Sharon Hays has called "the ideology of intensive mothering" in her study of the experiences of twenty-first-century American professional women (9); Dow's *Mothering While Black* provides an important corrective to the normalization of White experience, drawing attention to the ways Black experiences reveal the racialized nature of many assumptions about contemporary motherhood.

the constraints and affordances of that representational system that shape the "affective elements of consciousness and relationship" (*Marxism and Literature* 132–133).

In *Silent Sisterhood* Patricia Branca argues that "the Victorian mother was not only the giver of life but the maintainer of life, teacher to her children, confidant and disciplinarian. She had to devote a great deal of her time and energy to the fulfillment of this complex role" (111–112). Scholars have long problematized Branca's relatively straightforward acceptance of ideology as experience, seeking to expand our understanding of kinds of maternal experience in the nineteenth century. I nonetheless want to underscore Branca's emphasis on "time *and energy*": The idealization of nurturing motherhood not only defined women—even childless ones—as mothers but also posited that childrearing be the primary object of their attention. Bailey's understanding of the gendering of parental "tenderness" between 1760 and 1830 is helpful here. During this period, she argues, praise for both parents connected this term to "kind concern, compassion and anxiety for another's good, susceptibility to soft passions, care not to hurt, and gentleness" (28). In the case of mothers, in particular, this parental feeling also connoted self-sacrifice, in part through the residual associations with both the Virgin Mary and Jesus (31). The anxious attention—the time and energy—of a tender mother is thus a felt manifestation of her loving care, a manifestation that directs that loving care away from herself and toward her children. This was part of a broader set of transformations of the family that are largely associated with the rise of the middle class and capitalist patriarchy: from broad and partially elective kin groups to patrilineal nuclear families organized around the consolidation of property.[10] These transformations produced an understanding of "family" as being centered on the conjugal unit and their children—that is, the nuclear family—as both an economic entity headed by the patriarch and as a corporate body organized around the transmission of social identity to the next generation (Nelson 46–49, 65–68). Perhaps paradoxically, the self-abnegating nature of maternal love that centers the Victorian familial ideal renders that figure passive as well as lacking in authority, the opposite of the key attributes of the Enlightenment individual that emerged at this time.

Writing Maternity focuses not on the representation of mothers or on the historical experience of individuals who identify as mothers, but on the

---

10. In addition to Bailey's *Parenting in England,* the work of Naomi Tadmor and Ruth Perry has been particularly important to my thinking about the history of the family in eighteenth- and nineteenth-century Britain. Other landmark texts on the history of the family in particular include Stone; Davidoff and Hall. Nelson provides a valuable overview for the nineteenth century.

affective-rhetorical effect of ever-more depictions, invocations, and narratives of what it is like to be (to feel and act as) a mother. This project therefore also contributes to a growing and important body of scholarship on the rhetorics of motherhood, infant-feeding, pregnancy, and childcare by providing the cultural formation such work investigates with a new historical point of origin.[11] This work typically takes as its starting point the beginning of the twentieth century; *Writing Maternity* provides important historical depth, and in doing so complicates some of the key terms. For example, in *The Rhetoric of Pregnancy* Marika Seigel reads pregnancy advice as a form of technical communication, arguing that it positions women and their pregnant bodies as always already passive and prone to malfunction. My reading of the companion genre shows not only the historical origins of this phenomenon—revealing that it has been (even) more durable than she suggests—but also draws attention to the role of rhetorically cultivated affect in the initiation and sustaining of such cultural forms. At the same time, studies such as Seigel's, Lindal Buchanan's *Rhetorics of Motherhood,* Amy Koerber's *Breast or Bottle?,* Mary Lay's *The Rhetoric of Midwifery,* and Kim Hensley Owens's *Writing Childbirth* present a picture that is nuanced in different but equally valuable ways. Their contemporary focus allows them to incorporate direct interactions of readers and texts, the kinds of responses and reactions I can only glimpse in the historical record. This may also explain why this recent work offers powerful arguments for empowerment or revision in ways that *Writing Maternity* cannot, whether in the form of exhortations to attend to experiential knowledge (Lay), reflections on the success of maternal rhetoric (Buchanan), or recommendations for pregnancy advice that empowers rather than infantilizes its readers (Seigel).

In both rhetorical and Victorian studies, discussions of motherhood are bound up in discussions of the relationship of public and private spheres, especially in relation to gender roles. But subsuming motherhood into discussions of domesticity and femininity—even in their political deployment as metaphor or rhetoric—obscures the extent to which the figure of the anxious nurturing mother actively centers bourgeois gender ideology. There has been much brilliant scholarship on the complicated development of domestic ideology, and the cultural work of those nineteenth-century conversations for the normalization of bourgeois values as well as the growth of both European and

---

11. The essays in Stitt and Powell analyze a range of contemporary interventions, as does the recent special issue of *Women's Studies in Communication* on "Mothering Rhetorics" (see Hallstein). Enoch's *Domestic Occupations* focuses on the relationship of women's work, mothering, and domestic space.

American empires.[12] *Writing Maternity* contributes to this project by focusing not just on maternity (as opposed to femininity) but on the cultural formation of maternal anxiety as part of the emotional logic of the cultural and political dominance of the (White) middle classes both in Britain and its colonies. Across a variety of genres invested in furthering the domestic ideal, the structure of maternal feeling evokes self-abnegating, "tender" concern for the current well-being and future of the Child as the figure of the nation, attaching maternal subjectivity to the direction of that attention outward and into the future.[13] In the chapters that follow, I develop the argument that this structure of maternal feeling became dominant in the early nineteenth century: First because of the emergence of the genre of childrearing advice literature, which not only represented maternal care and concern as identical to one another but also collapsed them rhetorically; and second, because that genre worked in stochastic concert with memoir and domestic fiction to attach the spatial and temporal movement of anxiety to topics that were the province of mothers. By attaching this fearful, watchful emotion to the economic and racial conditions of middle-class childrearing, this ecology of genres focuses female attention on the domestic sphere as the vulnerable center of the current and future nation.

Advising Mothers

Books offering advice on the home treatment of childhood illness, advice on well-baby care, and an overview of the physical development of children, mostly written by medical men and aimed explicitly at a maternal audience, first appeared *en masse* in the early nineteenth century.[14] Figure 2 provides an overview of childrearing advice literature's emergence as a genre between 1740 and 1860. We can see here the numbers of texts published by decade, which includes subsequent editions: Thus Pye Henry Chavasse's *Advice to Mothers* is included once in the count for 1830–1839 and twice in that for 1840–1849 since editions were published in 1839, 1842, and 1843. I also disaggregate unique

---

12. On the development of the ideology of separate spheres and contemporary complications of it, see Armstrong; Chase and Levenson; Cohen; Corbett; Davidoff and Hall; Langland; McKeon; Poovey, *Uneven Developments*; Stern; Tange. These all connect this phenomenon to the rising dominance of the middle classes in Britain. On the relation of domestic ideology to empire see Archibald; David; Kaplan; Stoler; Tompkins.

13. On reproductive futurism, see Edelman; Sheldon.

14. Until now, this was most comprehensively documented in Attar's annotated bibliography; see also Hardyment; Branca 76–77. See Davis on twentieth-century England; and Murphy and Hulbert on the nineteenth- and twentieth-century US, respectively.

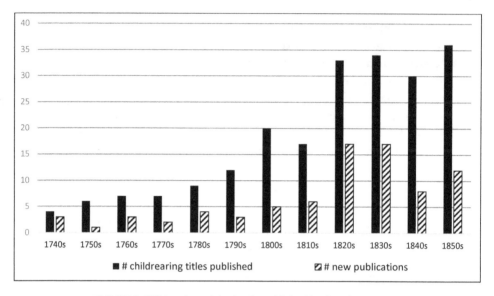

FIGURE 2. Childrearing advice books published by decade, 1740–1860

titles, indicating the number of new publications in each decade. (In this case, Chavasse's *Advice to Mothers* is only counted once, in 1830–1839.) Both of these metrics give us a sense of popular demand: Publishers could clearly sell updated versions of previously published texts, but also were clearly able to sell—or thought it worth trying to sell—works by new authors.[15]

There was only slow growth during the first half-century I've tracked, with a noticeable increase both in total publications and in new titles starting in the early 1800s. The period of 1820 to 1829 seems to have been a pivotal decade: During this time, the overall number of books published nearly doubles (from 17 to 33), and a significant portion of that increase is driven by the number and rate of appearance of new publications. New titles constituted 25% to 35% of publications for each decade between 1790 and 1820, but account for 50% between 1820 and 1840. The total number remains high into the 1850s, although the rate of new publication drops again. In addition to providing us with a picture of the development of a genre, these data give us a quantitative glimpse of the medical profession's move into the domestic sphere via publishing. Most of those authors were medical men: physicians, surgeons, or apothecaries. Of my entire sample of 215 texts, 18 (8%) were published anonymously, and 28 (13%) were published under female names or author-

---

15. Kathryn Hughes has observed a similar, slightly later, explosion of manuals offering advice both to governesses and their employers between the 1840s and 1860s. See Hughes xii, and my discussion in chapter 4.

designations. Both of these two categories were reprinted less often; 80% of the author sample is identifiably medical and male.[16]

Childrearing advice emerged from several much longer traditions of written advice: (1) *conduct literature* prescribing behavioral norms and practices, typically by social status and gender; (2) *domestic guides* detailing recipes and practices for managing a household; and (3) *medical treatises* describing diseases and their treatment, typically for a professional or student audience. Drawing on but also departing from these, the content of childrearing advice literature as it developed in industrializing Britain offered information about diet, clothing, cleanliness, and early discipline (that is, well-baby care) alongside descriptions of childhood illnesses and their appropriate treatments. Some texts include information on menstruation, pregnancy, and breastfeeding; others include guidance on moral and early academic education. These topics are also covered in separate volumes, sometimes by the same authors. Glossed generically as "advice to mothers," the genre addresses itself primarily or exclusively to female parents.

In the first forty years that I have tracked (1740–1780), the emergent genre is dominated by concern about breastfeeding: William Cadogan's *An Essay Upon Nursing and the Management of Children* (1748) and Hugh Smith's *Letters to Married Women; on Nursing and the Management of Children* (1767) dominated the field, and established a logical trajectory from the medicalization of women's bodies during pregnancy and childbirth to the medicalization of well-baby care. Cadogan published his 34-page pamphlet at the request of the Governors of the London Foundling Hospital; its central project is to convince both male and female readers that breastmilk is the only adequate infant food, although it makes a number of other recommendations—against swaddling, for example, and for fresh fruit soon after weaning (10, 30). Most significantly and influentially, however, it established rhetorically the authority of the medical profession over questions of early infant care and feeding; it was therefore a crucial first move in the development of pediatrics as a distinct discipline. While philosophers had long considered education and socialization their province (think of both John Locke's *Some Thoughts Concerning Education* [1693] and Jean-Jacques Rousseau's *Émile* [1762]), this medical intervention was new. It reframed questions not just of infant care but also, as Ruth Perry has brilliantly argued, women's bodies: In the middle of the eighteenth century, the female breast was drafted to the service of the nation ("Colonizing" 206–207; see also Fildes, *Breasts* 115–117). Smith's

---

16. In the count of works published anonymously, I include those for whom authors have since been identified. The latter category includes, for example, Margaret King Moore's *Advice to Young Mothers* since its title page reads, "By a Grandmother."

Letters, published twenty years after Cadogan's *Essay,* extends its rhetorical project by addressing women directly. Both publications discuss a few aspects of well-baby care as well as infant feeding. By the 1820s, the titular focus of the genre had broadened: The medicalization of childrearing now encompassed all aspects of well-baby care (breastfeeding, introduction of solid food, bathing, diapering, and so on) and normal physical development (for example, teething), as well as childhood illness and disease. This combination relies for models not only on the breastfeeding literature and the antecedent genres mentioned above but also on William Buchan's *Domestic Medicine* (first published in 1769). Addressed to a general and implicitly female audience, Buchan's text combines aspects of two previously extant genres: the curative (which offered medicinal prescriptions to cure disease, as the name suggests) and the longevity guide (which focused on preserving health). Domestic medical guides such as Buchan's remained enduringly popular throughout the eighteenth and nineteenth centuries, in part because they allowed families to avoid paying a doctor's fees for smaller issues.[17] We cannot know definitively whether medical practitioners began publishing childrearing advice in response to a significant demand on the part of the market or as an intervention that created the market it then addresses; it's essential to the genre that there always *seem* to be preexisting demand. Regardless of that initial motivation, however, the generic intervention established a broader sphere of influence for the profession, as well as quite possibly generating additional work for its individual members.

Genre and Situation

My understanding of genre comes from rhetorical genre theory, an interdisciplinary field that draws on applied linguistics, rhetoric and writing studies, sociology, and literary theory. Rhetorical genre theory takes several notions about genre as axiomatic: (1) that the set of possible genres is infinite rather than finite, (2) that genre is a category of social-rhetorical action, as well as a category of text, (3) that genres have a dialectical relationship to rhetorical situation, both emerging from and constituting it, and (4) that genre therefore has an interpellative relation to individual subjectivity.[18] Here I explain

---

17. For further discussion of the importance of domestic medical guides see Murphy 7, Attar 48–49, and Rosenberg. I have not included these in my sample because they do not specifically focus on childcare.

18. Bawarshi and Reiff's *Genre: An Introduction to History, Theory, Research, and Pedagogy* is an indispensable introduction to the field.

the concepts that undergird my argument that the historical emergence of childrearing advice literature both responded to and helped to constitute the situation—and therefore the subject position—of normative motherhood as anxious.

Understanding genre as a category of social action requires seeing the study of rhetoric not as the examination of speech or writing's persuasive capacities, strategies, and techniques but as the study of how meaning is made in and through human communication, specifically but not exclusively through language.[19] Successful rhetorical action depends on and cultivates shared assumptions—consensus regarding concepts, theories, facts, and even the nature of reality itself. This understanding invites a mode of reading that is not only attentive to context but also sees text as both emerging from and generating its own rhetorical situation(s). Rhetorical situation, as influentially defined by Lloyd Bitzer, is "a complex of persons, events, objects, and relations presenting an actual or potential exigence which can be . . . removed if discourse . . . can so constrain human decision or action as to bring about the significant modification of the exigence" (304). A rhetorical situation is comprised of people as well as circumstances both temporal and material; most importantly, it is a set of circumstances *in which language effects change*: when you ask someone to open a window and they do so; when political protest persuades legislators to change a law; when a doctor prescribes a particular course of treatment.[20]

Exigence is specifically the problem, puzzle, tension, or question that impels that rhetorical action: the hot and stuffy room, the unjust law, the mysterious symptoms. It can be positive as well as negative, as when one feels impelled to congratulate a colleague or wish a loved one happy birthday. Rhetorical action resolves the exigence, which dialectically gives rise to a new one: A happy birthday wish requires an expression of thanks in response; a new or changed law must be enforced. Carolyn Miller therefore emphasizes the social nature of exigence, insisting that it is "a form of social knowledge—a mutual construing of objects, events, interests, and purposes that not only links them but makes them what they are: an objectified social need" (157). We can see this operate in the following example, which I've chosen in delib-

---

19. The Classical understanding of rhetoric, following Aristotle, emphasized persuasion. Burke built on this concept by expanding the concept of persuasion, offering a definition of rhetoric as "the use of words by human agents to form attitudes or induce actions in other human agents" (*Rhetoric of Motives* 41). See also Bitzer.

20. The debt to J. L. Austin's work is evident. Todorov's and Bakhtin's discussions of the utterance echo these terms from the perspective of literary theory (see Todorov, *Genres* 13–26 and Bakhtin 66–103).

erate homage to Louis Althusser's thinking about interpellation: Two people, previously acquainted with one another, walking in opposite directions on the crowded sidewalk of a city street, is not a rhetorical situation until and unless one of them looks up and sees the other. Once person A sees person B, there is exigence: a problem of recognition that in Western culture demands speech or other rhetorical action. The particular form that resultant action takes—a wave, a smile and nod, "hello," "hey," or "yo"—will be shaped by A's background, preferences, knowledge of and relationship to B, and the particular ambient circumstances of the street (noise level, visibility, their proximity to one another, and so on). A's recognition of B exigently triggers A's rhetorical action; that action then creates a relationship to and new rhetorical situation for B—that of being hailed. In addition, A's action is the result "not of 'perception,' but of 'definition'"—A did not simply *perceive* themselves and B to be in a rhetorical situation requiring a greeting, but *defined* it as such (C. Miller 156). That act of definition leads to a rhetorical action which in turn results in a mutual construing of the situation. Situation thus provides a way of understanding social experience in terms of narrative, temporal patterning.

This particular situation is one that recurs, and we can understand any specific instance of it as one of a recurrent type, which we might call *Two Acquaintances Running Into One Another.* Typification occurs when we perceive similarity, when we consciously or unconsciously mobilize tacit knowledge and previous experience in order to act or think or feel in a situation that is both new and yet somehow familiar (Bawarshi and Reiff 66–67; see also Todorov, *Genres* 17–18).[21] *Two Acquaintances Running Into Each Other,* the giving of medical advice, the assigning of a research paper, the protest, and the conference presentation are all examples of recurrent situations that have over time become culturally recognized and structured exchanges. *Genre* is a name for the typified or codified categories of utterances that belong to recurrent situations: the greeting; the prescription; the essay assignment and the research essay; the protest speech, sign, and chant; the conference paper, and

---

21. In Western culture, we experience the phenomenological lifeworld as a series of situations; in order to perceive those situations, we have to be able to categorize them—to identify various *types* of situations that recur with variation (Bawarshi and Reiff 66–67). Amy Devitt approaches this from a different angle, drawing on linguistic and literary theory rather than sociology: "The socialization *to* genres implies socialization *through* genres. This means that the genres carry a world picture (Whorf), an *ideology* (Bakhtin/Volosinov), a doxa (Barthes), or a tacit culture which is forced upon the user through the communication" (Ongstad 23–24, qtd. in Devitt, *Writing Genres* 61–62). There are clear resonances between this line of thinking and S. Tomkins' script theory. Stewart's *Ordinary Affects* and Berlant and Stewart's *The Hundreds* are stunning enactments of this: "The everyday is a radical empiricism where things are not examples of anything but a profusion of forms performing their capacities in a situation" (Berlant and Stewart 109).

its slides or handouts, its questions and answers. For rhetorical theory, genres are not simply texts or utterances but also actions that create relationships. With the greeting, for example, A puts themself into a relationship with B by hailing them, by apprehending the exigence of crossing paths with someone you recognize as requiring that genre, and A and B are now momentarily defined in relation to one another, as gree*ter* (A) and gree*tee* (B). Carolyn Miller meditates on the implications of this for subjectivity:

> What we learn when we learn a genre is not just a pattern of forms or even a method for achieving our own ends. We learn, more importantly what ends we may have: we learn that we may eulogize, apologize, recommend one person to another, instruct customers on behalf of a manufacturer, take an official role, account for progress in achieving ends. (165)

To enact a genre, in other words, is to take on its structural assumptions and to participate in the rhetorical situation from which it emerges and which it (re)enacts (see also Artemeva). While this appears fairly neutral in the case of *Two Acquaintances Running Into One Another,* it has significant implications for authority and hierarchy: To prescribe a remedy is to take on the author- ity of physician; to seek advice is to adopt a position of both uncertainty and need.

Rhetorical genres are thus evidently ideological, interpellating individu- als as subjects in Althusserian terms: "You and I are *always already* subjects, and as such constantly practice the rituals of ideological recognition, which guarantee for us that we are indeed concrete, individual, distinguishable and (naturally) irreplaceable subjects" (117). They operate affectively, as any act of interpellation must. Rhetorical genre theory has recently begun to empha- size the emotional experience of generic stocks of knowledge, questions of apperception and apprehension, modes of conduct and appropriateness that evoke bodily, felt experiences. Silvan S. Tomkins provides a way to think about this; his theatrical metaphors have clear analogues in rhetorical genre theory's terms: We can substitute Tomkins's "scene" for rhetorical theory's "situation," and productively understand apperceptive stocks of knowledge as affective scripts that shape felt experience.[22] Genres both mobilize scripts and are

---

22. Tomkins offers the lifeworld as a series of *scenes,* which are Stimulus-Affective Response sequences. *Scripts* are the sets of flexible, always-in-progress rules for the appercep- tion, apprehension, interpretation, prediction, and management of scenes. Although I do not have the space to extend this insight fully here, I would argue that we can see *scene* as analogous to *rhetorical situation* and *script* drawing on both *genre* and *uptake.* See 179–197. On affect and emotion in rhetorical studies, see Chaput et al.; Emmons, *Black Dogs*; Kurtyka; Propen and Schuster.

part of them, since there is an iterative and reciprocal relationship between genre and situation: "Genre is a reciprocal dynamic within which individuals' actions construct and are constructed by recurring context of situation, context of culture, and context of genres," explains Amy Devitt (*Writing Genres* 28–29). Once again, we can illustrate this with *Two Acquaintances Running Into One Another*: A defines the rhetorical situation as requiring the genre of greeting; A's hail pulls B into a recurrence of that rhetorical situation, which calls for the same genre with a slightly different inflection. We can thus see that the relationship between genre and situation is mutually determinative and cyclical, as well as that it draws on individual memories: Situation determines genre (the exigency demands or invites a particular range of categories of response), but genre also determines situation (by invoking its context and pulling the addressee into a particular relationship with the rhetor) (Devitt, "Generalizing" 578).

"Emotions operat[e] precisely where we don't register their effects, in the determination of the relation between signs, a relation often concealed by the form of the relation," argues Ahmed (194). She calls this "determination 'stickiness,'" focusing on how "'signs' become sticky or saturated with affect" through circulation (194–195, see also 10–12). The temporal space of this determination is that of what rhetorical theory calls *uptake*, the responsive motion forward that (re)constitutes a relationship between bodies. Ahmed explains: "Rather than using stickiness to describe an object's surface, we can think of stickiness as an effect of surfacing, *as an effect of the histories of contact between bodies, objects, and signs*" (90, emphasis in original). Drawing on psychoanalytic and Marxist traditions as well as queer and feminist theory, Ahmed argues that emotions "accumulate over time," coming to shape social forms and structures—including subject positions in relation to one another—through repetition (11–12). She "read[s] texts that circulate in the public domain" in order to show how they "work by aligning subjects with collectives by attributing 'others' as the 'source' of our feelings" (1). Her opening example analyzes how nonwhite immigrant bodies trigger a version of national pride that is rooted in fear. This accumulative repetition happens through circulation; "emotions can move through the movement or circulation of objects" as these "objects become sticky, or saturated with affect, as sites of personal and social tension" (11). The racialized Others that trigger both fear and pride in her example are not inherently anything; they are constituted (as objects, as Others, as fear-bringing, as pride-engendering) through this process. Emotions, then, emerge from and generate relationships, situations, experiences, and structures through movement in time. In bringing Ahmed's insight into rhetorical genre theory, Faith Kurtyka uses the example of a student who feels nervous when a research paper is assigned in her first-year writing class. The emotion "does not reside solely in the student," Kurtyka explains; instead, it's "a mediated result of *contact* between the student and the assignment, which is based on [her] history with this genre, as well as her past contacts with . . . writing assignments, teachers, and the educational system" (emphasis in original). Emotions thus emerge from and generate interactions between individuals and situations, rather than inhering in either or in particular genres.

Branca describes the Victorian middle-class mother as being caught in a "vicious circle" of generically perpetuated anxiety: "She was anxious about her health and the health of her unborn baby, she sought advice, but for the most part all the advice did was to confirm all her anxieties while offering very little in the way of constructive advice" (77). Although for Branca concern precedes recourse to medical counsel, the movement she describes is that of anxiety itself, whose rapid temporal rhythm acquires objects and imbues them with the emotion. While I imagine that Branca's description is reflective of the individual, self-conscious experience of many early nineteenth-century mothers, I remain agnostic as to whether the collective experience of motherhood as anxious-making preceded or followed the emergence of childrearing advice literature. Genres as typified social actions work temporally, carrying forward the affective conditions and other intersubjective structures associated with the exigency that first called them into being. They mediate between individuals and ideology, giving individual subjects scripts for how to talk, write, act, and feel in particular scenes and situations—and therefore how to apperceive themselves and their roles in relation to the larger cultural world.[23] Advice literature, memoir, and domestic fiction shape the probability of infant death and the complexities of paid childcare according to the rhythms of constantly moving temporal and spatial attention. In doing so, they generate apperceptive schemes for mothers that attach anxious awareness to that subject position and its recurrent situations.

---

23. Bailey draws on the work of Robyn Fivush to point out that "when people talk or write about themselves they produce 'a life narrative in relation to the cultural script, whether it is conforming or deviating from it'" (51, qtd. in 8; see also Susan Miller, *Trust in Texts*). Angela Davis' oral history of motherhood in twentieth-century Oxfordshire confirms this specifically regarding the relationship between women and childcare advice, noting that many of the women she interviewed recalled a sense of needing to live up to specific "standards" (136, see 112–137; see also opening discussion in Mechling). Adam D. I. Kramer et al. have shown, in a controversial study that manipulated the News Feeds of over 680,000 Facebook users, that emotional contagion occurs through text- and image-based, depersonalized interaction. This all echoes the insights of affect theory in the tradition of Silvan Tomkins.

The Genre Ecology of Victorian Motherhood

In chapter 2, "Of Mothers and Medical Men," I use this understanding of genre and uptake to offer the first rhetorical genre analysis of childrearing advice literature. There, I contend that anxiety is a significant uptake of advice literature because of how the genre constitutes its rhetorical situation and exigence. In other words, the possibilities and constraints encoded for maternal readers by childrearing advice literature associate anxiety closely with the scene of mothering. This is not to suggest that we should take this—or any—genre's protestations at face value; genre theorists have long emphasized individual agency within generic constraints (see, for example, Bawarshi, "Between Genres"; Reiff; Spinuzzi). Without the necessary felicity conditions, no speech act has performative power—and, in any case, no one always takes all the advice they are given. My question in this chapter, then, is not whether the consumers of childrearing advice literature lanced their teething babies' gums as advised; it is how the increasing barrage of expert medical advice shaped how motherhood was imagined and its consequent emotional horizons.

The emergence of medically authored childrearing advice accelerated the rise of the structure of maternal feeling in part by suturing anxiety to the childcare situation. While the contours of the tender, attentive mother were laid down in the Augustan period, and the eighteenth century witnessed that cultural formation's rise to dominance, the naturalization of maternal anxiety accelerated between 1800 and 1840. Influence rather than authority became ideal, and the intensity and quality of maternal attention shifted accordingly.[24] Over the course of these decades, maternal emotion as defined for and by the middle classes came to be lastingly sutured to worry. It is one of *Writing Maternity*'s central claims that the emergence of childrearing advice literature as a significant genre at this time helped enact this shift—from authority to influence, from rhetorical confidence to rhetorical anxiety.

It's something of a truism in both rhetorical and literary genre theory that extrapolating from relatively simple instrumental genres like the greeting to complex literary genres is difficult. While I meditate on this challenge directly in the Coda, I take it up throughout *Writing Maternity*, thinking about the particular generic affordances of not only childrearing advice literature but also memoir and domestic fiction. I do this by focusing in chapters 3 through 5 on what I am calling—loosely following the work of Clay Spinuzzi—the genre ecology of Victorian motherhood. This concept invites attention to rela-

---

24. Sarah Stickney Ellis's *The Mothers of England* (1843) offers a paradigmatic discussion of maternal influence. Her vision contrasts directly with the eighteenth-century phenomenon of "maternal authority as a fixed, written discipline" (Davies 2).

tionships not just between pairs of genres but within larger constellations. In refining the concept, Spinuzzi argues that the ecological metaphor allows us to think beyond the instrumental relationships that enact the most likely or easiest uptakes: Instead of responding with, "Hey, how are you?" B might make eye contact with A and then look away and speed up; instead of administering all of a foul-tasting medicine, a mother might only give her child half the prescribed amount. Spinuzzi's research is on workplace genres, particularly in technical communication; he's therefore interested in how individual users put genres into unexpected and unanticipated conversation to accomplish specific tasks and in the "relatively stable" relationships particular genres have created over time (48; see also Spinuzzi and Zachry).

In *Writing Maternity,* I adapt genre ecology analysis for rhetorical-literary historiography, focusing on the relations between advice literature, memoir, and domestic fiction. My focus is not on how an individual user drew on and adapted available genres in order to complete a particular task, although there are moments in my analysis of autobiographical accounts that draw on this logic. Instead, I am using this method to name and understand the dynamic, overlapping, interactive, interdependent, and distributed context of genres that operated at a historically distant moment. My version of genre ecology analysis in a sense inverts Spinuzzi's emphasis; I am focused on the cultural formation(s) generated by genres' only semi-predictable uptakes. My archive makes it difficult to trace direct uptakes; in addition, I am invested in a kind of radical comparability of literary and non-literary genres, which leads me to read memoir (for example) as constituting as well as responding to the rhetorical situation. In this, I am following Tzvetan Todorov's argument in *Genres in Discourse* that while "readers read in function of the generic system . . . they do not need to be conscious of this system" (19). In other words, I am interested in the ways advice literature, memoir, and fiction read and reread one another from a distance, working in stochastic concert to iteratively develop, perpetuate, and normalize the subject position of anxious mother. These are not for the most part sequential or identifiably causal relationships. Following chapter 2's detailed analysis of advice literature, chapters 3, 4, and 5 take up specific topics that that genre makes especially sticky, particularly saturated with causes for concern: the likelihood of infants and children dying (chapter 3); the supplemental presence of paid caregivers (chapter 4); and the persistent rumor that such paid caregivers might dose babies with opium (chapter 5). In each of these chapters, I consider how the topic circulates through the genre ecology; my analyses emphasize generic affordances and consider what these formally and rhetorically patterned representations contribute to a broader discursive—intertextual, intergeneric, and intersubjective—situation.

Although *Writing Maternity* as a whole gives pride of place to advice literature, these individual chapters take the logic of a genre ecology seriously. In each chapter, I take up fiction, advice literature, and memoir in different orders and put the genres in different relations to one another in order to draw attention to how anxiety is generated through the circulation of topics, situations, and subjects. In contrast to my archive of literally hundreds of advice books, these chapters draw on select representative examples from mid-century fiction and life-writing. This allows me to focus on more intricate aspects of these genres' patternings, but also to acknowledge the different weight historically that has been given to literary versus non-literary texts.

In chapter 3 I emphasize the temporality of anxiety. In "Probability and Premature Death: Child Mortality, Prolepsis, and the Serial Novel," I argue that nineteenth-century representations of infant and child death operate by a proleptic logic, importing future probable tragedy into the present emotional moment. Little Nell's death in Charles Dickens's *The Old Curiosity Shop* (1840–1841) offers a paradigmatic example of this. Despite the fact that Nell is actually a young teen, Dickens's infantilization of her along with the serialized postponement of her death—always dreaded and yet almost always deferred—attaches prolepsis to child death. Advice literature takes up and transforms this suspenseful logic, affording motherhood as a kind of statistical stress through its relentless association of the aggregated likelihood of babies and children dying with maternal ignorance (see Woodward). This narrative patterning is then reinforced and extended in the writing of mothers watching their children die: *The Life of Mrs. Sherwood* (1854) and *Catharine and Craufurd Tait* (1879) lament mortal illness, seeking to reconcile faith in God's preordained plan with the writers' desperate desire to save their children. Both in the case of Mary Martha Sherwood, two of whose children died of whooping cough (also known as pertussis) and dysentery in British India in the early 1800s; and in the case of Catharine Tait, five of whose seven children died of scarlet fever over the course of a single month of 1855, narratives of religious faith offer comfort while at the same time reinforcing the proleptic fatalism of the other genres. In conclusion, I briefly consider the case of Elizabeth Gaskell and *Mary Barton* (1847), the novel she famously wrote to work through her deep sadness after her nine-month-old son's death from scarlet fever. That novel's critical and yet fatalistic depiction of the mortality of working-class children further associates the death of a beloved child with an obstructed agency that can anticipate but not prevent tragedy. Child death is thus an imminent and yet perpetually postponed narrative telos that is statistically probable, a proleptically experienced tragedy that defines maternal experience through her (doomed) responsibility to prevent it; and an axis of emotional identification across classes. By tying maternal identity to the preservation of child health, life, and morals, these genres thus work individually and in concert to attach the nurturing temporality of mother love to the fearful temporality of anxiety.

I then shift focus from temporal to spatial dimensions. In chapter 4, "Supervisory Attention and Maternal Management: Paralipsis, Paid Childcare, and Novelistic Perspective," I turn to questions of employment, race, and social class by taking up advice literature's persistent suspicion that paid caregivers might not be (or be doing) precisely what they are hired for. By focusing on the servants who provide "maternal" care—governesses and wet nurses—as paid employees, I draw attention to the role of feeling in domestic management. I argue that advice on how to limit servants' influence in the family is a rhetorical paralipsis that emphasizes the fundamental impossibility of doing so. In this chapter, I draw attention to direct uptake cycles, moving between advice literature and *The Life of Mrs. Sherwood* in order to see how worry, prescription, and struggle extend the rhetorical situation by positioning the paraliptic alterity of paid caregivers as both essential and dangerous to the White middle-class family. Predicated upon the possibility—if not likelihood—that all is not as it seems, and that the individual women hired to deliver childcare will do so with their own insights, values, and perspectives, this formation produces anxiety as the emotion that maintains elite women's attention on (and in) the home. Maternal anxiety thus becomes the productive suspicion of the managerial class, the affective motive for the supervision that maintains social and imperial control. *The Life of Mrs. Sherwood* enacts this with particular clarity in the colonial context, narrativizing the difficulties of managing a diverse staff made up of real people whose biases, beliefs, and conflicts have real (and perhaps fatal) consequences. I juxtapose these genres with three novels of the 1840s that feature paid caregivers—Anne Brontë's *Agnes Grey* (1847), Charlotte Brontë's *Jane Eyre* (1847), and Charles Dickens's *Dombey and Son* (1846–1848). As fictional autobiographies of governesses, *Jane Eyre* and *Agnes Grey* place the caregiver at center stage, giving readers the phenomenological experience of seeing things from the employee's (critical) perspective. *Dombey and Son*'s heteroglossic narrative also inhabits multiple perspectives, and takes as its emotional and narrative climax the likelihood and consequences of inadequate supervision. Together, these literary texts extend and deepen the spatialized attention advice literature and memoir cultivate by drawing attention to the impossibility of erasing employees' individual cultures, memories, values, and desires.

Questions of death collide with questions of supervision in chapter 5, "Godfrey's Cordial and an Opium Pill: Empire, Family, and Maternal Attention." In this chapter, I examine how warnings that paid caregivers would dose babies with opium or opiate-based patent medicines figure the middle-class home as porous, perpetually on the verge of extinguishing itself by the very structures on which it relies for social and physical reproduction. Emphasizing opium's role as a common medicine, exploitative and illegal global commodity, and synecdoche for class and racial difference, I show how the repetition of this warning across all three genres extends the vision of anxious maternity as never-ending supervision I developed in chapter 4. This chapter juxtaposes advice literature's warnings with narrative infant-doping episodes in *The Life of Mrs. Sherwood* and Charlotte Yonge's *The Daisy Chain* (1856). The dense symbolic and metonymic meanings of opium follow it as it circulates through the genre ecology, speaking the classed and racialized difference of paid caregivers in the British middle-class home. The warning invokes both the temporal and the spatial vigilance described in previous chapters; fictional and lived stories of infant-dosing enact both the danger and responses to it, narratively converting the vulnerability of White middle-class homes in Britain and British India into exigency for constant, productive, disembodied, and total authority of empire. This chapter thus identifies the perhaps paradoxical (re)productivity of maternal anxiety: Rather than marking the neurosis or failure of particular women, this emotion is precisely attached to the arrangement and control over temporal and spatial processes that is the managerial role in the neoliberal economy. Focusing the attention of those who identify as mothers to the future of the Child and the space of the domestic sphere, maternal anxiety is an essential, affective component of the patriarchal capitalism of empire, engineering its production and (re)production through genres and generations.

In the Coda, I reflect briefly on the theoretical implications of *Writing Maternity*'s argument that genre and affect are sutured to one another in uneven and stochastic alliance. Neither literary nor rhetorical genre theory has yet grappled with the challenges and complications literary texts pose for rhetorical readings. I seek to bridge this gap, briefly drawing out some of the fertile possibilities of rhetorical genre theory for literary scholars. What if, I wonder, instead of thinking that genres categorize or totalize or enact, we understand them to *advise?*

•

When did mothers start worrying so much? Why do they keep worrying so? Writing Maternity seeks to answer these intertwined questions by offering a rhetorical-literary history of maternal anxiety. While I'm confident that mothers worried well before the turn of the nineteenth century, the felt sense that good mothering *must* involve worry rose to dominance with the rise of the middle class, and is attached to its various material conditions. Maternal anxiety, as we will see, is complicit in reproductive futurism's relentless figuration of the fragile Child to enact the political; and in global capitalism's exploitative faith that some bodies (and babies) are more valuable than others. Emerging at a time when the Child is newly figured as both precious and vulnerable, the anxious mother is overwhelmed not simply by too many choices right now but also by the future implications of each decision.

As we will see, the persistent stickiness of "mother" and "worry" develops not simply through the emergence of a single genre, but through intergeneric circulations that iteratively constitute different versions of an anxious rhetorical situation that is nonetheless the same, arranging subjects, objects, and exigencies in ways that attach the emotion to the cultural formation. Advice literature, life writing, and narrative fiction circulate topics and forms, borrowing, repurposing, shifting, extending, and repatterning the rhetorical situation of motherhood, naturalizing its affect and collapsing the imagined and experiential differences between care and concern.

CHAPTER 2

Of Mothers and Medical Men

Advice as Genre

*A*DVICE TO A MOTHER. *Hints to Mothers. A Grandmother's Advice to Young Mothers. The Mother's Practical Guide.* The books themselves are small and relatively cheap. I've looked at 215 childrearing advice books published between 1740 and 1860. Most are a few hundred closely-printed pages and measure roughly 4.5 x 7.5 inches; technically, they are duo-decimos or octavos. The price lists I've located indicate that they sold for about sixpence. During the latter half of this period, book-buying became commonplace for the first time in British history; it makes sense that this genre couldn't develop until producing its material form was comparatively inexpensive. These are not family Bibles, imposing tomes meant to last generations. Nor are they solid volumes of novels by Sir Walter Scott or Jane Austen, traveling between vast numbers of readers through circulating libraries. But they are sturdier than the tracts printed to help educate and convert the poor, so it becomes easy to imagine them in regular use. One of these books would easily fit into an apron or skirt pocket—or rest on a table by an invalid's bed—within easy reach. Almost all of the texts include detailed tables of contents, and many have extensive indices. They are books for quick reference when circumstances call for a recipe or a recommendation: They don't seem to invite the immersive reading of leisurely afternoons. As Leah Price laments, the original users of books tend to leave few material traces (19). It's therefore unsurprising—if disappointing—that I can find no underlinings or marginal notes, no dog-eared corners or sentimental inscriptions. I cannot discern which prescriptions readers found the most or least useful. I wonder not only what the original readers *did* with these books, but how this historically new barrage of advice made them *feel*.

Historians caution against taking advice books' content as evidence for their impact in the world. Jay Mechling, for example, warned in 1975 that childrearing advice literature should be understood neither to represent contemporary childrearing practices nor to reliably articulate a time period's childrearing values. The genre itself has a tradition, he argues: "The simple fact is that *child-rearing manuals are the consequents not of child-rearing values but of child-rearing manual-writing values*" (53, emphasis in original). In other words, there are things advice books say because they are advice books, rather than because it was a pressing concern for parents at the time of a specific book's writing or publication. While we can trace changes in medical knowledge and doxa—the growing acceptance of chloroform for childbirth, advances in the best nutrition for bottle-fed babies—the books themselves do not reveal the extent to which their readers acceded to their self-conscious, even self-important, authority. In any case, the notion of a content- or values-based tradition doesn't help us understand the emotional impact of the emergence and rapid development of this genre. It doesn't explain a new genre's effect on *feelings*—or, for that matter, how the repetitive textual arrangement of doctor-advisor and mother-advisee contributed to the formation and sedimentation of those structural roles.

The content of the advice—how to interpret babies' cries, how to handle the fevers associated with teething, what to look for in a wet nurse—is part and parcel of the rhetorical situation the texts both respond to and enact.[1] The relatively abrupt historical emergence of this genre typified and thereby reified the rhetorical situation of a young mother in need of expert advice, carrying it forward as the genre reconstitutes its requisite exigence, audience, and purpose. Any particular text is a unique utterance, but its typical characteristics position audience and writers in a structural relationship—in this case, that of advisor and advisee. In this chapter, I read for childrearing advice literature's affective uptakes, showing how the genre sought to interpellate motherhood as an anxious subjectivity. I first offer a study of the genre as a whole—that is,

---

1. Nineteenth-century physicians understood teething as a dangerous time for infants, and recur to the likelihood of it bringing on dangerous fevers and even convulsions. In fact, it's likely that complications attributed to teething were from weaning (which typically occurs during the same age range), and which was a medically precarious time when children were likely to get infections from contaminated water, milk, or other foodstuffs. My thanks to Perri Klass for helping me think this through.

an exploration of its defining formal and rhetorical features and main topical foci. This discussion emphasizes how the genre enacts an intersubjective relationship between mother and doctor, and how that relationship typifies the rhetorical situation of motherhood as uncertain, in need of (expert) guidance, and therefore chronically anxious. I then turn to analyses of specific examples of the genre, identifying some of the ways individual enactments contribute to these anxious affordances.

Generic Prescription

Both Anne Freadman and M. M. Bakhtin emphasize the responsiveness of genre. Each genre gestures backwards in time, shaped by the utterances that have preceded it; and each gestures forwards, offering constraints and affordances that shape the avenues of possible response. In doing so, they are intersubjective, reliant on and enacting the common stocks of knowledge that make up the phenomenological lifeworld. In "The Origin of Speech Genres," Bakhtin writes:

> Both the composition and, particularly, the style of the utterance depend on those to whom the utterance is addressed, how the speaker (or writer) senses and imagines his addressees, and the force of their effect on the utterance. Each speech genre in each area of speech communication has its own typical conception of the addressee, and this defines it as a genre. (95)

A genre is thus shaped by the response(s) it anticipates—by how "the speaker (*or writer*) senses and imagines" those who hear or read the words. Freadman's notion of *uptake* builds on this logically, as it is rooted in an understanding of genre as not inhering in individual texts (or categories of texts) but in pairs— in the same way that the game of tennis consists not in the exchange of balls but in the exchange of shots ("Tennis" 43–44). The possibilities of any individual shot, she explains, are constrained and enabled by the shot that preceded it and that it now returns: Genre (shot) is always interactive, always crucially shaped by its position in a Bakhtinian chain of utterances. Building explicitly on J. L. Austin's work, Freadman calls the possibilities allowed by one shot for the next "uptake" (in the sense that one or more of those possibilities is "taken up"). *Uptake* thus names the role genre plays in the social, rhetorical, intertextual, and intergeneric circulation of utterances (see also "Uptake"). The uptake *profile* of a genre is the range of appropriate responses it delimits (Bawarshi and Reiff 86).

The concept of uptake has had particular traction in rhetorical theory because of how it helps us name and theorize relationships between genres and, as a result, the iterative relationships between speakers or writers and audiences. Dylan Dryer has pointed out that uptake's very popularity has led to significant imprecision in its usage, in part as a result of the field's principled understanding of genre as a flexible term—as category and social action, genre is both noun and verb. In "Disambiguating Uptake," Dryer distinguishes between several aspects of uptake; for my purposes right now, the most significant of these are a genre's *uptake affordances*—the responsive possibilities and constraints it encodes—and its *uptake captures*—its cognitive or affective *effects* on the audience that then generates some sort of response (65–66). If we recall my example in chapter 1 of *Two Acquaintances Running Into One Another,* the *uptake affordances* are the generic possibilities A's greeting makes possible for B's response (a return greeting, an invitation to pause and chat, a ghosting, and so on); the *uptake captures,* on the other hand, include how being hailed makes B feel (happy, surprised to be recognized, alarmed, embarrassed, and so on).[2]

Rhetorical genre studies has tended to emphasize the ways in which genres shape *actors,* who are sometimes glossed as the "users" of genres; I want to emphasize another significant implication—how genres are shaped by and therefore shape those who *receive* them, whether we consider them readers, audience, or addressees; rhetorically invoked or existing historically.[3] I therefore draw on both uptake theory and Bakhtin's work emphasizing the relationality of genre and the extent to which any genre is defined by its "typical conception of the addressee" (Bakhtin 95). Childrearing advice literature is shaped as a genre by its uptake affordances, by the responsive stance it enacts for an audience in relation to the text itself. This relationship is hierarchical; the relationship between text and addressee is homologous to that between expert medical practitioner and inexpert maternal reader. Over the course of the genre's first fifty years, it goes from addressing male audiences—both medical and lay—to addressing a female—and specifically maternal—one. We

---

2. Dryer also identifies *uptake artifacts* (the genres produced in response to a particular genre—in this case the greeting itself); *uptake enactments* (the speaker's or writer's act of producing such a genre—in this case, the *act* of greeting); and *uptake residues* (the long-term naturalization of affordances and captures, which shape cultural and personals scripts, patterns, memories, and other phenomena—for example, whether it's appropriate to bow or wave when hailed on the street by an acquaintance; or whether being singled out in such a way makes you happy or scared).

3. See Applegarth, "Bodily Scripts"; Bawarshi, *Genre* and "Between Genres"; Bazerman, *Shaping Written Knowledge*; Berkenkotter and Huckin; Brandt; Emmons, "Uptake"; Nowacek; Spinuzzi.

can see this shift happen early in the period: William Cadogan's 1748 *Essay* is offered "in a Letter to one of the Governors of the Foundling Hospital" while Hugh Smith's 1767 advice is a set of *Letters to Married Women*. If in the 1740s childrearing advice was addressed to men but circulated among women, by 1840 it was the reverse; Andrew Combe writes that his *Treatise on the Physiological and Moral Management of Infancy* is addressed "chiefly to parents" and also to "the younger and more inexperienced members of the medical profession" (xix). The titles stipulate audience clearly. There is *Advice to the Young Mother* and *Advice to Young Mothers,* as well as *Advice to Mothers* and *Advice to Wives.* One author offers *Instructions to Mothers and Nurses* while another offers *A Guide to Mothers and Nurses* and a third tenders *Hints to Mothers.* Some books—such as *The Mother's Medical Assistant* or even *The Mother's Medical Guardian*—offer themselves as explicit substitutes for embodied medical attendants.[4]

The titles alone do significant work to frame the rhetorical situation, defining not only the relationship between text/author and reader but also the exigency that brings the reader in: To read the book, after all, is to seek information, knowledge, or insight that one doesn't possess. To advise is to "give guidance or suggestions . . . as to the best course of action" or "to counsel" (*OED*). The action relies on inequality: For the counsel to be worth anything, the advisor must have knowledge or insight that the advisee lacks (and from which they may benefit). Although Samuel Johnson's first definition of *advice* emphasizes that it "may be given by equals or inferiors," it seems that he understands this strictly in terms of social status. His definition of the noun emphasizes "counsel" and "instruction"; that of the verb emphasizes the provision of information.

Medical texts specify whether or not the author has an M.D. (the degree of physicians but not surgeons), as well as membership in the Royal Colleges of Physicians and Surgeons, as appropriate. Frequently they also include mention of specific hospitals and other sites of practice. For example:

> Thomas Bull, M.D., Physician-Accoucheur to the Finsbury Midwifery Institution; and Lecturer on Midwifery, and on the Diseases of Women and Children.
>
> Pye Henry Chavassse, Member of the Royal College of Surgeons, London.

---

4. Respectively: *Advice to the Young Mother in the Management of Herself and Infant* by a Member of the Royal College of Surgeons; Moore; Chavasse, *Mothers* and *Wives;* Kennedy; Jenner; Bull, *Hints;* Clarke; and Vandeburgh.

Andrew Combe, M.D., Fellow of the Royal College of Physicians of Edinburgh, Physician Extraordinary in Scotland to the Queen, and Consulting Physician to the King and Queen of the Belgians.

H. H. Goodeve, M.D., M.R.C.S.L., Professor of Midwifery, &c. Medical College, Calcutta.

Medical texts without named authors specify some professional credential: The
anonymous *A Domestic Guide to Mothers in India* describes its author as "a
medical practitioner of several years' experience in India." Texts by nonmedical authors still assign the text authority over its readers: In the case of *Advice
to Young Mothers on the Physical Education of Children. By a Grandmother*,
that of age and experience. Across the genre, titles and author-descriptions
are formal elements that assert the dominance of text over audience before
a reader has begun examining the actual content of the book. These paratextual elements draw on and reinforce multiple hierarchical relationships:
between expert and novice, between experience and inexperience, between
age and youth. Explicitly medically authored texts in particular elevate male
over female knowledge and rely on the authority of the professional over that
of the amateur. Instead of competing, these hierarchical forms reinforce one
another. Texts with female authors similarly invoke the writers' authority,
drawing on maternal experience rather than medical training. Although these
female-authored books complicate elements of the rhetorical situation that I
lay out here, they largely conform to the features of the genre more generally,
particularly the subordination of readerly to textual expertise. To pick up or
purchase one of these books is to admit that there is knowledge you need—or
might need—but don't already have.

The books' prefatory self-justifications elaborate this exigency more fully.
Most books strategically emphasize the absence of similar advice, projecting
an information vacuum onto their readers' rhetorical situation. "Many valuable works are extant," notes the anonymous medical author of *Advice to the
Young Mother* in 1821, "but they are either too voluminous, or not adapted
to the general reader" (v). Pye Henry Chavasse and Andrew Combe echo
this concern roughly two decades later: Although both authors concede that
many other texts had already been published, "none . . . have been sufficiently
explicit, or have entered enough into minutiae" and "few of them are cal-
culated to supply parents with the kind of information which . . . is especially needed" (Chavasse, *Mothers* iii–iv; Combe xv). Every individual work
promises more accessible and precise information, suggesting an asymptotic
relationship between pediatric knowledge and maternal need. Thomas Bull's

Maternal Management (1840) goes beyond this, emphasizing the physical consequences of not knowing enough:

> The young and inexperienced mother . . . with that information which the
> experience and observation of some years convince the author, young moth-
> ers, almost without any exception, do not possess; and yet, from ignorance
> of which, the constitution of many an infant has received irreparable injury,
> and life itself but too frequently fallen a sacrifice. (v)

Bull opposes reader and author, mother and doctor: Her "inexperience" contrasts with his "experience," her "ignorance" and "youth" (the latter repeated twice) with his "observation of some years." The final clause makes the stakes clear, as children are harmed "irreparably," with death as the result. Here—as is typical—women's lack of essential knowledge is opposed to the professional expertise that saves lives. Prefatory moves such as this not only make the hierarchy between mother and medical man explicit but also use the fragility of infant life as the urgent circumstance that motivates both writing and reading. (I take this topic up in more detail in the next chapter.)

The genre thus creates a rhetorical situation in which ignorant mothers seek medical advice in order to save the lives of their children. Reading, apparently, will ameliorate their deadly lack of knowledge and experience. In doing so, it moves information about pregnancy and childcare from the realm of female experience to that of medical scientific knowledge and inserts—or tries to insert—a textual authority into the daily, repetitive work of childrearing. The genre thus interestingly and totally elides the possible presence of older women in the young mother's home. Its characterization of its readers as uninformed and likely to make deadly mistakes rhetorically isolates them: These mothers do not, apparently, have knowledgeable mothers or grandmothers or aunts to whom to turn; they apparently do not live within easy range of sisters or female cousins who have already given birth and raised babies. When they are cautioned against taking the advice of older women, that advice is most often associated with hired nurses rather than relatives: *Advice to a Young Mother* explains that it hopes that through its intervention, "the trammels of ignorance (in nurses) may be broken" (v). These ignorant young mothers are thus decidedly middle class—able to employ servants— and perhaps living in newly isolated nuclear family units. Ruth Perry has argued persuasively that the eighteenth century saw a shift from the consanguineal to the conjugal family as an individual's primary kin group, and that this both rendered young women more vulnerable economically and separated them more decisively from their natal families upon marriage (*Novel Relations* 38–77). In the rhetoric of childrearing advice literature, we see another consequence of that separation: the disruption of the transmission of childrearing knowledge between generations of women. Whether or not anxiety resulted from such changes in generational practice, the newly repetitive insistence in published material that new mothers in particular were ignorant and worried creates a kind of affective social reality.

Ann Hulbert's and Angela Davis's studies of twentieth-century childrearing advice books have emphasized the agonistic movement of the genre's content between poles of flexibility and control. By contrast, the nineteenth-century genre was characterized by overwhelming consensus, the appearance in publishing not of debate but of collective wisdom. This may be another manifestation of the professional conditions that facilitated the emergence of the genre itself—specifically, in this case, the rising status of medical knowledge in general, and specifically regarding the health and illnesses of infants and children. At the same time that motherhood was increasingly understood as a social institution organized around the paradoxically passive preservation of child life and cultivation of the national future, childhood itself was being created as a domain of expert and therefore male knowledge through the rise of pediatrics as a medical specialty. In a sense, this is a story about the "evolution" of the family doctor, who provides secularized pastoral care as well as medical advice (see Digby, *Evolution*). This process began in the eighteenth century with the medicalization of childbirth, with medical expertise extending not only to children's diseases but also to well-baby and child-care starting in the first quarter of the nineteenth. As Lisa Forman Cody, Anne Digby, and others have shown, the elaboration of this nurturing and knowledgeable persona was an essential aspect of professional medicine.[5]

Before the 1750s, Cody explains, pregnancy and childbirth were exclusively female domains, with knowledge rooted in women's social and bodily experience. Childbirth was framed as a time and space apart, guarded and overseen by a community of women; pregnancy was understood as beginning not with biological conception but with quickening—the moment when the

---

5. In the late eighteenth and early nineteenth centuries, the medical profession was organized very differently than it is now, or was even by the 1860s. Before 1858, there were loosely three categories of "medical men." In order of prestige and typical income they were: physicians, surgeons, and apothecaries. Lumped together as "medical men," then, we have categories significantly divided both in terms of class and in terms of medical paradigm. See Peterson, *Medical Profession* and M. J. D. Roberts on the professionalization of medicine; see Loudon as well as Digby's *Evolution* on the development of the general practitioner or family doctor; Sparks traces that figure's representation in literature. Brown discusses the importance of gentility in the development of medical professional identities.

pregnant woman first feels the fetus move; the course of labor was gauged in terms of felt experience (such as a laboring woman's need to push) rather than quantitative measures (such as cervical dilation). By the early nineteenth century, however, "a matrix of reproductive facts seemed to exist in the domain of obstetrics, population theory, political economy, and reproductive biology . . . and the wonder of birth [had] changed from being a feminine mystery to a simple, almost mechanical topic within the purview of modern science" (Cody 27).[6] Irvine Loudon has argued that it was the eighteenth century's man-midwives and surgeon-apothecaries that developed into the general practitioner and family doctor (2; see also Digby, *Making* 13–15).[7] Pediatrics soon followed obstetrics, both as an area of practice and as a domain of medical (male) versus experiential (female) knowledge.

This involved an effective extension of the medical market, as professional expertise—for which one paid a fee—came to be central to the care of illness and disease. Loudon cautions against reading the professionalization of medicine as a "coherent movement dedicated to the improvement of medical education and medical care" (2–3). Anne Digby's economic history emphasizes the importance of patient choice in the selection of medical attendant—or the decision not to have one. Her analysis therefore also underscores the early nineteenth-century tensions between "regular" and "irregular" medical attendants within that rubric; they were competing, quite literally, for patients' fees (*Making* 6–7; see also 199–224).[8] While fees for attending births were relatively low in the early nineteenth century, practices with a significant obstetric component were economically desirable: "Childbirth gave an entrée to the household and then to employment as both the woman's doctor and the family doctor" (Digby, *Making* 254; see also Peterson, *Medical Profession* 99–100). Personal interactions fostered an ongoing relationship: The doctor who is understanding when it comes to a headache is more likely to be called in for a fever; and sympathetic man-midwife is more likely to be consulted regarding an infant's rash.

The heterogeneous variety of medical professionals practicing in the early decades of the nineteenth century had reason to look widely for opportunities

6. For other accounts of the medicalization of childbirth and the replacement of midwives with doctors, see Donnison; Wilson. Lay provides a contemporary case study.

7. This gave rise to new representations of masculinity and fatherhood in the Georgian and Victorian period; the Victorian paterfamilias—and his professional counterpart, the family doctor—were loving, sympathetic, and emotionally invested (Cody 304–305; see also Sparks). The classic text on Victorian masculinity is Tosh.

8. This narrative follows the work of Roy and Dorothy Porter in focusing on the agency of individuals and families, and on the role of personal relationships and doctor-patient rapport in expanding practices. See *The Patient's Progress* and Roy Porter, "Reforming the Patient."

not just to make money but to expand their domain of influence and practice. At this time, doctors outnumbered available practices nearly two to one, by some counts (Brown 114). The profession had no mechanism by which to regulate the numbers of men qualifying for practice, and with the end of the Napoleonic Wars in 1815 a large number of newly discharged medics sought civilian practices (Digby, *Making* 43, 136–137).[9] As a result, there was a significant tension between entrepreneurship and professional disinterest in shaping medical identities in this context: Whether they were paid for their advice, a specific procedure, or for dispensing medicines, it was essential that patients' health and well-being motivate the prescription, not the doctor's need for a reliable income. Several historians have noted that publication may have been a way both to supplement an individual income and to expand the profession's sphere of influence, despite a countervailing emphasis on the noncommercial nature of medicine.[10] This was possible because industrialization had reduced the cost of paper and printing, along with speeding up printing processes, resulting in an "explosion of printed ephemera" (Penner and Sparks 4). In advertising a doctor's services in a competitive marketplace, the rhetorical construction of his medical persona takes on particular importance and meaning.

Projecting a knowledgeable demeanor in writing may well have been essential to expanding not only one's own but also the profession's sphere of influence and practice. Carolyn Steedman has noted with surprise the genre's consistent adherence to a relatively narrow set of recommendations (*Strange Dislocations* 67–68). Contemporary reviews routinely praise a specific publication's "good sense," a phrase that suggests particular texts confirmed the reviewers' own convictions: They note approvingly that the advice is "just such as might be expected from a sensible man" (Review of *Advice to a Mother, Dublin Quarterly Journal of Medical Science* 474). It seems that what was valued was an accessible style and the reproduction of medical doxa; while Bull's *Hints to Mothers* (1837) is praised for bearing "strongly the stamp of scientific and experimental knowledge," it is more common for such books to be lauded for offering advice that is "judicious," "plain [and] simple," and

---

9. Ackroyd et al. provide a comprehensive discussion of military medics during this period. Loudon discusses the implications of overcrowding at length; see 208–211. On the financial pressure facing early nineteenth-century medical men, and its role in shaping medical identity, see A. Tomkins.

10. Morrison approaches the question of textualized medical professional identity from another perspective, specifically focused on policing the boundaries of professional certification. Digby references medical authors (*Making* 43), as does Peterson (*Medical Profession* 252–254).

"marked throughout by good sense and good taste."[11] My own survey found strikingly little disagreement either in how to treat various illnesses and complaints or how to care for infants. Some of the consistency results from the common practice of reproducing and "updating" earlier authors' works, while some is the result of authors reproducing one another's text verbatim. Outright accusations and confessions of plagiarism appear to have occurred with some regularity. Sarah Boone has argued that there was substantial copying during this period in such inexpensive and popular genres; she tracks the phenomenon in sexual advice books, noting that in some cases the copying is silent—what would now be coded as outright plagiarism—while in others quoted material is marked but not attributed, and in still others attributed carefully, but so extensive that the work no longer meets current standards for appropriate originality.

This consistency of content does important rhetorical work. The circulation and reproduction of not just childrearing truths but earlier authors' language and anecdotes is one way the genre creates and perpetuates authoritative medical community. We can see this by tracing the afterlife of a warning against opiate medicines that first appeared in the edition of Michael Underwood's *A Treatise on the Diseases of Children* that was published in 1827 with additional "notes and observation" by Samuel Merriman.[12] (Such warnings are the focus of chapter 5.) At over 1000 pages, the Underwood-Merriman *Treatise* was clearly not intended for a lay audience; in addition to being overly technical for nonmedical readers, it would have been prohibitively expensive. It did, however, serve as a reference for many authors writing for the (female) public, as we can see by tracing quotations and references to this text in later publications. Merriman expands on Underwood's recommendations for the

---

11. See Review of *Hints to Mothers*, *The Monthly Review* 142; Review of *Advice to Mothers* and *Advice to Wives*, *Provincial Medical and Surgical Journal* 25; *The London Medical Review* (qtd. in Hardyment 42); and Review of *Hints to Mothers*, *British and Foreign Medical Review* 215, respectively.

12. Michael Underwood (1737–1820) was appointed to the Royal College of Physicians in 1784, the first physician-accoucheur to be so honored. His 1797 *Treatise on the Diseases of Children, with General Directions for the Management of Infants from Birth* has long been considered essential to the establishment of pediatrics as a medical specialty (see Colón; Nichols et al.). Underwood's *Treatise* went through at least six editions before his death in 1820, with posthumous editions appearing in 1827 (by Samuel Merriman), 1835 (by Marshall Hall), and 1846 (by Henry Davies). This was and remains a common practice: Pye Henry Chavasse's *Advice to Mothers* (1839) was posthumously reissued by George Carpenter in 1898 and 1906; by Thomas David Lister in 1906 and 1913; by an anonymous "leading physician" in 1911; and by Charles C. H. Chavasse in 1939 and 1948. Perhaps most famously in the twentieth and twenty-first centuries, Benjamin Spock's *Baby and Child Care* (1946), whose author died in 1998, was reissued with significant "updates" in 2004, 2012, and 2018.

treatment of "morbid snuffles," specifying not only that "recourse to opium has been attended with good effect" but suggesting specifically syrup of white poppies or a patent medicine called Dalby's Carminative (Underwood 52; Underwood and Merriman 133–134). He then adds a footnote paradoxically warning against such medicines that centers on an anecdote by a Dr. Clarke in which a woman "living near Fitzroy-square" not only accidentally kills her own baby with a dose of Godfrey's Cordial, but is also responsible for the death of a neighbor's child (134n; Godfrey's Cordial is another opiate patent medicine). Merriman avers that he was told this story by the surgeon called in to attend the second child, signing the footnote with his initials. This footnote is then included in its entirely in Marshall Hall's 1835 edition of Underwood's *Treatise* with two additional warnings appended to it.

This layering of medical opinion, so that an 1835 reader has the benefit of five physicians' opinions on a single page, explicitly depicts a kind of inter-generational medical conversation and consensus. In addition, both the original warning against opiates and the illustrative anecdote were subsequently recirculated by other authors. In *Maternal Management* (1840), Thomas Bull quotes the Godfrey's Cordial passage in full and provides a version of the textual history that I offer here. Fourteen years later, the story is included in a posthumous edition of Andrew Combe's *Treatise on the Physiological and Moral Management of Infancy* updated by James Coxe (see Combe and Coxe). Coxe includes a slightly abbreviated version of the anecdote without quotation, noting that "Dr. Merriman mentions one or two instructive examples" and citing Bull in a footnote. (There is no reference to Underwood.) These moments of citation help to establish the authority of a specific text and its recommendations by offering outside corroboration. In addition, the explicit creation of an intellectual lineage—such as when Bull cites Merriman's version of Underwood; or when Coxe, updating Combe, cites Bull's citation of Merriman—creates the impression that there is a long-standing, largely unanimous, professional community building medical knowledge. By enacting professional consensus through not just repetition but citation, the genre thus makes medical knowledge rhetorically reliable. In doing so, it helps to develop a kind of corporate, disciplinary authority for the field of pediatrics.

Anxious Uptakes

The genre's uptake affordances seem to leave little room for autonomy or agency: The confident hierarchy, the careful and extensive elaboration and enactment of medical authority, and the force of professional consensus seem to narrow the uptake profile relentlessly, rendering maternal readers Foucauldian docile bodies. But uptake is necessarily more complicated than this suggests, both because individual addressees have experiences and memories on which they draw in apperceiving the rhetorical situation, and because no extended utterance is wholly consistent or monologic. (Recall Kurtyka's example of a student made anxious by their previous experience of research assignments, English classes, or school.) The limits of the archive make it impossible for me to track enough readers' responses to this genre to safely generalize about uptake enactments. Instead, I turn to an illustrative area of content in order to show how the genre's rhetoric affords anxious uptake capture. One of the few direct responses I have found, which shows how the consensus I describe above was perceived, is the diary novelist Elizabeth Gaskell started in 1835, when her eldest child was six months old. In this diary, Gaskell describes Marianne's character and habits, as well as a range of her own childcare decisions and struggles: Marianne "goes to bed *awake*"; and her mother struggles with jealousy over the baby's fondness for her nurse, Betsy (51, 56). Early on, Gaskell puzzles over crying, writing with frustration that it "has been a great difficulty for me":

> Books do so differ. One says, "Do not let them have anything they cry for"; another (Mme Necker de Saussure, "Sur L'Education Progressive," the nicest book I have read on the subject) says: "Les larmes des enfans sont si ameres, la calme parfait de l'ame leur est si necessaire qu'il faut surtout epargner des larmes." So I had to make a rule for myself, and though I am afraid I have not kept to it quite as I ought, I still think it a good one. (52)

Contrary to her complaint that books "differ," my survey of texts published near the time Gaskell was writing at first seems to reveal less variety of professional opinion than she suggests. We can start with Gaskell's preferred source. Albertine Adrienne Necker de Saussure (1766–1841) was a Swiss educational theorist whose *Progressive Education* was published in volumes between 1828 and 1838; a partial English-language translation was published in 1835, with complete translations appearing between 1839 and 1843. (Hardyment notes that it circulated in both Britain and the United States before being translated [37].) I have not been able to locate an edition with precisely the language Gaskell quotes, which suggests that she is working from memory; the closest moment is: "*Le calme intérieur se produit au moyen du calme extérieur, et, pour cette raison entre mille, il est encore très nécessaire d'épargner des pleurs aux petits enfants.*"[13]

---

13. *L'éducation progressive, ou Étude du cours de la vie*, I: 170. As translated in the first English edition, published in 1839: "Inward tranquility is produced by outward tranquility; and for this reason, among many others, infants should, as much as possible, be prevented from

For Necker de Saussure, "cries are the true language of infancy" (I: 60). From this principle, she argues that "a watchful mother" should "always presume that there is a cause for the infant's tears" and should seek to identify it. This is strikingly similar to the "rule" Gaskell "makes for [her]self":

> We must consider that a cry is a child's only language for expressing its wants. It is its little way of saying, "I am hungry, I am very cold" . . . [if] it is to have the object for which it is crying, I would give it it *directly* . . . But if it is improper for it to obtain the object . . . I think it right to withhold it steadily. (52)

In addition to seeming deeply indebted to Necker de Saussure's thinking, Gaskell's approach seems humane and logical to twenty-first-century eyes. (It also aligns interestingly with the sympathetic desire for real communication between individuals and classes that her fiction demonstrates.) But this communicative theory of infant crying falls well within the orthodoxy of the time. In *Advice to Young Mothers. By a Grandmother* (1823), for example, Margaret King Moore writes that "the crying of an infant should never be disregarded; it is the sign of some pain, or some want which ought to be attended to" (60). In *A Treatise on the Physical and Medical Treatment of Children* (1825), William Dewees similarly emphasizes that crying is "intended very often as an appeal to the tenderness of the mother, when the child is impelled to make its necessities known" (114). Andrew Combe echoes this in his *Treatise*: An infant "can indicate its discomfort only by its cries . . . [C]rying ought to be considered simply as a sign of distress; . . . we should endeavor to discover the real exciting cause, and seek the surest means of relief in its immediate removal" (197–198).[14] While various authors provide different details regarding what the potential issues might be, there is consensus that the child's cries are a communicative act, indicating that something specific is wrong—and that the thing wrong should not always be assumed to be hunger.

But some of these same texts offer competing interpretations alongside this communicative theory of crying. Combe tells his readers that "as a passing

---

crying" (I: 69; subsequent references are to this edition). Gaskell's recollection of the passage translates to: "Children's tears are so bitter, the perfect calm of the soul is so necessary to them, that one must above all spare their weeping" (my translation).

14. Although Combe's *Treatise* was published after Gaskell kept her childrearing diary, it's evident in the text that she was influenced by Combe's earlier publication, *The Principles of Physiology Applied to the Preservation of Health* (1834): "It is quite astonishing to see the difference bodily feelings make in Marianne's temper & powers of endurance. I was in a great measure prepared for this by Combe's Physiology, but I had no idea how every change of temper might be deduced from some corresponding change in body" (55).

and occasional occurrence, [crying] serves to exercise and develop the lungs" (197), while Dewees suggests that babies should not always be hushed at all costs because tears are a "'waste gate' to an excess of excitability" (120). In the 1827 edition of *Treatise on the Diseases of Children,* Underwood and Merriman encapsulate these contradictions over the course of a few pages. Initially, they insist that that "moderate, and not too frequent crying . . . ought not to be alarming" (91), and note that a baby's first cries are in fact essential to its health. But in reflecting further on the question, they then note:

> The cries of infants, however, it must be confessed, are, very commonly, plaintive; and, as they seem to argue distress, cannot but create it in every person of sensibility around them, and merit a strict inquiry into the particular occasion of them. The nurse, therefore, who can with calmness hear an infant cry, without attempting to pacify it by every proper means, is a monster in human shape. (92–93)

The internal inconsistencies of these discussions of infant cries help us understand the stress Gaskell reveals with her frustrated, "Books do so differ." On the one hand, the authors emphasize the communicative nature of infant cries and the importance of careful interpretation of them—they don't *all* mean that the baby is hungry, after all. On the other hand, they present those same noises as important bodily, cardiovascular, and emotional release. There is no guidance in telling the two categories apart, in definitely knowing whether you should pay attention to a particular cry or ignore it. Understanding whether your baby needs food or a clean diaper, is being pricked by a pin, wants to roll over onto its other side, has gas, is sleepy, or quite simply needs to let off steam, appears both essential and difficult. There are many options, many apparently arbitrary signs, and yet a clear indication that experts have the key to the code—after all, they can enumerate and reflect on the different possibilities. Gaskell frets not because the books differ from one another, but because any one book offers competing diagnoses—and hence prescriptions—for the same issue in infant care.

The problem is both that of excess and that of opposition: The baby's cries can mean too many different things and they cannot mean some of those things at the same time. This opens up a variety of responsive possibilities—what we can call, following Dryer, uptake *enactments*—affording maternal agency by inviting, or perhaps forcing, readers like Gaskell to make their own "rules." The genre does this by enacting rhetorically the rapid mental movement of anxiety. If cries mean different things, they call for different actions. The cognitive work interpreting the cry is therefore forward-looking in that it requires forecasting the result of a particular response. Maternal agency lies both in creating a principle for action, as Gaskell does, and in moment-by-moment decisions in response to any particular cry. This excess of interpretive possibilities within a framework that at once insists on the importance of making the right choice and the difficulty of doing so without professional training is essential to the genre's cultivation of maternal anxiety. The authority of the author and text, and the projected "inexperience" (and hence helpless tendency to err) of the maternal reader conduce to make anxiety one of the most significant uptake captures.

Prescribing Anxiety

My analysis has hitherto emphasized continuities between texts in order to provide the portrait of a genre that was historically new in the 1820s and '30s, and whose emergence at that time made anxiety a definitional component of the new ideology of nurturing motherhood—and, as a result, a defining element of the experience of mother love. My portrait has emphasized not simply an area of content—early infant and well-baby care, and the nonprofessional diagnosis of and care for childhood diseases—but also the rhetorical situation that the genre enacts as a defining formal element. This rhetorical situation not only arranges mothers and doctors in hierarchical relation to one another, but saturates that structural relationship with anxiety. As genres (re)enact and typify situation, these relationships, subject positions, and emotional contexts become sticky. Individual enactments of a genre, in turn, allow us to see the genre's uptake affordances and afforded captures in more detail, as well as to better understand the variety of individual texts or utterances that fall under the generic umbrella.

This section first explores two of the genre's most common rhetorical strategies—lecture and question-and-answer—by analyzing examples from the two medical authors who dominated the mid-nineteenth-century market: Thomas Bull, author of *Hints to Mothers* (first published in 1837) and *Maternal Management* (first published in 1840); and Pye Henry Chavasse, whose *Advice to Mothers* (1839), *Advice to Wives* (1842), *Counsel to a Mother* (1869), and *Aphorisms on the Mental Culture and Training of a Child* (1872) created a kind of pediatric oeuvre. I then consider the complicated rhetorical relationship advice literature creates between maternal and medical authority, between deep day-to-day knowledge of a particular child and scientific knowledge about health and disease. Here, I also consider two books authored by women—Margaret King Moore's *Advice to Young Mothers. By a Grandmother*

(1823) and Mrs. J. Bakewell's *A Mother's Practical Guide* (1836)—in order to better understand the complexity of this rhetorical relationship and the emotions it mobilizes and (re)circulates.

I should note at the outset that the four authors were quite different. Pye Henry Chavasse (1810–1879) was a Birmingham surgeon in private practice. Thomas Bull (1807?–1858) was a London physician at the Finsbury Midwifery Institution. Mrs. J. Bakewell was an Evangelical writer and editor active from the 1830s to the 1860s. A generation older than the others, Margaret King Moore, Countess of Mount Cashell (c. 1772–1835), was an Anglo-Irish aristocrat with republican sympathies; she was notorious in her own lifetime for leaving her husband for another man, and for disguising herself as a man to attend medical school in Europe.[15] Chavasse and Bull's childrearing advice texts were among the most popular in the middle third of the nineteenth century (Hardyment 42–43; Steedman, *Strange Dislocations* 67–68). Moore's and Bakewell's books were less so, but were among the few by women to appear in multiple editions (two and three each, respectively). Chavasse's *Advice to a Mother* and *Advice to a Wife* were the only of these texts to be updated by other physician-authors after his death, à la Underwood. The latest editions appeared in 1948 and 1921, respectively.

MATERNAL MANAGEMENT'S ANXIOUS ADDRESS

Thomas Bull (1807?–1858) had a hospital-based practice in London from the 1830s through the 1850s. He appears to have obtained his medical degree from the University of St. Andrews, and was a licentiate of the Royal College of Physicians by 1842. His first publication—*Hints to Mothers* (1837)—built on his obstetrics practice at the Finsbury Midwifery Institution and promised to be a guide for young women "for the management of health during the period of Pregnancy, and in the Lying-in room." Between 1837 and 1861, *Hints to Mothers* went through thirteen editions, most of them advertising "careful revision" as well as expansion. The companion volume, a childrearing guide called *The Maternal Management of Children,* was first published in 1840 and went through seven editions before Bull's death in 1858. The *Gentleman's Magazine* reports Bull dying in Brighton on 31 May 1858, at the age of 51 years ("Deaths"

---

15. I follow the convention of library catalogs and refer to the author as Moore rather than by her title of Lady Mount Cashell.

92); it seems that this was two years after he retired from practice, since he stops appearing on the Royal College of Physicians membership lists in 1856.[16]

Bull's *Hints to Mothers* and *The Maternal Management of Children in Health and Disease* dominated the market in the 1840s and '50s, with editions of one or the other appearing, on average, every two years. Their rhetorical stance is both monologic and totalizing; the structure that of lecture or informational treatise: Both the menstruation and pregnancy guide (*Hints*) and the childrearing guide (*Maternal Management)* appear to provide comprehensive surveys of possible pitfalls and dangers in order to advise ways to avoid or address them. *Maternal Management*—my focus here—progresses from general care (infant diet, weaning, children's diets, sleep, clothing, and so forth) to home medicines (calomel, opiates) to teething and, finally, illness (with sections on "Hints for the Early Detection of Disease" and "On What Constitutes the Maternal Management of the Diseases of Children"). The 300-page text is detailed, informative, and apparently comprehensive. It moves rapidly from danger to danger, from symptom to illness, from common practice to deadly consequence.

After the introductory material positions the maternal readers as constantly on the verge of making deadly mistakes, the text itself forces her to move *in the act of reading* quickly and repetitively between puzzling present and tragic future. The book is divided into parts ("On the Dietetics of Infancy," "Weaning," and so on) and then into chapters (in the first section, for example, "Maternal Nursing" and "Wet-nurse Suckling"). Chapters are then subdivided further by topic: In "Maternal Nursing" these include "Plan of Suckling," "Deficiency of Milk," "The injurious Effects to Mother and Infant of undue and protracted Suckling," and "Mothers who ought never to suckle." Each topic is clearly marked and typically includes: (1) An opening statement of the guiding principle and its medical basis, sometimes articulated in negative (against common prejudices) and sometimes in positive terms; (2) a description of the severity of the problem, often in the form of an anecdote that illustrates the danger of not following the doctor's orders; and, finally, (3) the medical prescription, often with reiterated warnings about the consequences of not adhering to it properly.

16. I have found no full obituary for Bull; this is surprising, given his professional success. On the RCP's membership lists, his professional address is listed as Blackheath (rather than Finsbury Square) starting in 1853. In addition to his affiliation with the Finsbury Midwifery Institution (established in 1823 "for the relief of poor married women"), it seems that in 1839–40 Bull may have been connected to Charing Cross Hospital. My thanks to Amelia Walker (Wellcome Library), Sarah Hutton (National Archives), and Elaine Garrett (Royal College of Obstetricians and Gynaecologists) for their efforts in helping me track down this information.

A rhetorical pattern emerges: Precept & Medical Basis—Illustration—Prescription. While it is not followed formulaically throughout the text, the basic ingredients appear consistently and they work together to create a climate of danger and fear. Advice and prescriptions are offered throughout, intertwined with statements of precept and medical principles, and at times reiterated through or at the conclusion of the illustration. There is never a moment when following the doctors' orders does not seem both necessary and urgent. The frequent articulation of the core precept in negative terms—combating prejudice or common practices—reinforces this by making it seem that mothers are always on the verge of doing it wrong. In the opening paragraph to the section on "Air and Exercise," for example, Bull follows the precept that "nothing is so prejudicial to [the infant's] health as sleeping in an impure and heated atmosphere" with the warning that "the practice, therefore, of drawing thick curtains closely round the bed is highly pernicious" (83). This suggests that a caregiver's default impulse might be dangerous: She is likely to harm her child in trying to protect it from drafts. The illustrative anecdotes that punctuate the text—sometimes drawn from Bull's own practice, sometimes from published (and footnoted) accounts, and sometimes simply retold as the observations of colleagues—intensify the drama.

The dire consequences of not precisely following the doctor's orders are articulated with increasing vehemence as the text moves from general issues of childcare into a discussion of medicines and other treatments and, finally, the detection and "maternal management" of disease. The chapters on medicines typically open with a description of the treatment that includes some discussion of its utility, a strategy that combines precept with medical knowledge. This is then quickly followed by a warning that readers should be careful in administering this treatment, that they should be sure to follow medical instructions carefully. While this can seem self-evidently necessary in the case of opiate-based patent medicines such as Godfrey's Cordial, it seems strange in the case of "Sea Bathing" (120–123): "When sea bathing can be obtained," opens Bull, "it is even more conducive to the health of the child than the fresh water plunge bath" (120). The next paragraph warns, however, that "*as a remedy,* sea bathing is highly serviceable. Its employment, however, requires much caution, and great mischief is sometimes committed by its indiscriminate use" (121, emphasis in original). Detailed conditions and instructions follow: Sea bathing is good for some children, but not for others; be careful to minimize the shock of the cold water; don't let them stay in too long; have them exercise beforehand, but not too much; and so on.

These detailed instructions, perhaps paradoxically, create the same double bind we saw with crying. They require careful scrutiny of ambiguous evidence; doing so without clear guidelines increases anxiety and ultimately inculcates increased dependence on the doctor even as they putatively educate the mother to make her own decisions. (Is my child of "a delicate and feeble habit," for whom sea bathing is positively "dangerous"? Or is she "of a weak and relaxed habit, but free from organic disease," in which case it would be "highly useful"? [see 122–123].) Responding appropriately—that is, taking this advice up in action—seems impossible at the same time that it seems essential to the task of keeping children alive and well. Even from this partial representation of a much longer passage, it's clear that reading through such nominally informative and reassuring advice is overwhelming and anxious-making. The rapidity of the mind in weighing options, possibilities, and consequences as well as the collapse of past, present, and future in these moments of consideration (re)create this as a scene of anxiety. Maternal care is transmuted into maternal concern.

Childrearing advice literature purports to allay anxiety by providing information; it is putatively an educational genre, implying that with time and study the reader will be able to progress to independence of the text (and its author). But the impossibility of identifying the correct course of action in moments such as these undercuts this narrative: These are not medical textbooks, seeking to train independent practitioners. Instead, the rhetorical and substantive goal is to inculcate dependence: "The essential province of the mother is the prevention of disease, not its cure," writes Bull (184). He continues:

> Medical treatment, for its successful issue, is greatly dependent upon a careful, painstaking, and judicious maternal superintendence. No medical treatment can avail at any time, if directions be only partially carried out, or be negligently attended to; . . . [N]ot only is a firm and strict compliance with medical direction in the administration of remedies, of regimen, and general measures, necessary, but an unbiased, faithful, and full report of symptoms to the physician, when he visits his little patient, is of the first importance. (184–186)

To this end, Bull separates his discussion of each disease into sections about the disease and its treatment, on the one hand, and the "maternal management," on the other. The distinction between a mother's and a doctor's care is thus delineated clearly, with periodic reiterations in the latter sections of the importance of "the strictest obedience to the directions given" (289).

The anxious uptake captures *Maternal Management* affords are rooted in the apparently impossible choices it requires mothers to make, extrapolating from their children's histories their likely futures as a result of choices in the present. The lecture format reinforces this, in particular in its characteristically negative opening which projects mistakes or misjudgments onto its readers as exigence. Proceeding through the book—or turning to a particular topic for information—a reader is confronted by the accusation that they have already done something wrong. (Or, even more frequently, allowed their paid caregiver to do something that will damage their child's health, as I discuss in chapters 4 and 5.) The overwhelming content aligns with a dominating stance to figure maternal readers as ideally passive and docile, their attention focused on their children's current and future health in order to execute the doctor's orders.

ADVICE TO MOTHERS' WORRISOME QUESTIONS

Pye Henry Chavasse published his first guide for mothers as a relatively young man, after he had been a practicing surgeon for only six years. Born in 1810, he apprenticed with his cousin in Birmingham and then attended University College, London before becoming a licentiate of the Royal College of Surgeons in 1833 ("Obituary"). For most of his career, he combined authorship with his medical practice; he wrote, revised, expanded, and reissued a variety of pregnancy and childcare guides between 1839 and his death in 1879, five years after he had retired from the practice of medicine ("Obituary"). His first advice book was *Advice to Mothers on the Management of their Offspring* (1839), followed a few years later by *The Young Wife's and Mother's Book* (1842), which added information on pregnancy and lactation to the first volume's advice on the care of infants, children, and youth. A year later, these two categories of advice were separated into different volumes, with *Advice to Wives* and *Advice to Mothers* appearing as separate texts starting in 1843. Both books were reissued with revised and additional material regularly. In 1869 Chavasse added a second volume of childrearing advice (*Counsel to a Mother*) to his oeuvre as well as a collection of *Aphorisms* three years later. By his death in 1879, *Wives* had gone through twelve editions and *Mothers* had gone through thirteen.

Advice to Mothers and Advice to Wives were initially published in 1839 and 1842, respectively. Apparently less popular than Bull's *Hints to Mothers* and *Maternal Management* through the 1850s, they took over from Bull's texts after that author's death in 1858 and dominated the market thereafter. (Chavasse only published six editions total between 1839 and 1854, while updated editions of both books appeared roughly every two years between 1861 and 1879). Chavasse's considerable stylistic innovation was to offer his counsel dialogically, staged as question and answer between maternal reader and medical expert. This approach reinforces the hierarchical address of the genre, for all that dialogue is a putatively more open form. In Bull's *Maternal Management* the maternal readers are silent, apparently filled with dangerous beliefs, opinions, tendencies, and practices, but never speaking them directly; by contrast, Chavasse's reader appears *in* the text, eager for information and asking questions to get what she needs. But while the doctor's lines function as a part of a fully developed role, fitted out with a name, credentials, and paternalistic concern, the lines assigned to the maternal subject are assigned to the reader. The effect is to put readers in the position of the maternal interlocutor: After the text poses a question, we receive the answer. Any form of first-person narration aligns the reader more closely with the subjectivity of the narrator, and that alignment is reinforced in these texts by the absence of a specific character for the fictive mother who keeps interrogating her doctor. These scripted exchanges are subject positions rather than subjectivities, stripped to their relative rhetorical positions of advisor and advisee.[17] By rhetorically aligning the reader with the ignorant, nervous mother represented in the text, Chavasse delineates that subject position more fully than other contemporaries, extending the invocation of readerly anxiety farther into the textual equivalent of the fourth wall. This fictive maternal interlocutor speaks for us and *as* us, as we read. Phenomenologically, the interpellated questions draw us into this maternal subject's anxiety: We anticipate possible dangers with her, moving rapidly between present and future, and between possible outcomes.

The first edition of *Advice to Mothers* is 148 pages long and consists of 203 questions and their answers; subsequent editions were longer and had more exchanges between fictive mother and authorial medical man. Unsurprisingly, these individual items invite advice on issues that range from the everyday to the deadly, the obsessively specific to the global, as this sampling shows:

> 1.—*Question.* Is the new-born infant to be washed, for the first time, in *warm* or *cold* water? (21)
>
> 21.—*Q.* What should be the diet of a wet nurse or of a mother who is suckling? (34)
>
> 35.—*Q.* At what time does dentition commence? (42)
>
> 62.—*Q.* What is the cause of Hiccup, and what is its treatment? (59)
>
> 86.—*Q.* Are you partial to puddings for children? (75)

---

17. My analysis assumes that we do not already know how the doctor is likely to answer the questions; reading Chavasse's texts with that information already in mind, as contemporary reviewers did, seems to require ignoring the rhetorical form of the questions themselves, and treating them more as topic headings.

108.—Q. Have you any more hints to offer conducive to the well-doing of my child? (83)

142.—Q. How may worms be prevented from infesting children's bowels? (105)

185.—Q. What profession or trade would you recommend a youth of a con-sumptive habit to follow? (131)

Even without the answers, we can see—as we saw in Bull's advice about sea bathing as well as the discussions of crying, above—that every bodily detail and aspect of the daily routine must be scrutinized for its contribution to the child's continued health (or the threat it poses to it). The questions also create a believable fictive frame. The format is convincing even if, upon closer inspection, some of the questions themselves seem staged. As a surgeon with a general practice, it was indeed inevitable that Chavasse routinely answered his patients' questions, some of which must have been minutely detailed, and some of which doubtless revealed blanket ignorance. If we understand these questions as representing a variety of interlocutors, they seem less overwhelming; the effect of the format, however, is for that multiplicity to condense, and for the interlocutor to seem—and to make us feel—like a single individual shaped entirely by her need for information. (Tellingly, with the fourth edition Chavasse silently consolidated the referent in his title: Instead of *Advice to Mothers*, in 1852 and thereafter he offered *Advice to a Mother*.)

Roughly one quarter of the questions in the first edition are what we might call open or informational questions, inviting or even requesting expert opinion or knowledge.[18] These sorts of questions bring the maternal reader into the text as a simple device to justify the delivery of information and operate much as topic headings do in other texts: "What are the symptoms of Red Gum?" initiates a description of what we now call *erethyma toxicum neonatorum* (a benign and self-limiting rash that primarily occurs in healthy newborns); "When does dentition commence?" is taken up as a developmental and physiological discussion of teething; "Have you any general observations to make on the washing of a new-born infant?" invites the delivery of basic and very general information (60, 42, 22). The lack of knowledge that moti-

18. I coded four different types of questions in the first edition of *Advice to Mothers*: (1) *open questions*, which invite the doctor to give his opinion on a general topic (12%, or 25); (2) *informational questions*, which seem to ask for facts rather than medical opinions (typically the symptoms associated with or causes of a particular illness) (14%, or 29); (3) *specific questions*, which typically seem to have a correct or desired answer embedded within them (28% or 56); and (4) *requests for recommendations* (50%, or 101), which ask the doctor for his opinion on how to handle a particular issue but do not embed a possible answer. The total number of questions in *Advice to Mothers* is 203, but some were counted in multiple categories.

vates the genre as a whole is thus dramatized; such questions project the fictive interlocutor's blanket ignorance onto the reader and reinforce the generic conviction that every mother is "liable to fall into prejudices and mistakes, and consequent dangers . . . from the want of some little work to guide her" (Chavasse iii). By consolidating the questions and concerns of the addressed readers (plural) into the questions and concerns of a single invoked readerly position, Chavasse narrows the profile of uptake captures available.

The typical addressee of advice literature is not simply uninformed, however. Her ignorance is coupled with enough self-awareness to seek answers— to do research, buy books, and ask specific questions of the experts. Nearly 50% of Chavasse's questions dramatize this rhetorical act of requesting a recommendation. For example:

> 7.—Q. Sometimes the navel is a little sore after the navel string comes away: what should be done? (24)
>
> 100.—Q. When a child is four or five years old, have you any objection to tea? (80)
>
> 130.—Q. When a child is delicate, and his body is gradually wasting away without any assignable cause, and where the stomach rejects all food that is taken, what plan can be adopted likely to support the child's strength, and thus, probably, be the means of saving the child's life? (95)
>
> 159.—Q. When should a girl begin to wear stays? (118)
>
> 199.—Q. How may Chlorosis [hypochromic anemia] be prevented? (145)

While some of these questions require simple yes/no or either/or responses (as in Question 100), most often they are requests for prescriptions—for specific instructions telling the mother what to do both in everyday care and in cases of illness: What to do when the umbilical cord falls off? When can a girl start wearing stays? What treatment for chlorosis? *How do you save a child's life?* Chavasse's text makes both necessary and startling juxtapositions; information about how to diagnose a disease is almost always followed by or combined with a prescription for how to treat it, and routine information about how to care for a child on a daily basis is periodically and abruptly interrupted by warnings that incorrect care can cause permanent damage. (Tea at the age of four or five, for example, "acts injuriously upon [a child's] delicate nervous system, and thus weakens the whole frame" [80].) It is unnervingly rare that the question itself explicitly indicates the possible gravity of the situation; the interlocutor reveals little awareness of danger, and the physician in response seems to take all issues of childcare as matters of life and death.

Even when the maternal reader is granted some knowledge, she is as likely as not to be guided by "prejudice" rather than reliable information. Fifty-six (28%) of Chavasse's questions suggest possible treatments, typically by presenting the doctor with a yes/no option: "Is it necessary to wash a new-born infant's head with brandy, to prevent him from taking cold?" (22). If we take this statement of practice as evidence of intention, Chavasse puts the interlocutor in the wrong roughly two-thirds of the time (in 38 out of 56 questions). At first glance, this seems to be a way for the medical expert to dismiss folk practices: Chavasse opposes washing newborns' heads with brandy (22) and wrapping the umbilical cord in a singed rag (23). He also argues against giving babies fruit while they are teething (45) and dismisses the fear that washing a child's head every morning will "make him more liable to cold, and weaken the sight" (70). As in the case of Bull's negative precepts, these questions and their answers consistently position the maternal reader in the wrong. As invoked by this text, mothers know little, and the little they do know is probably dangerous to the health of the child.

Chavasse's question-and-answer format thus affords the same anxious uptake capture as does Bull's lecture. In both cases, refusing to worry while reading this book is an act of resistance—one that, of course, admits the concern. In both cases, maternal ignorance appears the greatest danger threatening child health, and therefore (for the most part implicitly) not only the futures of those small citizens but the future of the nation. Rhetorically positioning maternal readers as perpetually on the verge of deadly error, childrearing advice literature focuses not just women's bodies and activity but also their attention and affective energies in the domestic sphere. These analyses of Bull's and Chavasse's texts have allowed us to see how the genre extends the hierarchical rhetorical situation it establishes through prefaces, titles, and other paratextual elements. Childrearing advice literature as a genre is thus in part defined by its simultaneous investments in replacing the authority of female practice with that of the medical profession and focusing female attention ever more narrowly on the realm in which they are no longer expert.

"Judicious" Mothers and Medical Men

This subordination of female to medical knowledge was neither simple nor uncontested, even within the genre. We can see this most clearly by bringing together discussions of the relationship(s) between mothers and medical men as portrayed in both male- and female-authored texts. The latter were neither common nor distinct enough to properly constitute a subgenre, but there are two cases that seem worthy of consideration: *Advice to Young Mothers on the Physical Education of their Children. By a Grandmother* by Margaret King Moore, Countess of Mount Cashell (1823, 1835), and *The Mother's Practical Guide in the Early Training of Her Children* by Mrs. J. Bakewell (1836, 1845, 1863). Like their male peers, female authors such as Moore and Bakewell have a vested—pecuniary and rhetorical—interest in establishing textual authority over the realm of childcare, and their advice is similarly formed by their typical addressee: the young, ignorant mother likely to make deadly mistakes. But in this increasingly competitive market, women authors insist that their own maternal experience sets them apart from the (male, medical) crowd. This is first evident in their prefatory claims, which preserve a place for the empirical if unscientific knowledge that comes from providing daily childcare. As I noted earlier, prior to this period pediatrics as a medical specialty could not be said to exist. In particular, well-baby care and "the prevention of disease" (Bull, *Maternal Management* 184) fell within the realm of female experience, rooted in practice-based knowledge that must have been primarily communicated orally between generations of caregivers working side by side.

While Moore and Bakewell are in generic alignment with the male-authored texts in the readership they invoke—ignorant young mothers in need of expert guidance—and the exigency they create—the fragility of child life—their subject positions complicate the hierarchical relationship between text and addressee. Moore's *Advice to Young Mothers* is offered as "by a Grandmother" and the first sentence of the Preface emphasizes that it is "*the work of an old woman*" (iii, emphasis in original). Both authors emphasize maternal experience rather than medical knowledge in their prefaces, thus maintaining the rhetorical hierarchy characteristic of the genre: Moore explains that, "having suckled many children, [I have] had the means of obtaining . . . a species of knowledge which professional men can derive only from the information of women" (iii–iv). Bakewell announces at the outset, "I am myself a mother" but also insists that the advice in her book does not draw solely on her own experience: "I have assiduously watched the conduct of other mothers . . . I have read with great attention many of the best works on the different branches of education" and "submitted [the manuscript] to the inspection of a medical gentleman, who gave it his unqualified and cordial approbation" (x, xi).

Moore was a public—or at least somewhat notorious—figure in the first third of the nineteenth century. (*A Guide to Young Mothers* does not seem to have been associated with her at that time.) The book was published when Moore was 51 years old and, as she claims, a grandmother; its anonymity kept it separate both from her other published works (including a series of pamphlets supporting Irish independence in 1799–1800) and from the notoriety of her romantic and marital choices. Born into the Anglo-Irish gentry in around 1772, Moore was educated by governesses, including Mary Wollstonecraft, before marrying Stephen Moore, Earl of Mount Cashell at the age of 19. (Wollstonecraft based the child in *Original Stories* on her; Moore credited Wollstonecraft as one of her significant influences.) After having seven children, Moore left her husband and family in 1804 to elope with George Tighe; they went by the surname Mason, after Wollstonecraft's fictional governess. Moore dressed as a man in order to attend medical school in Germany, and later ran a health clinic and studied surgery in Italy. During this time, she hosted her former governess's daughter and the young woman's husband, Mary Shelley and Percy Bysshe Shelley. With Tighe, Moore had an additional two children; they married in 1826, four years after her first husband's death. *A Guide for Young Mothers* was not published under her name until the year of her death in 1835. Reviews of the initial publication appear ignorant of the author's identity; they describe the author as being evidently "a very clever and a very well-informed old lady" and note appreciatively that *A Guide for Young Mothers* supplements the advice offered by "medical men; who cannot, however, be competent to furnish all the details which the subject [of childcare] requires."[19]

Bakewell, an Evangelical writer and educator, was active between 1836 and 1864. She edited and contributed fiction to the *British Mothers Magazine* from 1847 to 1864, and ran "an educational establishment for young ladies" in London until 1862 (qtd. in Law). *The Mother's Practical Guide in the Early Training of Her Children* was first published in 1836, with subsequent editions appearing in 1845 and 1862. Reviews of the first two editions describe it as "one of the best works yet published" and recommend it as being "worthy of careful perusal by parents" ("Physical Exercise of Children" 294). "Such works as this are much needed," notes that in the *Metropolitan Magazine*; "for though many and successful efforts have of late been made for the promotion of education, still, that particular branch which devolves upon a mother, has not been considered of sufficient importance" (407). *The Mother's Practical Guide* places more emphasis on the ideological importance of maternal care than the works of the other authors I discuss in detail; it also provides less information on childhood illness and more on moral training and early education.

The first edition of Moore's *Advice to Young Mothers* is over 400 pages long and provides brief introductory chapters on pregnancy and childbirth before offering comprehensive and detailed childcare guidance. This is divided roughly by age: Part I covers "Treatment of infants from their birth till after

---

19. See reviews of *Advice to Young Mothers* in *Monthly Review* ("Education") and *Lady's Monthly Museum*. I've drawn this brief synopsis of Moore's biography from Todd; Garman; and Gordon.

two months old"; Part II from two months until two years; and Part III after the age of two. Part IV, accounting for more than half of the total length, discusses "diseases common to children of all ages," and proceeds from fevers and "eruptive fevers," to diarrhea and dysentery, to scrofula and rickets.[20] As in the books by medical men, there is minimal treatment of moral training or education. By contrast, those categories form the bulk of Bakewell's 250-page *The Mother's Practical Guide* (1836). Although Bakewell offers "advice to the expectant mother" in the second chapter, she moves more quickly through the physical care of infants and spends the bulk of the volume discussing the training and physical care of children over the age of twenty months. This includes not only sleep, food, clothing, and physical exercise but also religious training, discipline, and how to handle the death of a child.

Bakewell explicitly defers to medical authority. We see this in the prefatory note that an unnamed "medical gentleman" has inspected and approved the guidance she offers specifically about physical education (xi). In the Preface to the second edition, she reiterates this process with a difference: "The corrected copy has been submitted to a Medical Gentleman of this town, who is himself a Father" (xi–xii). *The Mother's Practical Guide,* unusually for my sample, does not include discussion of specific childhood illnesses. Bakewell explains that she defers discussion of disease entirely to the medical profession: "Convinced, as I am, that none but Medical Professors can with propriety write on these subjects, I have studiously endeavoured to avoid encroaching on their department" (xii). This explicit deference to medical authority both in what Bakewell includes and in what she has chosen to omit is part of a rhetorical strategy that cedes territory in order to consolidate ownership over a particular domain. Conceding expertise in the physical realm of childcare to the medical profession, she reinforces maternal precedence in the moral and emotional realm. Bakewell emphasizes that her advice draws not only on her own experience mothering but also her observation of "the conduct of other mothers in their young families" (x). Rather than competing with medical advice, she emphasizes a market niche that she attempts to fill: "I have not met with one [treatise], *written by a mother,* that has comprised what seemed to me the requisite directions for the *early* training of children" (xi, emphasis in original). Reviews of the book also value this perspective, noting that "such works as this are much needed" (*Metropolitan* 407).

Bakewell's approach embraces the logic of separate spheres. Rather than setting maternal knowledge against medical expertise, she elevates moral

---

20. Also known as the King's evil, scrofula is an infection of the lymph nodes caused by tuberculous or nontuberculous mycobacteria. It is characterized by abscesses in the neck. Rickets, typically the result of vitamin D deficiency, results in weak or soft bones.

training to the same level of importance as physical care: It is not enough, she contends, to simply keep the children alive and healthy. Her title promises "practical" guidance across the realms of "physical, intellectual, and moral education"; and the epigraph to the book articulates the temporal principle that unifies these three domains of childrearing: "Train up a child in the way he should go, and when he is old he will not depart from it" (Proverbs 22:6). This sets the focus. The goal of Bakewell's text is not simply to advise mothers on how to protect their children from illness and ill-health; it is to "lay . . . the foundation" of health *and* morality for their future lives (x):

> It is during infancy and early childhood that those impressions are most easily made which are necessary to the development and cultivation of the mental faculties and affections; it is during childhood that habits of observation, attention, and obedience are to be formed, and that the principles of all the moral virtues are to be inculcated. (1)

This logic permeates the genre as a whole: Maternal care is important because it establishes the lifelong bodily, moral, and intellectual trajectory of the child. This takes up the eighteenth-century educational paradigm, modified by the Romantic Evangelical ideology of childhood, and creates a fantasy of a controllable future. Carefully raised children will not simply be healthy; they will reproduce in the future their parents' values and ambitions. The temporal meaning of the Child that underwrites reproductive futurism is thus mobilized here to reimagine maternal care. That care, therefore, forecasts future possibilities as though they result directly and solely from decisions and actions in the present moment. This mental movement in time, coinciding with the mental movement navigating double binds, focuses maternal attention and emotion on the domestic sphere and the figure of the Child. By elevating the importance of maternal childrearing at this ideologically future-oriented level, Bakewell thus extends the anxious temporality of the genre. The temporal horizon of maternal care and concern is extended indefinitely, as they are responsible not just for their children's mortal lives but their immortal souls.

Although *A Guide for Young Mothers* never explicitly reveals Moore's medical training, her authorial position confidently combines medical and maternal expertise. A generation older than the other authors in this quartet, Moore also seems to be drawing on late eighteenth-century paradigms of maternal *authority* rather than the early nineteenth-century framework of maternal *influence* that undergirds Bakewell's claim to distinctive maternal experience (see Davies). Insisting throughout the book that close adherence to her recommendations will allow families to avoid illness, discomfort, and physical frailty, Moore articulates a complicated relationship between maternal and medical authority. The hierarchy between scientific knowledge and day-to-day intimacy she presents is shifting rather than rigid:

> The disadvantages under which a medical man labours, in his attendance on infant patients, are many . . . but the greatest is the difficulty of obtaining accurate information from the sick . . . Even where a physician, by being the father of a numerous offspring, may appear to have had the best means of studying those maladies incident to the early years of man, it is impossible that he should ever have such experience of the momentary changes to which the infant frame is liable, as may be acquired by an observing mother or an attentive nurse; and which, were it combined with a moderate degree of scientific knowledge, would often prove the surest guide to the medical attendant. (v)

The "observing mother" and "attentive nurse" conjured here are themselves empiricists, watching and tracking symptoms over the long term. Even in a relatively narrow interpretation, this knowledge appears indispensable to the doctor, because it provides data that he cannot gain himself but which instrumentally shape his prescriptions for the child. Indeed, Moore later notes that physicians are often consulted too late, as a result of women's lack of medical knowledge.[21] More globally and ambitiously, however, she suggests that pediatrics as a field—even when supplemented by paternal experience—can never compete with the information and experience of the women who provide daily care. Her ideal caregiver is not the physician who is also a father, but the mother with medical training.

This challenge to male authority persists throughout *A Guide to Young Mothers*. Moore opposes her advocacy of gradual weaning, for example, to the more abrupt process she claims is recommended in some "medical books" (122). She routinely reveals her conviction that she has the authority to evaluate doctors and their advice by referring to "medical men of real merit" (ix) and emphasizing the importance of seeking "the assistance of a *really skilful* physician": "Be sure that he is a clever man before you consult him," she cau-

---

21. See vii. This was a characteristic lament of the genre, and one of the ways authors motivate their intervention in the field: The books, it was claimed, could educate mothers to be doctors' assistants, their proxies in the home. Chavasse's Preface to the 1852 edition of *Advice to a Mother* emphasizes this: "A medical man well knows, that it is much more satisfactory to treat the child of an *intelligent* than of an *ignorant* mother: that the former will enter into his views, and co-operate with him; while the latter will thwart him by her prejudices, and defeat him by her obstinacy" (vi–vii).

tions (83, emphasis in original; 352). At the same time, she cautions her readers against listening to "a vulgar apothecary, . . . an old nurse," or "ignorant pretenders" (xi, 83). This simultaneous reliance on and judgment of medical advice is enacted with particular formal repetition in the fourth section of the book, which is organized into chapters according to different diseases: fevers, smallpox, measles, scarlet fever, and so on. In each chapter Moore, like Bull, follows a consistent format. She begins with a detailed description of the characteristic symptoms that is either punctuated with or concluded by reference to the symptoms that indicate a sufficiently serious turn to call in medical expertise; this is then followed by detailed prescriptions for home treatment, including follow-up treatment after the initial crisis is passed. Moore is more explicit and direct about the symptoms that indicate an urgent need for professional expertise than either Chavasse or Bull. In discussing whooping cough, for example, she notes: "When there is great redness of the face, difficulty of breathing, or much fever, a professional man should be immediately consulted" (218). In a chapter on "Convulsions," Moore explains that she goes into so much detail for the sake of readers who cannot afford to regularly call in a qualified physician: In those cases, she explains, "it is but just to point out . . . the means of curing slight indispositions, and of retarding (and perhaps removing) danger in severe maladies" as well as "to mark the period when the aid of a physician must, if possible, be obtained" (83).

But while Moore's careful distinction between the respective provinces of mothers and "professional men" seems intended to empower her readers, particularly those who are less financially secure, it creates the same double binds as we saw in other texts' byzantine directions. Immediately after describing the whooping cough symptoms that require a doctor, Moore cautions that "appearances, however, are sometimes alarming to mothers when there is in fact no danger" (218). Although reassuring in tone, the effect is to make decisive, confident action more difficult. Once again, future outcomes proceed from current data and decisions, but the data are difficult to interpret—or difficult to recognize through the text's description. Even when maternal care has an authority comparable to that of the medical practitioner, the movement and temporality of care are anxious.

"Judicious" mothers and medical men are invoked throughout the genre as ideal cases, and "judicious" care is repeatedly imagined as not simply curing but preventing the diseases and difficulties endemic to life in early nineteenth-century Britain. In describing the different results of two siblings who both came down with scrofula, for example, Bull argues that early detection and "judicious medical treatment" might have prevented one child from becoming lame; in discussing scarlet fever, he insists that "by judicious treatment, the

duration and violence of the disease may be both shortened and greatly miti-
gated" (183, 249). Moore contends that "the most delicate infants may grow up
healthy, with constant and judicious attention" (358). She opposes the "learned
and judicious physician" to both the "vulgar apothecary" and the "old nurse"
(ix), echoing an earlier author's distinction between the "regular and judicious
practitioner" and "the illicit and confident pretender to medical knowledge"
(Grigg 305–306). Bakewell characterizes "every judicious thinking mother" as
"necessarily somewhat both of a philosopher and a metaphysician" (19).

Johnson's 1797 *Dictionary* defines *judicious* as "prudent; wise; skilful," and
we can see these various meanings operating here. The word is also offered to
help explain terms that reinforce these associations, while also adding conno-
tations of judgment and careful, detailed observation: It appears to help define
"clearsighted," "critical" (in the sense of "exact"), and "distinctive: having the
powerful to distinguish and discern." Moore credits her readers with both
the self-confidence and the financial security to be able to choose a doctor,
rather than simply accept the nearest or cheapest medical man available. They
therefore have a degree of agency that is unusual for the genre. In the final
chapter of *Advice to Young Mothers,* Moore initially underscores obedience to
medical orders: "When a physician is called to a sick child, it should be with
a full reliance on his skill, and a determination to follow his advice" (351). In
emphasizing that this is a conscious decision, Moore draws attention to the
agency involved in taking up prescriptions, agency that the genre otherwise
elides. As she continues, she extends this possibility:

> If, however, he should happen to prescribe any thing that the child par-
> ticularly dislikes, or which has before disagreed with it, explain all this, and
> a judicious practitioner will either substitute another mode of treatment
> equally applicable, or tell you if the case be such that no other than the
> medicines already directed can benefit. (351)

Here, the doctor's judgment—his judiciousness—manifests in his willing-
ness to concede that the mother's assessment is comparable in authority to his
own. Later Moore offers this formulation again: "When it is possible to save a
sick child from the pain of crying and agitating his nerves, it is always better
to do so; this may frequently be effected by changing the form of the medicine prescribed, which a judicious physician will always be willing to do, if it
be in his power" (355). The assessment of the caregiver—the individual who
administers the treatment—has an authority that is different from but comparable to that of the expertise of the physician. In life-threatening cases, Moore
emphasizes the importance of consulting with the physician and deferring to

his judgment; but these moments reveal the extent to which this is a case of conscious deferral and not the automatic docility of a trained body and mind. Although she cedes dominion over "expert" knowledge, she—like Bakewell, and unlike the male authors—reasserts female knowledge within the domestic sphere. Rather than marginalizing and infantilizing women, anxious domestic attention in the hands of female authors grants them authority.

Chavasse and Bull also acknowledge the possibility that a mother's perspective might differ from that of a medical man. Chavasse only includes eleven questions in which the fictive mother resists or challenges the doctor's orders; in every instance, the doctor reiterates and reemphasizes his point without compromise. In response to question 29, for example, "But vaccination does not always protect a child from smallpox?" (40), Chavasse concedes momentarily ("I grant you it does not always protect him") before insisting that the infection will be milder: The child who gets smallpox after vaccination "is seldom pitted, and very rarely dies" (40). The tone is reassuring, but indicates that the doctor has already considered every possibility. A more direct challenge receives a sterner response:

> Do you not consider that medical men are generally too apt to give larger doses of medicine, or order a greater number of leeches, to a child, from knowing how prone mothers are to administer less medicine, or apply fewer leeches, than have been ordered?
> Most certainly not. (97)

This is followed by more than three full pages of anecdotes demonstrating the deadly consequences that come "of disobeying a medical man's orders, or only adopting half his measures" (97). Such flashes of skepticism or resistance in the maternal interlocutor add realism to Chavasse's fictive frame, making that figure more effective as an invoked reader. They also provide occasion for the doctor to not just reiterate his recommendation but also underscore the stakes: In Chavasse's anecdotes illustrating the dangers of medical noncompliance, the child in question typically *dies* because the parents failed to follow the prescription.

Bull reiterates the deadly consequences of such failure and elaborates on the hierarchical partnership essential to the maintenance of child life and health. "Not only is a firm and strict compliance with medical directions in the administration of remedies, of regimen, and general measures, necessary," he insists, "but an unbiased, faithful, and full report of symptoms to the physician . . . is of the first importance" (185). An "unintentional but erroneous report of symptoms" can mislead the doctor, which may "prove seriously injurious to the welldoing of the patient" (185). He concludes: "The medical man cannot sit hour after hour watching symptoms; hence, the great importance of their being faithfully reported" (186). Bull both underscores Chavasse's insistence on "firm and strict compliance" with orders and suggests a respectful awareness of the knowledge accrued in "hour after hour" observation. But in Moore's formulation maternal observation and medical knowledge were both complementary and competitive; in his, a mother's information serves simply to assist the medical man, just as her action enacts his orders: "Careful and judicious maternal superintendence" "give[s] effect to the measures prescribed by the physician" (Bull v).

Genres, Uptakes, Ecologies

Advice can, of course, be taken, revised, ignored, and laughed at—often in strange combination. But the uptake profile of a genre nonetheless delimits a rhetorical and affective range, imposing a constraint that shapes the directionality of both acceptance and rejection, makes some avenues of response possible and others impossible, and renders some feelings more and some less likely. In examining childrearing advice literature's invocation of its readers, I have identified generic affordances—the formal and substantive deployment of hierarchy, the interpolation of an ignorant and maternalized addressee, and the repetition of scenes of significant future-oriented choice between options at once contradictory and nearly indistinguishable—that facilitate an anxious uptake capture, which in turn sutures worry to the scenes, situations, activities, and feelings of motherhood. Whether or not maternal readers took the advice these books offered, then, may well bear little correlation to the extent to which the cultural institution of motherhood came to be spoken of as needing it. As we have seen, advice literature's persistent and effective invocation of maternal anxiety relies on a complex representation of motherhood as a state of both professionalized knowledge and blanket dependence, of discerning, judicious judgment and indulgent, overwhelming love.

In addition to uptake affordances and captures, Dryer names *uptake residues* as an important and distinct category (66). These are the long-term naturalization of affordances and captures, which through sedimentation shape cultural and personal scripts, patterns, and memories—and through that process of sedimentation, constitute cultural formations (66–67). Uptake always implies at least a pair of genres, and I would argue that a single genre cannot take credit for a significant change in culture, or even a structure of feeling's increasing dominance. To understand maternal anxiety as a naturalized uptake residue, the next three chapters juxtapose advice literature with two other, at least putatively nonprescriptive, genres: the domestic novel and memoir. These chapters offer three studies of the genre ecology in order to illuminate the topical, rhetorical, and generic collisions that shape the structure of maternal feeling as it became dominant, and to emphasize the role of anxiety in that cultural formation. This also allows me to further theorize maternal anxiety itself, considering its temporal and spatial aspects as well as its productive role in middle-class, imperial identity. As we turn to consider how other genres participate in initiating and perpetuating the stickiness of maternal care and concern, we are looking not for direct uptake enactments but diffuse, oblique, rhizomatic, and circulatory connections, overlaps, and sedimentations. In each chapter, I seek to illuminate a particular aspect of maternal anxiety as it developed as part of the consolidation of middle-class motherhood as an institutionally sanctioned and sacralized role. Generic affordances shape the ways in which representations circulate through the genre ecology, naturalizing uptake residues and making them stick—to particular scenes, situations, roles, and objects . . . and to one another.

CHAPTER 3

=====

Probability and Premature Death

Child Mortality, Prolepsis, and the Serial Novel

A DVICE LITERATURE motivated its interventions into the female domains of pregnancy, birth, breastfeeding, and childcare in terms of the life and death of the child.[1] Pye Henry Chavasse's Preface to the first edition of *Advice to Mothers* (1839), for example, opens by invoking the axiomatic fragility of newborns: "When it is considered that the first years— nay, months—of an infant's life frequently determine whether he shall live . . . it would appear that too much attention cannot be paid to the subject" (iii). Mrs. J. Bakewell treats the subject at greater length in "Domestic Affliction," the penultimate chapter of *The Mother's Practical Guide in the Early Training of Her Children* (1836), confessing that she has "hitherto . . . spoken of the precious objects of maternal solicitude as though health and life were assured to them, if mothers only performed their duty" (198). Reminding readers of the limits of medical knowledge and maternal care—that babies and children do, in fact, die—Bakewell offers concrete advice, the consolations of religious faith, and an empathetic understanding of maternal grief and love. The last disrupts the narrative logics of the former, with expressions of proleptic grief interrupting both the scientific reassurance of following the doctor's orders and the fatalistic teleology of maintaining faith in God's will: "None but a mother, none but a bereaved mother, can conceive what a mother's feelings

---

1. This chapter is for Tamara, Mackenzie, and Anya.

are . . . And oh, when those accents can be heard no longer, . . . who can tell a mother's agony!" (202). By enacting a rhetorical situation in which experts are impelled to write by the urgent probability that children will otherwise (and in any case) die, advice literature forcefully directs maternal attention toward a hypothetical and threatening future. The genre anticipates future illness and death as already having occurred—or already being sure to occur—in the present moment in order to proleptically diagnose, discount, or somehow otherwise contain the tragedy.[2]

In turning to infant and child death, this chapter takes up advice literature's most consistently invoked exigency, the dire possibility that shapes the rhetorical situation, that motivates—at least within the fictive rhetorical frame—not only reading and writing the genre itself, but also the temporal orientation of maternal care and concern. We saw in the previous chapter how maternal ignorance was figured in advice literature as a mortal danger, an actual threat to children's health that could only be ameliorated by reliance on professional medical knowledge. The prospect of infants and children dying recurs throughout the genre, a material probability mobilized rhetorically. At times it appears as a specific and localized danger—it is something to consider in most discussions of childhood disease, from measles to scarlet fever to whooping cough. At other times it is normalized as part of a developmental stage of life: When children are teething or being weaned, for example. But it is also part of the overarching rhetorical context, a defining feature of the genre: Most of the advice books in my sample include at least a passing reference to persistently high rates of infant and child mortality, and most of those associate it with the failures of the children's day-to-day care.

"Mothers" are invoked as those who must—but perhaps cannot—keep their children alive. The proleptic experience of grief for a dead child *while the child is ill but still alive* transforms the present moment of maternal care by associating it with the likelihood of tragic failure. Maternal anxiety is the temporal inverse of Freudian mourning, making meaning from a future (rather than a past) tragedy that could already have been prevented, if only it had been anticipated earlier. In this chapter, I first explore how the attachment of anticipatory grief was rhetorically attached to the death of a beloved child by analyzing the serial affordances of Dickens's *The Old Curiosity Shop*, which appeared weekly from April 1840 through February 1841. I then return to advice literature, focusing on how that proleptic attention was attached to

---

2. This rhetorical sense of *prolepsis* extends the logic of its literary critical definition. While typically glossed as foreshadowing in literary analysis, rhetorical prolepsis involves crafting an argument such that possible objections are anticipated and disproved *before* they can fully develop.

maternal care, before turning to the fatalistically anxious memoirs of women whose children have died. With a concluding meditation on Elizabeth Gaskell's moving invocation in *Mary Barton* (1848) of the power of maternal "wishing" to keep a child alive when its time has come, I argue that the genre ecology structures the rhetorical situation of motherhood as one of anxious, resistant grief for the premature death of a child.

It seems that during much of this period there was an overall child mortality rate of 27–32%, and that this was consistent with previous centuries. Historical demographer Robert Woods argues that between the 1580s and 1940s, "in general, and from the best available estimates, it appears that 20 to 30 per cent of all live-born infants were likely to have died before reaching their first birthday, while 30 to 35 per cent would have died before reaching their tenth birthdays" (*Children* 44).[3] This stasis is perhaps surprising in that it happened during a period when overall life expectancy increased, and while material and highly publicized advances were being made in the realm of baby care and childhood disease: Breastfeeding rates started increasing in the 1750s, while smallpox mortality decreased in response to increased rates of vaccination after 1798 (Fildes, *Breasts* 115–117; Woods, *Demography* 251; Davenport et al.). In addition, the fertility rate increased during the second half of the eighteenth century (Woods, *Demography* 109–112); in that context, static infant and child mortality rates mean that more babies and children die. Between the 1750s and the 1820s, it came to be axiomatic that infant and child death *ought to be* preventable.[4] Invocations of the high rate—and preventable nature—of infant mortality are a generic feature of childrearing advice literature, justifying publication and exhorting maternal readers to employ the authors' colleagues (and perhaps themselves). Demographic facts are thus used simultaneously

---

3. Infant and child mortality rates are especially difficult to capture for the seventy years before 1840, when civil registration of births was legislated in England: Historical demographers have largely had to rely on parish registers, but the increase in nonconformity in the 1700s as well as massive population movement render these incomplete and unreliable. Wrigley et al.'s *English Population History from Family Reconstitution, 1580–1837* is one valuable resource but its data set includes only 26 rural parishes. Galley and Shelton draw on more regionally varied data in order to deepen the picture, as does Woods. Infant and child mortality rates were significantly higher in London and other urban centers, and among poorer families (Woods, *Children* 33–48; Galley and Shelton).

4. In *Centuries of Childhood*, Ariès offers what Woods glosses as "the parental indifference hypothesis," positing that before the seventeenth century the likelihood of children dying before their parents meant that people did not invest emotionally in their children (*Children* 9–10). While some scholars—most notably Lawrence Stone and Randolph Trumbach—took up and further popularized this hypothesis, it has long been challenged as a misleading oversimplification (see Pollock; Cunningham; Bailey). Woods summarizes this history in "Après la mort des enfants" in *Children Remembered*.

to justify serious scientific attention to a topic hitherto deemed too domestic, to idealize and sentimentalize motherhood, and to figure the helpless dependence of maternal care on medical expertise. Child death—as anecdote, statistic, or generalized probability—is a rhetorical trope that pulls mothers into a subservient alliance with medical men to protect the national future.

Serial Anxiety

Charles Dickens's early serial *The Old Curiosity Shop* (1840–1841) associates the temporality of anxiety with child death specifically, attaching readers' emotional investment in a character's future to the question of whether she will live or die. In this section, I argue that *Shop*'s serialized deferral of little Nell's death affords anxiety, contributing a temporal orientation to the genre ecology's suturing of that emotion to the scene and situation of motherhood. This novel is an ideal example of this because of its own indelible association with child death both during its publication and in its reception history. In her 2011 biography of Dickens, Claire Tomalin notes that "it is [Nell's] death that made [the novel's] fame" (114), glossing the observation of generations of scholars. (Theodor Adorno writes, for example, that "the novel is nothing but the story of Nell's sacrifice" [173].) I follow these critics in considering Nell Trent's death that of a child, despite the character's chronological age (13); it is, indeed, one of the most commented-upon literary child deaths, along with those of Paul Dombey (*Dombey and Son* [1846–48]), Jo (*Bleak House* [1852–53]), and Little Eva (*Uncle Tom's Cabin* [1851–52]).[5] *The Old Curiosity Shop* anticipates those others and offers a new narrative paradigm for the topic by combining, concentrating, and repurposing Romantic and Evangelical narratives of child death in a serial format (Winter 147–148). Nell's death was immediately controversial, with one reviewer complaining that the character "deserve[d] a better fate" and others writing publicly or privately of being overcome (qtd. in MacPike, "Part I" 34). At the conclusion of its serial run, *The Old Curiosity Shop* was selling 100,000 copies; whether readers liked or hated either the fact of Nell's death or the way Dickens lingers over it in the

---

5. See, for example, Lerner; Jalland. There is a historical logic in this—for all that it is also important to recall that the character is an adolescent—in that the term "infant" was frequently used for children under the age of seven in the nineteenth century, and "child" for any individual older than that but not yet deemed an adult. I would argue that the anxious anticipation that I map in *The Old Curiosity Shop* also operates in *Dombey and Son* and *Uncle Tom's Cabin*, among others, so that *Shop* is a specific instance of how serial fiction operated in the genre ecology to attach novelistic suspense to the proleptic temporality of anxiety.

final installment, then, it seems that the probability of her demise was motivating. In other words, the question of whether or not Nell would die kept Dickens's contemporaries anxiously awaiting, buying, and reading the next installment, wondering together whether or not Nell was already dead. *The Old Curiosity Shop* as a serial fiction patterns the probability of child death in temporally anxious terms.

Nell was at the center of both author and readers' interest in *Shop* from the beginning, although Dickens did not conceive of the plan to "murder" her until halfway through the novel (*Letters* 180). Dickens had not planned to write a novel in 1840, having decided to move away from the pressures (and lack of editorial autonomy) of serial publication and into editing a weekly periodical, *Master Humphrey's Clock*. But while the first issue sold well (70,000 copies), sales dropped off precipitously; "the public had [initially] flocked to *Master Humphrey* under the impression that it was another Dickens novel" (Johnson 1: 298). *The Old Curiosity Shop* begins in No. 4 (25 April 1840) as a standalone story, but in order to rescue sales Dickens brought the story back in No. 7 (16 May) and thereafter. The serial follows the always diminutive "little" Nell Trent and her grandfather from London through a precarious journey launched by the grandfather's gambling debts to the predatory, grotesque Quilp who repossesses the pair's home and shop, and whose continued desire for Nell motivates their continued flight. The novel cuts between their repeated frightened departures from what had seemed safe havens and the efforts of their pursuers to find them—both the alarming pursuit of Quilp and the attempted rescue missions undertaken by Kit Nubbles (their former servant) and the "single gentleman" later revealed to be the younger brother of Nell's grandfather. Roughly halfway through the novel Nell begins to fall ill—exhaustion, malnutrition, hypothermia—and her death is clearly foreshadowed long before it occurs in the opening to the final installment, which appeared on 6 February 1841.

Loralee MacPike's 1981 pair of articles, "The Old Cupiosity Shape" parts I and II, document the extent to which readers' responses to the novel since its publication have been divided along the lines of their feelings about little Nell and her sentimentalized deathbed scene. This focus has continued through the present, with more recent work variously arguing that rigorous historical contextualization mitigates accusations of "excessive" sentimentality; seeking to understand the function of the novel's emotional impact; or, most recently, using *Shop* to better understand the relation of feeling and literary form. Laurence Lerner argues that the emotional impact of Nell's death "derives from iconographic, pictorial elements and from the accumulating, pervasive atmosphere that leads us to think about death all through the book" (95). Similarly,

Helen Small suggests that the novel thematizes mourning for "young loved ones" quite early, aligning readers with the emotional activity of mourning and creating a world in which premature death is a fact of life (554). I follow William Lee Hughes in finding the novel's form saturated by affect, but where he reads the breaks between serial installments as instantiating pauses that disrupt the progressive relationality enacted by mourning, I contend that they afford the anxious uptake capture readers experienced, in Margaret Oliphant's words, as "def[ying] augury and cl[inging] to hope for her" (458). The emotional impact of Nell's death and the scene at her posthumous deathbed, then, lie less in Dickens's crafting of those images themselves than in the narratological anticipatory process that makes readers anxiously anticipate a probable but not certain tragedy. Rather than pauses, then, I see the breaks between installments as filled with anxious interpretive energy.

In *The Victorian Serial*, Linda K. Hughes and Michael Lund emphasize the temporality of the serial, which they cogently define as "a continuing story over an extended time with enforced interruptions" (1). In chapters on serial poetry as well as fiction, Hughes and Lund draw attention to the ways in which seriality shaped the reading experience, and how the affordances of the serial itself fostered certain practices and habits of mind in readers: The patience and persistence to continue reading over the course of a year or more (15–59); the relationship between forward progress and reflective, anticipatory pause in experiencing the week- or month-long wait for each new installment (59–109); and so on. Reading a novel serially radically extends the time period it takes—from a few weeks, say, to ten months in the case of *The Old Curiosity Shop*—fostering a differently intense engagement with the story as well as an enhanced sense of intimacy with the author. In addition, the periodic nature of serial publication patterns the reading experience to include pauses, as Mark W. Turner emphasizes: "Built into the notion of seriality is necessarily some conceptualization of waiting. The pause is a constitutive feature of periodical-ness, of all periodicities—there must be a break in time. What is important about this break is that it is the space which allows us to communicate" (193). We know that for Victorian readers, serial fictions were shared, communal experiences: Families read the latest installment aloud to one another, and copies were passed from hand to hand. Breaks or pauses in the story, then, stand as incitements to social reflection, curiosity, speculation, anticipation—and worry (Goodlad; Turner). Dickens's original readers lived with the probability that Nell would die for nearly four months, wondering from week to week whether or not she would have survived. Such prolonged anticipation of premature death attaches the surprise of prematurity to the apprehensive, Janus-faced emotion of anxiety.

The Old Curiosity Shop makes Nell's death a narrative probability roughly two-thirds of the way through the novel, in a three-installment sequence focused on her and her grandfather (Parts 29–31, published 17, 24, and 31 Oct. 1840).[6] I rehearse the plot steps in some detail in order to draw attention to how they play out over the breaks between installments. This sequence begins with chapters 42–43 (17 October), in which Nell discovers that her grandfather has continued gambling and that he is being pulled into a plot to rob their host, Mrs. Jarley. The two flee and find passage on a canal boat; Nell spends two nights on deck in bad weather. In the next installment (No. 30, chapters 44–45, 24 October), they come to an industrial town, where they find temporary shelter but continue on their journey. Dickens builds Nell's resulting illness slowly, noting that she is "cold" and "poorly clad" on deck and then describing her the following day as "shivering with the cold and damp, ill in body and sick to death at heart" (332). After a night's respite by a factory furnace, she mentions "pains in all my limbs" (339). Soon thereafter, Nell begins to think about death:

> So very weak and spent she felt, so very calm and unresisting, that she had no thought of any wants of her own, but prayed that God would raise up some friend for *him*. . . . [E]ven hunger was forgotten in the strange tranquility that crept over her senses. She lay down very gently, and, with a quiet smile upon her face, fell into a slumber. It was not like sleep—and yet it must have been, or why those pleasant dreams of the little scholar all night long!
>
> Morning came. Much weaker, diminished powers even of sight and hearing, and yet the child made no complaint . . . She felt a hopelessness of their even being extricated together from that forlorn place, a dull conviction that she was very ill, perhaps dying; but no fear or anxiety. (341).

Lingering over the progress of Nell's symptoms from her perspective, Dickens emphasizes not only her passivity but also the gradually wasting effects of poverty and poor care. But I am pausing on this moment in order to draw attention to the narrative as well as symbolic energy invested in this initial moment that puts Nell on her journey toward death. Building to this moment

---

6. Ginsburg reads this shift as that from a "narrative of survival" that is motivated by flight and characterized by monotony and repetition to a "narrative of homecoming," which is shaped by its telos (414). At this point, she contends, "death is glossed as a returning home, as joining one's true 'kith and kin,' that is, as the victory of innocence over a corrupt world rather than the defeat of a fragile body by an indifferent world" (415). While I concur about the shift in narrative focus and pacing, I think that even such a notion of Nell's death as an allegorical victory needs to take into account the extent to which the serial narrative invites readers to anticipate it as tragic sorrow.

over the course of several chapters, Dickens invests readers emotionally as well as intellectually in the likelihood of Nell's death. This intensity builds over the course of the next several pages; No. 30 concludes with Nell collapsing "senseless" at the feet of a fellow traveler whom she and her grandfather overtake on the road. The opening of No. 31 (31 October 1840) quickly reassures readers that the traveler is the schoolmaster who had taken them in early in their journey; within a very few pages he has taken over paternal care of Nell, providing both the presence of mind and the funds her grandfather lacks. Warmed and fed by the landlady at a nearby inn, Nell recovers. But the narrative offered no guarantee that this would be the case; the collapse at the end of No. 30 could well have been final instead of temporary. While readers no longer experience the chronological delay of the week's break between serial installments, this sequence still occurs over the break between chapters. The affordances of the form still enact the emotional movement through dreading anticipation, precise fear, and then relief and release.

The emotional impact of this sequence is further enhanced by its framing, as Dickens shifts between plots to enhance intensity as well as narrative pacing. In No. 28 (10 October), the single gentleman approaches Kit with the news that Nell and her grandfather have been located with Mrs. Jarley, and he departs London with Mrs. Nubbles to reclaim them. In turning to No. 29 a week later, readers might well have anticipated a happy reunion; instead, Nell and her grandfather sneak away from Mrs. Jarley's in the middle of the night, leaving no indication of where they are going. When we return to the would-be rescuers in No. 32 (published on 7 November), we know that they are safe but unlikely to be found—and that Nell's health remains uncertain. Peter K. Garrett has argued that a defining tension of the Victorian multiplot novel is that between inclusivity—representing a various, densely populated world—and coherence—the development of individual plotlines and character arcs (2). Drawing on Bakhtin, he offers the concept of "dialogic form" to name this, insisting that this genre is shaped formally by the intersections, juxtaposition, and collisions of its opposed impulses. In this, his mode of reading has important similarities to the notion of "collision" that Caroline Levine offers in *Forms*: "the strange encounter between two or more forms that sometimes reroutes intention and ideology" (18). Both scholars mandate an analytic focus on narrative (which, as Levine contends, "is the form that best captures the experience of colliding forms" [19]). Serialization affords moments of delay, while the multiplot novel necessitates abrupt shifts in focus. Dickens exploits these two aspects of the serial form to draw out a reading experience of anticipation and surprise. When the rescuers set off, they are heading for the place readers know Nell to be; by the time we return to their journey (and their arrival there), we know her to be already gone.[7] Indeed, it seems that the time of Nell's journey to safety is precisely that of her rescuers' disappointed journey to find her. As we will see in the statistical accounts mobilized in advice literature and the experiences recalled in memoir, saving Nell is thus something to be anticipated, but always with the real possibility of disappointment.

The final third of the novel repeats the movement with a difference: Once again, the narrative arcs of Nell's death and that of her possible rescue jostle and intersect in order to foster a sense of suspense and anticipation in readers. In Nos. 34 and 35 (21 and 28 November) the novel invests heavily in the possibility of Nell's death, staging multiple conversations and contemplations of mortality, its meanings, and its consolations. No. 36 disrupts this focus by launching a long sequence in which—among other significant plots—Kit is framed for robbery, imprisoned, and ultimately exonerated; Dick Swiveller falls ill and is saved by the Marchioness; and Quilp and the Brasses are punished. The first two plotlines are largely unexpected, and this interruption of Nell's story lasts for seven numbers—which translates, of course, into nearly two months of serial publication. Rather than simply the week-long pause between Nell's collapse and rescue on the road, then, there are seven weeks during which the original readers would have gone through an iterative cycle of expecting to know what happens to the heroine and being disappointed. (Dickens noted on 24 Nov. 1840 that he was "inundated with imploring letters recommending poor little Nell to mercy" [*Letters* 153; see discussion in Bachman 306–307].) Kit's release and return coincide with the discovery of Nell's location, but the subsequent installment (43) narrates the journey and concludes by extending the suspense: Kit arrives at night and sees a light on, but there is no answer to his knock on the door. The final sentence leaves him (and, by extension, readers) stepping over the threshold.

This time, of course, Nell does not recover. As Sarah Winter notes, "the revelation of Nell's death is delayed," with the death itself taking place offstage (161); even within the scene of discovery, Dickens installs repeated delays,

---

7. Dickens draws attention to these shifts in ways that are uncharacteristic of his later serials: At the beginning of chapter 42 (No. 29), after the previous installment had closed with Kit watching the chaise carry his mother and the single gentleman off toward Nell, the narrator justifies the change in focus: "It behoves us to leave Kit for a while, thoughtful and expectant, and to follow the fortunes of little Nell; resuming the thread of the narrative at the point where it was left some chapters back" (316). And then, after settling Nell and her grandfather in their final home near the churchyard, chapter 47 (No. 32) begins, "Kit's mother and the single gentleman—upon whose track it is expedient to follow with hurried steps, lest this history should be chargeable with inconstancy, and the offence of leaving its characters in situations of uncertainty and doubt" (355). It's worth noting that apart from these unusual interpolated justifications there is no acknowledgement of the temporal coincidence of these plots.

postponements, and misdirections, in part through the grieving grandfather's confusion, insisting in response to Kit's questions that "she is asleep—yonder—in there" (534). Over the course of the next four pages, the explicit revelation of Nell's death is repeatedly postponed, the grandfather's references to her "sleep" becoming increasingly overdetermined by the metaphorization of death as a final sleep or rest. Discussion of this scene has centered on the revelation of Nell's dead body, the rhythmic repetitions of "She was dead" and the extended meditation on her angelic qualities (528–529). William Lee Hughes reads this scene's elongation of "the realization of Nell's death over as much time as possible" as saturating the form of the text with grief; "while others have argued that reading the representation of Nell's death in its historical context demonstrates that it is not excessively sentimental," he writes, "I would insist that this death can only be meaningful, can only signify, to the extent that its representation is excessive" (96–97). The notion that the death of a beloved child is—or must be represented to be—inherently excessive echoes Mrs. Bakewell's sentimental exclamation in "Domestic Affliction": While religious and medical narratives variously recuperate and explain such tragedy, the sentimental permits and affords the excessive, disruptive, unproductive experience of grief. But rather than grief itself saturating the fictional form in this installment, the prolongation formalizes the prolepsis of child death: In this scene, Dickens gives his readers an approximation of what it feels like to *anticipate* such a tragic disruption. The four pages between the old man's first insistence that Nell is sleeping in the other room and the narrative exclamation that "she was dead. There upon her little bed, she lay at rest" build readers' and characters' understanding ahead of the grandfather's and before decisive revelation: Sleep is "all with her" and "it is a good and happy sleep" (538, 536). "We will not wake her," he later admits, and reflects, "I should be glad to see her eyes again, and to see a smile upon her young face now, but it is fixed and changeless . . . We will not wake her" (537). By invoking and postponing Nell's death over weeks and then here over sentences, Dickens attaches the anticipated and yet dreaded death of a child to the experience of novelistic suspense, the present apprehensiveness that draws both on past experience and imagined futures.

Winter shows how Dickens's fiction "incorporate[s] associationist theories of memory" in which reading "lay[s] down serial memories in the form of associations that are reinforced and reorchestrated . . . through repeated reading" (13, 16). The intensified apprehension of Nell's death at this moment has been shaped by the earlier moment of anticipation and rescue. In addition to exploiting the serial's cliffhanger potential, however, Dickens has also conditioned *Shop*'s readers to expect specifically unpleasant surprises. We can see this with particular clarity in his deployment of Daniel Quilp as a kind of rhetorical effect. One of Dickens's early grotesques, Quilp is played both for comic effect and to heighten the climate of threat that surrounds Nell: His proportions are exaggerated—"so low in stature as to be quite a dwarf, though his head and face were large enough for the body of a giant"; his features terrifying—his eyes are "restless, sly, and cunning," and he has a habitual "ghastly smile, which . . . constantly revealed the few discoloured fangs that were yet scattered in his mouth"; and his body in perpetual, disruptive motion—standing on his head, or contorting himself to torment others (29). He is also sadistic: The chapter after his initial introduction focuses entirely on his abuse of his wife, and he has a casually cruel relationship with his errand-boy. His power over Nell—and therefore in the novel—derives from his function as her grandfather's primary lender, presenting himself as an ally in order to ruin the old man financially. (In fact, he takes full possession of their home and shop and all its effects, catalyzing their initial flight.)

Quilp operates narratively through surprise. Early on, it appeared that he would occupy a significant portion of the plot, but he soon becomes marginal to the activities he sets in motion. Instead, he maintains a malevolent and threatening presence by appearing at unexpected intervals and in unanticipated ways: He appears, like a gargoyle come to life, on the first night Nell stays with Mrs. Jarley (212); he is in chapel when Kit goes to fetch his mother so that she might accompany the single gentleman on the quest (311); he's already at the inn where Kit's mother and the single gentleman stop while on that search (361–362); and he is watching nearby when Kit is framed for theft and arrested (449). For each of these characters, the moment of seeing Quilp is not just surprising but alarming. The novel emphasizes the effect on Nell, in particular:

> As her popularity procured her various little fees from the visitors on which her patroness never demanded any toll, and as her grandfather too was well-treated and useful, she had no cause for anxiety in connexion with the wax-work, beyond that which sprung from her recollection of Quilp, and her fears that he might return and one day suddenly encounter them.
>
> Quilp indeed was a perpetual nightmare to the child, who was constantly haunted by a vision of his ugly face and stunted figure. (223)

As we'll see, references to child death appear in advice literature both in expected contexts and apparently at random; Quilp operates by the same logic in *The Old Curiosity Shop*. His danger is apparently not just a result of his instrumental actions—and his explicit verbal or physical threats—within the plot, but also of his habit of appearing unexpectedly. The repetition of this means that we start to expect him; Quilp—for readers, as for Nell—is a memory but also a possibility. Nell's anxiety comes as an anticipation of (yet another) surprising appearance, and Quilp's appearance (in both senses) is inherently threatening. Dickens distributes this effect across characters: Quilp surprises and therefore disturbs not just Nell and Kit, with whom he has distinctive histories, but also Kit's mother. This allows him to operate as a rhetorical effect, rather than a narrative feature. In other words: It isn't simply that Quilp's sudden appearances make characters anxious or fearful; Quilp's appearances contribute to the anxious effect of the narrative of *The Old Curiosity Shop* as a whole. Readers become "prepared to be taken unawares," as Paul Saint-Amour phrases it in *Tense Future* (93). The novel thus allows us to see the extent to which anxiety is the uptake capture of the recollection of the likelihood of an unpleasant surprise; the uncertainty of whether or not that surprise will recur—and what material difficulty it will bring—is part of what renders anxiety objectless, the emotion an effect of the movement between past, future, and present, as well as between various future possibilities, rather than the specific concern.

In this section, I've emphasized the association of that loomingly possible tragedy with anxious temporality, with "apprehensiveness" as Saint-Amour glosses it: "The uncanny condition in which some still-forming thing appears to take hold of us, as if from a future that has itself become prehensile" (93). The symptoms of that "still-forming thing," he explains, "appear to lead both backward and forward in time—back to past shocks that help set one on edge, and forward to the disaster that may be about to arrive" (93). *The Old Curiosity Shop* creates a climate in which tragic probability looms and yet cannot be fixed because it both has already been set in motion and is repeatedly postponed. Advice literature takes up this logic directly, iteratively enacting the surprise of unexpected danger in a climate of statistically likely death. By addressing mothers as those primarily concerned with this likelihood as well as those somehow at fault for it, this genre attaches anticipation of the "still-forming thing" that is premature death to the rhetorical situation of motherhood.

Tragic Probabilities

Statistics were an important strategy for many advice literature authors' proleptic moves in that they create a generalized context of precarity. As early as 1767 Hugh Smith's *Letters to Married Women* offers quantitative data: "Almost two thirds of the children born in this metropolis and its environs are intirely lost to society: 16283 are, upon the average, the annual births; 10145 the infant burials" (v). In this section I consider the most extensive statistical treatment of this topic, which appears in Andrew Combe's *A Treatise on the Physiological and Moral Management of Infants,* first published in 1840. Combe posits a causal relationship between inadequate female education and infant mortality: Babies are dying, in other words, because women are not being properly trained to be mothers. The author was already well known at the time of publishing his *Treatise on the Physiological and Moral Management of Infants.* His 1834 *Physiology Applied to Health and Education* sold widely, and with his brother George, Combe was one of the foremost British proponents of phrenology. (The Combe brothers founded the Phrenological Society in 1820, and Andrew Combe's publications evince a lifelong interest in the association of physiology and character.) He considered *Physiological and Moral Management* the culmination of his life's work (Bettany). "The Extent of Mortality in Infancy" is the book's second chapter; it draws extensively from the first *Annual Report of the Registrar General of Births, Deaths, and Marriage in England,* which was published in 1839 shortly after being presented to Parliament.[8] In other words, the question of "extent" that Combe emphasizes in the title is statistical: "ONE-THIRD OF THE TOTAL DEATHS OCCUR UNDER TWO YEARS OF AGE" he proclaims early on; he explains that this amounts to 342.54 per thousand (9). Comparing the data to those for other countries, as well as analyzing those for Liverpool in more detail, he concludes that this provides "unquestionable evidence of that fact, that a great mortality prevails in infancy, even among the most civilized communities, and under what are considered the most favourable circumstances" (11).

As we've seen, the infant and child mortality rates seem to have been relatively consistent across England as a whole for decades if not centuries, but this would not have been known, since there was no method to aggregate the data. The first *Annual Report* made the death rate *knowable* in a fundamentally new way, and Combe's emphasis—announcing it in capitals, and subsequently wondering whether or not it is God's will (11)—presents it as a dire, calamitous problem. This allows him to create the causal link that justifies publication, insisting that it is "the first duty of parents . . . to make themselves acquainted

---

8. The Act for Registering Births, Deaths, and Marriages in England of 1836 (6 & 7 William IV, c. 86) created the Office of the Registrar General in 1837 and established civil (as opposed to ecclesiastical) registration. This facilitated the collection, analysis, and presentation of vital statistics in annual reports. For an overview of the Act's establishment and impact, see Cullen. For a broader account of statistical thinking in the Victorian period, see Poovey, *Making a Social Body.*

with the general nature and treatment of the infant constitution" (11): "Even in the best regulated families," Combe laments, "it is rare to meet with a mother, who, before becoming such, has devoted the least attention to the study of the infant constitution, to the principles on which it ought to be treated, or to the laws by which its principal functions are regulated" (27). Although Combe later suggests that he doesn't want to blame his maternal readers individually for "the defects of their own education" (28), he argues that their lack of professional knowledge is ultimately responsible for the deaths of their children. Positioned after the title page's presentation of his credentials and before his extensive discussion not just of childcare strategies but of the underlying principles of his recommendations, this chapter weaponizes the available statistics, using them to document failure to align childcare "to the laws of its constitution": "Where the treatment and laws are not in harmony, failure, disease, and untimely death may be expected as the most frequent and certain results" (7). Combe builds his case not only with disturbing demographic data, but also with compelling case studies, including accounts of changes in childcare and hygiene practices in hospitals in London and Dublin that made significant changes in mortality rates (20–21). It's difficult to argue with the basic notion that hygiene, diet, and medical treatment have a material effect on health and the progression of disease, but my interest lies not in the underlying truth but in the probabilistic logic such invocations of infant death use.

Although occurring earlier than the period she studies, these statistics do work analogous to those Kathleen Woodward discusses in *Statistical Panic*— indeed, maternal anxiety takes part in what she calls "statistical stress" (211). Statistical stress, Woodward contends, is produced by the saturation of public discourse with medical probabilities, a saturation in which "bodies are figured as being in a perpetual state of risk" (196). "Even when the citation of statistics is meant to provide assurance," Woodward explains, "it may more often than not produce its opposite: a sense of foreboding and insecurity" (210–211). The phenomenological effect of reading medical statistics is to experience risk to oneself, to feel the likelihood of danger (even danger averted, if only barely) on the temporal horizon. But it catalyzes this sense of precarity by drawing on the past: Medical statistics use past facts to forecast future probabilities, proleptically pulling those potential futures as affective truth into the present moment. Understanding maternal anxiety as a form of statistical stress draws attention to how that emotion enacts a collapsed temporality in which past and future are felt in the present moment.

The statistical stress of Combe's "Extent of the Mortality in Infancy" affords a sense that *the mother's* present-day decisions produce (or fail to ward off) future danger. Despite the caveat that he doesn't wish to "throw unmerited blame on mothers" (28), Combe's emphasis throughout is on a radical revision of middle-class girls' education, effectively insisting that the prevention of childhood death is a fundamentally female responsibility. Invocations of the deadly danger of maternal ignorance and unpreparedness serve as a generic feature of childrearing literature. An 1840 review of *Physiological and Moral Management* in the *Athenaeum* echoes this, noting in its rueful opening that "we have been so frequently called on to notice works of this description, and to force upon public attention the defects in female education, and the consequent helpless ignorance of young mothers, that we must not again enter upon the subject" ("Our Library Table" 570). If maternal ignorance is at fault, then the only way to prevent personal and familial tragedy is to read. Childrearing advice literature promises both medical expertise and education, but to do so it must reiterate the very dangers that motivate its readers: Maternal concern catalyzes maternal care.

The genre cultivates maternal reading as an anxious experience through statistical stress, not simply accusing mothers of deadly ignorance but also providing ample data making the deaths of their children seem probable. Its dominant patterning is repetitive rather than narrative; whether through Chavasse's catechistic approach or the more dominant treatise and lecture format of Bull, Moore, Bakewell, and Combe, the logic of the genre is that of problem-response repeated for 200 or more pages. Illness, symptom, puzzle, danger, or habitual practice is followed by diagnosis, warning, and treatment. In this way, each individual moment—each specific concern or recommendation—is experienced phenomenologically as both typical and different; the rhetorical situation recurs. These books are roadmaps to the physical and moral pitfalls that dot infancy and childhood, from everyday challenges like crying and getting children not to lie and those of particular developmental stages (teething, weaning), to the health challenges of particular conditions (jaundice, rickets) and the care for specific diseases (red gum, scarlet fever, measles). In addition to the statistical overwhelm that creates an overall probabilistic expectation of tragic surprise, the genre's reliance on formal repetition takes readers through that experience locally. All of the topics covered by this genre become equally subject to expert medical opinion, but all are evidently not equally dangerous or deadly. Scarlet fever can kill, but eating raw or underripe fruit before the age of two is unlikely to permanently damage a child's digestive system. The typifications on which generic patterning and uptakes rely can never fully predict or constrain the context of a specific piece of advice (any more than they do so for the content of a greeting or a lyric poem), but the perpetual *likelihood* of a deadly threat that only periodically appears keeps readers—like Nell—"constantly haunted" (Dickens, *Shop* 223).

Combe's discussion of *convulsions* helps to illustrate this, in part because the treatment of convulsions as a distinct disorder—as opposed to a symptom of a high fever or an epileptic seizure—is usefully strange to twenty-first-century readers, and in part because convulsions operate rhetorically in ways oddly similar to Quilp's appearances in *The Old Curiosity Shop.*[9] Many authors discuss convulsions as a specific condition or issue. Moore, for example, devotes two chapters to them in *Advice to Young Mothers,* one in a section on infant care and another in the section organized around individual diseases (it falls after "Hydrocephalus" and before "Worms"). For others, convulsions are a dangerous symptom. In Bull's *Maternal Management,* for example, convulsions appear as a concerning symptom variously produced by the wet nurse or nursing mother's mood or other problems with feeding; or as a corollary to specific times of life or conditions. Combe lists convulsions as one of the common causes of deaths, alongside measles, whooping cough, pneumonia, diarrhea, and teething, and offers three underlying causes: "breathing impure air . . . the irritation of teething, and . . . improper diet" (156, 40). "If we neglect to discover their exciting cause," he warns, "we shall not only fail to put a stop to them, but may actually leave their causes in full operation" (40). Convulsions thus appear to confirm the danger of one of Combe's pet concerns: The dangers of "impure air" (specifically referring to the air in overheated, poorly ventilated rooms). The juxtaposition of impure air and (deadly) convulsions appears in multiple places throughout the book: in an early contrast between "enlightened" and "ordinary" maternal management, in his recommendations for nursery design and architecture, in his discussion of raising children in cities, and in his argument for wire fireplace gratings (32, 159–50, 164, 169). But convulsions also appear a danger during teething and weaning and—most unexpectedly—when an infant is exposed to "loud and sudden sounds" (210, 245; 262). Such specific threats to child life and health pop up unexpectedly throughout these texts. The rhetorical logic is one that repetitively enacts the dangers described in the statistical aggregate and illustrated with the telling case study and anecdote. This logic forces readers to approximate the experience they describe: As different objects (dangers) appear and then recede from view, all that is left is the emotion generated by the rapid, fearful movement that adheres to the maternal situation itself. In this way, advice literature sutures the tragic probability of child death to the scene of motherhood, conditioning that topic generically. Through statistical stress and convulsive surprise, the maternal script is (re)written as anxious, its attention rapidly

9. Perri Klass notes that convulsions associated with other illnesses may have been an effect of dehydration, a connection that was not identified until the twentieth century (private communication, 19 July 2019).

flickering between future, past, and present in a constant effort to prevent the danger(s) that are foreordained and only belatedly preventable, always on the horizon and around the corner.

Anxious Grieving

The concept of a genre ecology decenters and destabilizes some thinking about clusters of genres, their interactions, and their impacts. Specifically, Spinuzzi and Zachry argue that the ecology metaphor moves away from the emphasis on *users* of genres installed at the heart of the concepts of genre sets and genre systems, both of which tend to organize genres at least in part on the basis of the subjects who generate particular instances of them. While I share their emphasis on contingency and transformation, as well as the notion that concepts, topics, forms, and narratives are continuing to (re)circulate through the genre ecology over time, I hold onto consideration of positionality because my primary interest lies in how the dispersion and circulation of uptake capture and residue accreted to the subject position of Mother—whether rhetor, audience, or topic of the text. I now turn to the memoirs of Mary Martha Sherwood (1775–1851) and Catharine Tait (1819–1878). At first glance, these texts are straightforward uptake artifacts: texts responding to the rhetorical context fiction and advice literature helped shape (Dryer 65). I also consider them, however, as active constituting participants in the maternal genre ecology, generating their own uptake affordances, enactments, captures, and residues—their own horizons of interpretive and affective probability. My analysis of this genre ecology emphasizes the positive—what is selected, what persists—rather than the negative—what is omitted or dropped—because my interest ultimately lies in the uptake residues: how the intergeneric circulation of child death as foreordained but preventable tragedy contributed to the durable attachment of anxiety to the cultural formation of motherhood.

Sherwood and Tait—a generation apart—both experienced and wrote about the mortal illnesses and deaths of some of their children, in circumstances at once shockingly tragic and not untypical of nineteenth-century motherhood. Both were deeply religious, so their memoirs also allow us to see the influence of that framework for understanding child illness and death in relation to the mother's self-conception. Sherwood was one of the most important children's authors of the first half of the nineteenth century, best known for "Little Henry and His Bearer" (1814) and *The History of the Fairchild Family* (published in three parts in 1818, 1842, and 1847). Born into a prominent Anglican family in 1775 (her father was chaplain in ordinary to

George III), Sherwood's marriage to her cousin in 1803 led to her move to
India two years later. (He was paymaster to an army regiment; the Sherwoods
were largely stationed in northern India.[10]) The Sherwoods had nine children.
Their first daughter was born in England and left with relatives when the cou-
ple moved to India; between 1805 and their return to England in 1816, they
had an additional six biological children and adopted two more. Henry and
Lucy Martha, the oldest biological children born in India, both died before
they turned two: Henry, born in December 1805, died of whooping cough in
the summer of 1807; Lucy, born in the spring of 1807, died of dysentery in the
fall of 1808. Sherwood had always been religiously serious and became Evangelical after these losses. In the final years of her life she wrote a memoir, relying heavily on the extensive diaries she had kept. *The Life of Mrs. Sherwood,
Chiefly Autobiographical* was published posthumously in 1854, edited by her
youngest daughter, Sophia (born in 1815).[11]

Catharine Tait was born in 1819. Although her family was Evangelical, Tait
was influenced by a brother-in-law's Tractarianism as a young woman. The
family lived near Rugby, and after the announcement of Archibald Campbell
Tait's appointment as head of Rugby School, she worried about his influence
because he had written against Tract 90 while a tutor at Oxford.[12] (They married in 1843.) Archibald Tait was appointed Dean of Carlisle in 1849, Bishop
of London in 1856, and Archbishop of Canterbury in 1868. Tait herself established a school for girls at Rugby, and throughout her life "used her position
to support and to organize more effectively a traditional style of philanthropic
work among the less fortunate and orphans" (Kollar). While the Taits lived in
Carlisle, five of their seven living children died of scarlet fever over the course

---

10. During this period, the Sherwoods were stationed largely in Bihar and West Bengal,
specifically Danapur (then called Dinapore by the British), Kolkata (Calcutta), and Baharampur
(Berhampore). Later they were stationed in Uttar Pradesh: in Kanpur (Cawnpore) and then in
Meerut.

11. For biographical information on Sherwood, see Royde Smith; Cutt; and Harvey Darton. Corbett discusses *The Life of Mrs. Sherwood* as spiritual autobiography. For discussions of
Sherwood's fiction in the context of Evangelical and Romantic writers, see Royde Smith; Cutt;
Demers; Vallone; and Middup. Ferguson; Bhattacharya; Mathison; Mascarenhas; Malhotra;
and my "Intimacy's Empire" focus on her work in the context of empire and postcolonial
studies.

12. John Henry Newman's Tract 90, "Remarks on Certain Passages in the Thirty-Nine
Articles" (1841), was the most controversial of the *Tracts for the Times*. In it, he examines the
39 Articles, which were the doctrinal foundation of the Church of England, and argues that
they are not incompatible with Catholicism. (This aligned with the Oxford Movement's larger
goal of redefining the Anglican Church as Catholic rather than Protestant.) Born in Scotland,
Archibald Tait grew up Presbyterian but decided to enter the ministry in the Church of England
as a young man. A tutor at Balliol College, Oxford, in 1841, he was one of "Four Tutors" who
formally protested Tract 90. The following year he was appointed head of Rugby.

of a single month in March 1856. (A newborn daughter and the only son survived; the Taits later had two additional daughters.) Soon after the tragedy, Tait wrote about the illness and deaths of the children to share the details of the tragedy with family and close friends. After her death in 1878, the manuscript was found along with a note encouraging her son to publish the account after both she and her husband had died: "As the suffering [we faced] is one which must recur over and over again while the world lasts, it may speak a word of help and comfort to those upon whom a similar burden is laid, and who are feeling that it is too heavy for them to bear" (qtd. in Benham 252). It was ultimately published in 1879 as part of a joint memoir of Tait and their son (who had died a few months before his mother) at the behest of Archibald Tait, edited by William Benham.

Published life writing like memoir and autobiography is generically messy: "impure, unsettling, and unpredictable," in Valerie Sanders's evocative phrase ("Life Writing" 212–213). Sherwood's and Tait's texts fall into slightly different categories. The latter is bereavement literature, written—or at least published—as an account of her daughters' illnesses and deaths, and with the goal of providing a sense of community and comfort, as well as a model of Christian mourning. The former is more generically complicated; it has elements of travelogue and spiritual autobiography, as well as being the professional autobiography of an author. In addition, while there is no indication that Tait's family edited her account before its publication, Sophia Kelly edited her mother's manuscript heavily. My discussion below relies primarily on the published text of *The Life of Mrs. Sherwood,* but I do draw attention to the emphases created by Kelly's editorial decisions by referring periodically to Sherwood's manuscript and diaries. Before moving into my analysis, however, I want to pause. Both women were devastated by their children's illnesses and deaths; it's clear that in both cases, the deaths also challenged their beliefs—even Tait, who writes with the greater consistency of religious conviction, notes shortly after the girls' deaths that both her and her husband's faith was "deadened," if only temporarily (403; see Jalland 135–136). However statistically likely or predictable, it seems that the actual death of one's children was an event that defied explanation or consolation. As in Bakewell's "Domestic Affliction" with which I opened, we see in these experiential accounts the excessive force of grief disrupting the tension between the active resistance (but possible fallibility) of medical care and the fatalistic acceptance of religious faith. In both cases, the imminence of tragedy transforms generalized anxiety into specific fear within the texts themselves; their contribution to the genre ecology is to confirm the affective and social truth that motherhood is emotionally as well as statistically likely to include the experience of grief.

•

Writing in the early 1850s about the death of her son Henry in 1807, Sherwood reflects, "Well do I remember that, although the death of infants is so common an event, I was utterly confounded when I was called upon to give up my infant baby. Oh, my baby—oh, my Henry! Teach me to do thy will, my God."[13] Infant mortality rates for British infants were even higher in British India than they were in Great Britain itself (Chaudhuri, "Memsahibs and Motherhood" 527–528); in her two years in India before Henry's death, Sherwood had already experienced the death of a child quite dear to her (the daughter of her servant, Betty Parker). But the death of her own child was different: surprising, *confounding,* a radical rupture. The interpolated cry illustrates the emotion she describes, but also enacts it rhetorically: After recalling her experience for readers, she cries out in pain twice before praying for help in reconciling herself to the grief she has not been able to domesticate. Writing about the grief takes her back into it, with the expression both disrupting and pausing the narrative. In her understanding, this experience is not idiosyncratic: "It is a new and terrible feeling when a tender parent first looks upon the corpse of his own child. Every father or mother possesses a sort of instinctive persuasion that his child is to outlive him" (*Life* 304–305). For Sherwood, the death of the child is a radical upset, a surprise that knocks the anticipated narrative off course despite—or in futurist defiance of—the fact that the possibility and *probability* of child death saturated early nineteenth-century culture. The anxious temporality of motherhood experiences both possible futures, and takes shape in the proleptic mental movement between the present and the two incommensurate worlds in which the child does or does not survive, has or has not already been foreordained to die.

The portion of Sherwood's autobiography recounting her early years in India has elements of travelogue. For the most part, the picaresque rhythms of that genre serve as a facilitating background to the teleological narratives of the deaths of her young children in 1807 and 1808 and her conversion to Evangelical Anglicanism shortly thereafter. These two narratives overlap and combine, particularly when she recalls and condemns the intensity of her grief and her difficulty accepting her children's deaths. By retrospectively anticipating the babies' foreordained deaths and, at the same time, identifying her own errors in Christian belief or child management, Sherwood takes up the narratives we see in contemporary advice literature and brings them together in

---

13. *The Life of Mrs. Sherwood, Chiefly Autobiographical.* Edited by Sophia Kelly, Darton and Co., 1854, pp. 304–305. Subsequent references will be made parenthetically to *Life.*

an internally contradictory narrative of consolation that both mandates and justifies maternal attention as at once totalizing and anxious.[14] Sherwood still actively grieved her children decades later, the emotion still raw when catalyzed by the act of rereading her journals and writing her memoir, but the narrative she offers is one that uses the telos of religious conversion and faith to contain the devastating possibility that the children's deaths could have been avoided. In Sherwood's writing, the tragedy of child death is both preventable and inevitable; it is both the result of mismanagement and the will of God.

Henry's life and subsequent death are described in more thorough detail than Lucy's, so I focus on them here. The boy was born on 25 December 1805, and seems to have been frequently ill; Sherwood tells the story of his life as a series of near-misses and adventures that are signs he will die young: A one-time dose of opium, her trouble nursing, and the decision to wean him at fourteen months appear as some of the "many, many things were against my infant boy!" (*Life* 299). In Sherwood's writing, these dangers are at least in part those of India itself, of contact with religious and racial Others. The narrative prolepsis intensifies when she comes closer to his fatal illness and death at eighteen months, lingering with particular intensity over his weaning:

> I began the month of February with plans for weaning Henry; there was no one to tell me that in so doing I was sacrificing him. I learned this lesson when it was too late to profit my boy. Everything was against my child; everything as it regarded his continuance on earth, everything in favour of his early admittance into a happier state of being. (*Life* 299)

Sherwood discusses the decision to wean Henry at some length, considering herself misled by her ignorant importation of English childcare practices to India as well as ill-advised by the surgeon (whom she believes was similarly misled by "our English notions" [*Life* 299]). In her manuscript, Sherwood describes conversations with Englishwomen of longer residence in India that make her realize that it was customary for them not only to hire Indian women as wet nurses but also to wean children later than was contemporary practice in Britain.[15] Nupur Chaudhuri's historical study confirms this ("Memsahibs and Motherhood" 528–529).

---

14. An important feature of Evangelical Anglicanism in the early nineteenth century was the realization of one's own sinfulness, as part of accepting personally the doctrine of Christ's personal sacrifice. See Bebbington 20–28.

15. Diary of Mrs. Sherwood, 1804–1808. Sherwood Family Papers (1437), box 2, folio 1, UCLA Special Collections, pp. 131–132. Although the UCLA catalog marks these volumes as Sherwood's "Diary," they are clearly written retrospectively and periodically refer to rereading

Although Henry ultimately dies of whooping cough months after his weaning, Sherwood remains convinced that the early weaning permanently weakened him. Medical advice and the English customs she brought with her were literally poorly adapted to the Indian climate; she appears at least in part to blame herself for her child's death, enacting the message of childrearing advice literature that maternal care requires anticipating physical dangers in order to avoid them—not to mention that a mother's lack of knowledge or inexperience can kill. But in telling the story, Sherwood minimizes her own agency—and therefore the extent to which she is to blame for her son's eventual death—by reading her decision as evidence that the child was predestined to die: "May we not, therefore, understand by faith, that the early death of this little boy was the best which could have happened to him, and thus my prayers for him were answered" (*Life* 299). Her retrospective narrative, in which errors can be seen and imaginatively corrected, jostles against the religious conviction that God doesn't make mistakes: Henry's death therefore *must be* "the best which could have happened to him." Sherwood thus toggles between agency (and self-blame) and resignation: Her son's death could be foreseen but not prevented; Henry was both destined to die and also "sacrificed" to maternal ignorance.

This tension comes into relative balance through the story of Sherwood's own conversion, another telos that provides her with an interpretive lens. Here, both Henry's and Lucy's illnesses and deaths are lessons for Sherwood herself, part of what brought her to the Evangelical faith that defined her adult life (as well as the writing for which she was famous). This pattern begins with another kind of self-criticism: "By many persons it will be thought that my grief for Henry was inordinate. I do not dispute the point," she writes, reflecting on her reaction to his loss; other mothers "may have suffered these losses with far more resignation, cheerfulness, and submission to the Divine will than I did" (*Life* 309, 329). In *The Life of Mrs. Sherwood* itself it is not always clear why Sherwood worries about this, because Kelly removed many of her mother's most intense expressions of grief over the loss of her son, including one in which Sherwood notes the intensity of her focus on her vulnerable children:

> Through all . . . the early part of my life in India God in his infinite goodness provided me with one protection—Namely, the presence of tender & most lovely infants. My Henry was a beautiful child . . . he probably never knew

the diary itself. I have therefore taken them as a manuscript of *The Life of Mrs. Sherwood*. Subsequent references will be made parenthetically with the abbreviation "Diary" and indicating folio and page numbers.

an hour of real health from the day of his birth to his death, & so entirely so deeply were my affections bound up in that child that nothing then had power to interest me deeply but my boy. ("Diary" 207–208)

Her attention glued to the child, focused on the care decisions that might or might not keep him alive, Sherwood was "preserv[ed] from the Dark & Luxury of India" ("Diary" 219). As the grief narrative is appropriated by the conversion narrative, Sherwood becomes increasingly passive, her helplessness in the face of tragedy converted into faith in Christ. Anxiety becomes the expression of maternal love that might want to but cannot ultimately defy the will of God. Mourning is a retrospective emotion just as anxiety is primarily an anticipatory one, but we see in maternal writing of grief that they collapse into one another around the figure of the Child. The demographic likelihood that the experience of parenthood would include mourning is further shaped by a religious paradigm in which individual choice has only limited efficacy in preventing tragedy.

●

Over the course of the month of March 1856, five of Catharine and Archibald Campbell Tait's seven children died of scarlet fever. Five-year-old Charlotte (called Chatty) fell ill a little more than two weeks after Lucy was born on 11 February; after four days, she was dead. By early April, all her other sisters— ages ten, eight, three, and one-and-a-half—had also died, leaving only the newborn baby and their brother Craufurd, about to turn seven. The children's birth and death dates are here:

Catharine Anna (Catty): born 15 Mar. 1846, died 25 Mar. 1856 (10 years old)
Mary Susan (May): born 20 June 1847, died 1 Apr. 1856 (8 years old)
Craufurd: born 22 June 1849, died in adulthood
Charlotte (Chatty): born 7 Sept. 1850, died 6 Mar. 1856 (6 years old)
Frances Alice Mason: born 29 June 1852, died 20 Mar. 1856 (3 years old)
Susan Elizabeth Campbell: born 1 Aug. 1854, died 11 Mar. 1856 (1.5 years old)
Lucy Sydney Murray: born 11 Feb. 1856, died in adulthood[16]

Tait seems to have written the account of her daughters' illnesses and deaths in the fall and winter of 1856 and 1857: The memoir is headed "written at Hal-

---

16. See Benham 253 for the death dates. I've reconstructed the birth dates from references in the memoir itself.

stead," where the family was living in September of that year; and in writing about three-year-old Frances's illness and death, Tait notes that "her birthday has come and gone since then" (320), the singular suggesting that it has not yet been more than one June since the March when the little girl died.

Scholars have noted that Tait's memoir provides one of the most comprehensive glimpses into the experience of parental love and loss available from the Victorian period, and Katharine Kittredge argues that by the 1850s, this genre of public maternal mourning was a staple (156). The genre—of which Tait's is a paradigmatic example—takes the tragic loss of a child as its exigency, and recounts the mother's progress from grief to acceptance. The 139-page account provides painstaking detail regarding the progression of each child's illness; the treatments recommended by various medical practitioners; the rounds of sincere prayer; and the complexities of arranging with friends and paid caregivers to isolate the still-healthy children from those who had fallen ill. Tait's devout religious faith appears to have provided her with comfort almost immediately—or at least frameworks to help her perform acceptance (although, as I note above, she describes temporary loss of faith in the immediate wake of the tragedy). The response to the published account suggests that the rhetorical certainty she expresses there provided comfort to others, as well.[17] The memoir is striking in the absence of medical doubt as well. The Taits never seem to question the medical man; indeed, it seems clear that Tait and her staff assiduously follow his prescriptions. He also seems to represent medical consensus. Mr. Page—the family doctor, and a surgeon by his title— is called in after Chatty has been sick for about 24 hours and soon diagnoses scarlet fever (284). He recommends quarantining her, separating all the other children to mitigate the spread of the disease. (This clearly fails.) After Chatty and Susan both die, the family calls in additional advice at the surgeon's own suggestion, both a local physician and a specialist from Edinburgh. There is no dispute over treatment: All three physicians agree with the course Mr. Page had prescribed (324–325). In fact, the methods they describe—cutting off the children's hair, steam baths and sweating, sponging with vinegar and water—are still considered appropriate ways to bring down fevers in the absence of antipyretics. (In the case of a bacterial illness like scarlet fever, one could only treat symptoms until antibiotics were discovered in the early twentieth century.)

---

17. Jalland notes that "the 1879 publication of the memorial volume of the deaths of Archbishop Tait's children and his wife was one of the most widely read Victorian books of consolation literature, and letters of thanks poured in from bereaved parents who found it helpful" (141). See also Lerner 14–17, 187–189; and Goldhill.

Tait's religious faith, like Sherwood's, provides a framework that allows for active efforts to prevent death to operate alongside acquiescence to its seemingly inevitable approach. In this writing, Tait draws on the spaces and rhythms provided by mainstream Anglican theology to make a kind of sense of the tragedy. They also make anxiety and love stick to one another and to the scene of grief. Although she, too, is writing retrospectively, Tait's story rejects any narratives that involve resistance or blame. For this writer, the deaths are God's will, but not a punishment; and while God sends tragedy, he also sends the strength to bear it. After Chatty dies, for example, she writes: "We knelt beside that form in agony, for it was hard to part with her; but strength was given: we felt Whose hand had given, and now had taken her" (299). After the death of Frances (the third child to pass away), this resignation is bolstered by an image of heaven as an extension of the family home: "I thought of the Home in Heaven to which Chatty and Susan were gone, and then thought of the very brightest home I might hope to secure for this little lamb on earth. If her Home in Heaven was ready, should I wish to keep her here? No!" (327). Tait's narrative turns the resistance of a tender mother into a rhetorical question, even as she documents the family's extensive and complex efforts to save the lives of their children.

Unlike Sherwoord, Tait doesn't create meaning out of her children's deaths for her own experience of faith, finding consolation in a personal conversion narrative. Tait's acceptance, instead, relies on the theological implications of the Romantic conflation of children and angels. When Catty is dying, the little girl points upward, and Tait recalls herself saying: "'She sees in heaven her Chatty, her Susan and Frances'" (357). This creates a spatial relationship between heaven and earth, as well as a vision of the afterlife as extending present relationships radically into the future. In Tait's memoir, the angelic aspect of the dying child serves an anticipatory narrative function. As she moves from child to child, each comes into focus as notably beautiful and sacralized as she comes closer to death: Chatty is a "sweet picture of heavenly beauty" (266) just before she becomes ill, and Susan's face is "lighted up with the beauty of heaven" (302). Even May's delirium, "heartrending to witness," is that of "a pure and holy child" (369).

The Anxious Temporality of Child Death

In the published memoirs of these two religious women, we see how life writing about mortally ill children shaped and was shaped by proleptic grieving even as it further associates that likelihood to the lived experience of (any) maternal subject. This possibility is reinforced by Anglican theology, which both provides the iconography that marks angelic children as always already fated to die and insists on a doctrinal truth that even tragic, premature death is the will of God. The genre ecology affords anxiety by associating motherhood with helpless responsibility for child life, and child life with the likelihood of death; collapsing past and future into the present moment, it generates the rapid temporal movement of anxiety, a movement that collapses concern into care, worry into nurture.

In a moving scene early in Elizabeth Gaskell's *Mary Barton* (1848), Alice Wilson whispers to Mary that they must get a dying baby away from his mother: "'He cannot die while she's wishing him.'" "'Wishing him?'" Mary asks: "'Ay,'" Alice explains, "'donno ye know what wishing means? There's none can die in the arms of those who are wishing them sore to stay on earth. . . . We mun get him away fra' his mother, or he'll have a hard death, poor lile fellow'" (116). The logic of "wishing" is the reverse of the resignation to God's will that we saw in Sherwood's and especially Tait's memoirs. It positions maternal love against the inevitable future, although in the case of the Wilson twins that inevitability is epidemiological rather than theological in nature. The grieving mother at first resists Alice's offer to take the child, but later succumbs: "'May happen yo'd better take him, Alice; I believe my heart's wishing him a' this while . . . I cannot help longing to keep him, and yet he sha'not suffer longer for me'" (117). Gaskell wrote *Mary Barton* while grieving for her son William, who died of scarlet fever at nine months old, and the deaths of babies early in the novel trigger both of its major plots: Jem Wilson declares his love for Mary as she comforts him after his siblings die; and John Barton's Chartist activism is rooted in a desire for "vengeance" against his employers for his son's death (also of scarlet fever) before the novel begins (118–119; 61).

The novel's first third abounds with babies who are dead, dying, or nearly so, whose lives end prematurely or are developmentally stalled; many of the novel's most moving moments turn on parental grief or anxiety for children even once they've grown to adulthood. Gaskell both mobilizes this context as a feature of working-class life and offers parental anxiety as one of the sentimental avenues of identification for her middle-class readers. Unlike Dickens, whose serial postponement of Nell's death pulls readers into the temporality of the emotion, Gaskell creates still, sentimentalized portraits of this doomed feeling. By figuring grief for the past or pending death of a beloved child as an essential point of identification for middle-class readers with working-class characters, *Mary Barton* normalizes that emotion as a universal feature of parental experience. Imaginatively fleshing out and personalizing the weaponized statistics of advice literature, *Mary Barton* (re)attaches hopeful—wishful—parental love to the devastating probability that children die.

Narrative, statistical, and experiential accounts of child death cut across and reinforce the generic forms that shape it, patterning the phenomenon according to the temporal rhythms of anxiety: moving toward the subject and yet always in the future, that approach implying both that it can be avoided and that it cannot, characterized by both a dreadful anticipation and the expectation of surprise. This chapter has sought to sketch out the temporality of maternal anxiety as it emerged in the public genres of advice literature, serial fiction, and published memoir in the nineteenth century. The affordances of each genre contribute a different aspect, emphasize and make available different uptakes: statistical stress, apprehension, passivity. But it's my central contention that they work stochastically and yet in concert to make the emotion of anxiety sticky to the scene of childcare, to make it not-entirely-separable from the experience of maternal love. Advice literature's probabilistic expectation of child death cultivates statistical stress as a feature of maternal reading, while the serialized anticipation of a fictional child's death transmutes that stress into an anxious temporality and normalizing axis of identification. Taking up both possibilities, the autobiographical writing of grieving mothers charts collisions between paradigms that offer comfort only to carry forward the anxious mental movement of anxiety by emphasizing the struggle for fatalistic acceptance of premature death as the foundation of character and the will of God. The statistical, biographical, and imaginative likelihood of child death accretes as uptake residue onto the subject position whose present body and attention are imagined as guaranteeing the reproductive future. Maternal love, which collapses and unifies care and concern, is thus a focused attention on the present in relation to the future, a projection of what-might-come (whether tragedy to forestall or desired outcome to produce) that shapes activities and choices in the present moment. The mother—as daily caregiver and as moral influence—undertakes a kind of temporal surveillance watching *now* in order to predict and control future *thens*.

CHAPTER 4

Supervisory Attention and Maternal Management

Paralipsis, Paid Childcare, and Novelistic Perspective

WANT TO RETURN to Émile-Carolus Leclerq's *The Physician's Verdict* (p. 2, fig. 1). It seems important to linger momentarily on the nurse who nearly fades into the wallpaper. Standing behind the mother's red velvet chair, she frames the central tableau, eyes downcast and face shadowed. Her arm and shoulder curve into the back of the chair, continuing the line begun by the physician's back and the baby's crib. She appears part of the furnishings that mark the family's wealth and status, but the urgent curve as she cranes over her employer suggests an emotional stake in the doctor's "verdict." The mother is more interested in the credentialed expertise of the medical man across the crib than the experiential knowledge of the professional caregiver who looms behind her. Gazing earnestly at the doctor who clasps her hand, the middle-class woman seems to take the nurse for granted. (Perhaps she assumes that her employee is also deferentially absorbed in the doctor's words). We can't tell, of course, what the nurse is thinking. Her gaze seems to rest on the clasped hands of her employer and the physician—on an alliance that excludes her. She might be worrying about the child, or be concerned about the extra work the doctor's prescriptions will entail. She might not be thinking about the scene in front of her at all; distracted by an aching back or feet, she might be wondering when she'll get to sit down for a spell. She might be remembering a similar moment, when another child—perhaps her own—lay ill without such a profusion of white linen or such expensive, expert care.

If the illness and death of children was one material aspect of middle-class family life in nineteenth-century Britain and the British Empire, another was having servants perform the bulk of children's day-to-day care. This chapter takes up that topic, exploring how the genre ecology's circulation of representations of paid caregivers generates maternal care as anxious supervision. We will look at advice regarding wet nurses and governesses; Mary Martha Sherwood's representation of her younger self struggling with managing her multiracial nursery staff; and the slippery impossibility of erasing the perspectives of domestic and professional employees as it appears in the fiction of the 1840s, here represented by Charlotte Brontë's *Jane Eyre* (1847), Anne Brontë's *Agnes Grey* (1847), and Charles Dickens's *Dombey and Son* (1846–1848). In turning from the probability of premature death to the present embodied alterity of paid caregivers, I am complicating our understanding of the anxious residues that constitute middle-class motherhood as a cultural form. I am also expanding our understanding of maternal anxiety itself. Child death mobilizes the emotion's temporal aspect, collapsing past, present, and future and suturing maternal love to the flickering apprehension of oncoming dangers that only might be avoidable. Paid childcare mobilizes a more spatial dimension by directing maternal concern toward what is (or might be) happening out of sight—around the corner, in another room, while her attention is elsewhere. Maternal care thus operates not just proleptically—by apprehending dangerous futures in the present—but also paraliptically—by manifesting *here* dangerous or disruptive possibilities that are potentially occurring *there*.[1] In the case of paid childcare, as we will see, the specific alternatives range widely. They are unified, however, in standing as evidence of the unsettling quality of the paid caregiver's psychological and cultural or racial difference. If temporal anxiety shapes maternal care's manifestation as nurture in the present moment, paraliptic anxiety shapes its effort to control the delegated activity of daily childcare. Maternal anxiety not only enacts a mother's love, then, but also channels its performance as the managerial oversight of staff.[2]

---

1. Paralipsis is the rhetorical strategy of emphasizing a point by professing not to mention it: *I won't mention that many of you still owe me that essay,* observes a teacher at the beginning of class; *I don't want to say my opponent meant to mislead you,* suggests a politician. It crosses spatial boundaries, bringing information or knowledge into view by overwriting the literal statement (*I won't mention, I don't want to say*) with an alternative, competing, and apparently more authentic truth.

2. This differs subtly from Ngai's brilliant theorization of the spatial dimension of anxiety in *Ugly Feelings.* Taking up the understanding of anxiety as "something 'projected' onto others in the sense of an outward propulsion or displacement," Ngai offers a theory of anxious subjectivity in which the emotion is less the effect of temporal or spatial distinction (here vs. there, now vs. someday) than it is "a structural effect of spatialization in general" (212). Ngai's reading of works by Herman Melville, Alfred Hitchcock, and Martin Heidegger compellingly empha-

Paid caregivers are consistently depicted as intimate strangers, interlopers whose supplemental presence both allows the upper-middle-class family to function and indicates that its ideological self-sufficiency is just or only ever nominal. There is broad historical consensus that for most of the nineteenth century, servant keeping was one significant marker of middle-class status (see Tange 6, 27; Stern 54–55).[3] With wealth increasing in the early decades of the century, more households employed staff to assist in the significant labor of keeping homes clean, with the maid-of-all-work typically the first servant hired. Historians note that "the relationship between waged domestic workers and their employers . . . was . . . the most widely and consistently experienced extra-familial relationship in the society" (Steedman, *Labours Lost* 36; see also Davidoff et al. 161–163). This is extended and complicated in the context of British India. Nupur Chaudhuri explains that the individuals Englishwomen hired as servants were the "only group of Indians with whom [they] had substantial contact" and that a middle-class family would likely employ five to six servants in India (versus three in England) ("Memsahibs and Their Servants" 550). The ubiquity of the service relationship, and the integration of that structure into the social reproduction of the English middle class both in Britain and British India installed a system of contract at the heart of the very social unit ideologically opposed to such logics.

Within the middle-class home, the hierarchies of gender, class, and race collide over the work—symbolic but also physical—of childcare. Over the course of the eighteenth century, as we have seen, motherhood was defined with increasing rigidity as the biologically and divinely mandated socialization and physical care of children. Symbolically, it hinged both on maternal breastfeeding and on a mother's "natural" ability to provide moral training. At the same time, however, a family's middle-class status depended on its ability to hire at least a maid-of-all-work, and in households with children her responsibilities included childcare. Nursemaids tended to change jobs frequently; Carolyn Steedman points out that, from the point of view of servants, "a good place was a place without children" (228; see also McBride 50–51): In a household with children, the maid would not only have to hump coal and water, empty chamber pots and clean outhouses, scrub floors and pots, and

---

sizes anxiety's connection to a particular type of intellectual masculinity. My thinking about maternal managerialism aligns with this in that I am connecting the middle-class mother's supervisory attention to that of the nineteenth-century professional man.

3. Although writing about later in the century, Davidoff et al. render the labor of domestic servants vividly: "both a full hod of coal and a jug of bath water weighed around 30 pounds, often to be carried up numerous flights of stairs" (160). On literary representations of servants more generally, see Robbins; McCuskey, "The Kitchen Police" and "Not at Home."

do laundry, but also—and quite possibly at the same time—make sure that a toddler didn't wander off, choke on a pebble, or burn themselves; change and launder diapers; and increasingly find the time and energy to *play*.[4] But while class hierarchies assign childcare to servants, gender hierarchies require that it be the province of the lady of the house, the middle-class woman whose simultaneous leisure and intensive nurturing labor centers domestic ideology. While middle-class mothers in the early nineteenth century were *responsible* for the physical care and moral education of their children, then, they did not necessarily *deliver* most of it themselves.

This ideological collision positions the servant's care as somehow extra, an addition to the structure of the nuclear family rather than an intrinsic component of it. I've found it useful to think through these complexities through Jacques Derrida's idea of the *supplement,* which he develops through his reading of Jean-Jacques Rousseau's thinking about motherhood. For Derrida, the supplement is "a surplus, a plenitude enriching another plenitude," but at the same time the supplement "adds only to replace. It intervenes or insinuates itself *in-the-place-of*" (144, 145). It therefore marks a void or emptiness in the original structure, while also being always already excessive to it. "Compensatory [*suppléant*] and vicarious," writes Derrida, "the supplement is an adjunct, a subaltern instance which *takes-(the)-place [tient-lieu]*" (145). Presence— which, in Derrida's reading of Rousseau, is both natural and maternal—"*ought to be* self-sufficient" and yet raising a virtuous man requires a complex and totalizing system of education, a system of "culture or cultivation that must supplement a deficient nature" (145, emphasis in the original; 146).[5] Maternal care is both enough, and not. *Non*-maternal childcare is both superfluous and essential, supplementing a self-sufficient middle-class nuclear family that cannot reproduce itself without an instrumental subaltern presence. This, we might say, causes problems. The enabling contradiction of middle-class famil-

---

4. Steedman describes the burden—and the filthy nature—of child-attending labor in *Labours Lost* (99–104 and 228–254). She notes, for example, that it's easier to embrace the philosophical importance of children mucking about in the dirt if you don't have to wash their clothes, and that the replacement of linen with cotton in the later eighteenth century significantly increased the work entailed by diapers (235, 237). On *play* as a marker of children's class status, see Frost 76–96.

5. Parker shows how the figure of the mother has been systematically suppressed in the canon of philosophy and psychoanalytic theory descended from Marx and Freud, distorting the conceptualization of knowledge those disciplines seek to provide. In thinking about the particularities of Derrida's development of the notion of supplement from Rousseau's thinking, I would draw our attention to the latter's influential sense that breastfeeding was a natural duty and yet required exhortation and incentive. If we accept Derrida's reading, then we can see that Rousseau helps to install a supplemental logic in the foundations of the ideology of nurturing motherhood.

ial ideology, then, is that the nuclear family both is and is not complete; it both does and does not raise children in its own image without supplemental aid. It falls to the mother of the family to manage this contradiction. In fact, I would argue, she must *manage* in a literal and interpersonal sense: Rather than exclusively delivering their children's care themselves, middle-class mothers direct, arrange, and oversee it. Understanding paid caregivers as supplementing the structure of the nuclear family allows us to see how the disciplinary, supervisory, anxious attention mobilized around such figures operates paraliptically—by drawing attention to the very things it purports to render irrelevant.

My argument in *Writing Maternity* has thus far implicitly posited that advice literature *preceded* the anxiety it addresses in historical if not biographical terms, calling the emotion into being by projecting it as the exigency to which individual advice-givers respond; but rhetorical situation is more cyclical than such causal directionality suggests. In what follows, I juxtapose life writing and advice literature—rather than treating them separately as I did in the previous chapter—before turning to domestic fiction. By curating representative interactions between Mary Martha Sherwood's memoir, on the one hand, and contemporary advice literature she may or may not have read, on the other, I zoom in on these two genres' uptakes of one another. This demonstrates one way to analyze uptake in a stochastic and diffuse public genre ecology as opposed to a bounded and goal-oriented activity system.[6] I subsequently turn to two subgenres of domestic fiction—fictional autobiography and the multiplot novel—in order to show how rhetorical context can inform literary analysis as well as to extend my earlier contention that fiction plays an essential role in the sedimentary process by which uptake residue accretes into cultural formations.

Milk, Morals, and Maternal Management

Before the late eighteenth century, wet nurses in Britain were predominantly hired privately by wealthy families, or by parishes and local governments to care for abandoned children. In both cases, they were typically artisan-class married women who continued to live in their own homes while caring for additional infants; they provided complete infant care, not just breastmilk, under a version of the feudal fosterage system. There was no assumption that

---

6. Some brilliant examples of historical scholarship examining rhetorical genre in the context of public activity systems include Applegarth, *Rhetoric*; Bazerman, *Languages* and *Shaping Written Knowledge*. See also Winsor. On public genre systems and ecologies, see Reiff and Bawarshi. Russell provides an excellent introduction to genre and activity theory.

the nurse would separate herself from her own children: Only the wealthiest families had space for a nurse to live in, in addition to a conviction that rural areas were healthier and safer for children. While children were integrated into the nurse's household-family, these women's relationships to their employers were shaped by geographic separation.

This changed as the ideology of nurturing motherhood became a dominant structure of feeling, in part through increased cultural attention to maternal breastfeeding in the middle of the eighteenth century. The earlier fosterage model for wet nursing was possible because breastfeeding was understood as a relatively straightforward bodily function that was distinct from maternal love and care; a wealthy woman could hire one less wealthy to provide this service without impact on her own maternal identity, and a woman who fostered children neither lost her claims to respectability nor was deemed to be selling what rightfully belonged only to her own children (see Fildes, *Wet Nursing* 79–81; Perry, "Colonizing" 220). But as motherhood was increasingly conflated with daily, time- and emotion-intensive, care, children could not be sent "out" for fostering; instead it was expected that wet nurses would live "in," with the families of their employers and apart from their own. This increased the total expense of a wet nurse, since a family had to not only afford her wages but also be able to provide room and board, and it also shifted the labor pool significantly, at least in Britain: Artisan-class married women with children were unlikely to be willing or able to leave their own families in order to live with their employers for six months, a year, or more. Instead, English wet nurses were increasingly poor, single mothers (Fildes, *Wet Nursing*, 191–192). This new location and profile—a resident employee who was a sexually experienced single woman—afforded increased supervision both logistically and emotionally. Living under a single roof facilitated scrutiny and control of the nursing woman's "diet, regime, care, and behavior," and also exacerbated anxieties about class contact and moral contamination (see Fildes, *Wet Nursing* 191–193).[7] While in Britain the increasing dominance of the ideal of nurturing motherhood reduced the numbers of wet nurses and transformed the spatial and supervisory relationship between them and their employers, middle-class Englishwomen in British India continued to hire wet nurses in large numbers through much of the nineteenth century. The latter were medically advised to hire Indian women to nurse their children; there is no discussion of their sexual history that I have been able to locate, and the discussion of what

---

7. Matus illuminates the specific ways in which sexuality and maternity came to be conceived of as incompatible aspects of the female body; see also Perry, "Colonizing" and *Novel Relations* 339–341; Bowers 163–93; Nussbaum 47–73. On mid-Victorian debates about wet nursing within the medical community, see Berry.

will happen to the wet nurses' own children is more explicit (see Chaudhuri, "Motherhood" 529–530). In both cases, the practice of incorporating a racially or socially Other woman at the center of the family's reproductive practice supplemented and destabilized maternal identity and mobilized considerable ideological and practical efforts.

The episodes I analyze from *The Life of Mrs. Sherwood* occurred between 1805 and 1807 and were revised into her manuscript memoir in the early 1850s before being published in 1854; the advice literature dates from the decades between experience and revision/publication. This allows us to read Sherwood as representative both of the historical or addressed audience advice literature claims—the historical analogue to the genre's constitutive addressee—and of the anxious maternal subject its address affords as an uptake capture. In addition, Sherwood's *Life* serves (as it did in the previous chapter) as what Dryer calls an uptake artifact, an example of a text produced in response to advice literature's anxious affordances (65). Bringing these genres into conversation allows us to see the cyclical movement of uptake, in which each genre responds to and (re)enacts the rhetorical situation. Emotion accrues and accretes with each iteration's repetition with a difference, generating the affective truth that paid childcare was inherently both supplemental and paraliptic.

As I described earlier, Sherwood's son Henry was born in December 1805 and died of whopping cough the summer of 1807. The child was sickly and fragile from birth; after nursing him herself for six months, Sherwood hired an Indian woman named Ameena as a wet nurse. She had Henry weaned at fourteen months (in February 1807), a decision that, as we've seen, she blamed for his death six months later. Shortly before her discussion of Henry's weaning, Sherwood recounts the consequences of an excursion in which Ameena took the baby to a "Poojah" (puja)—which she glosses parenthetically as an "idolatrous service"—and brings him home with "some idolatrous daub or spot on his forehead" (298) (likely a tilak). The fact of the outing seems to have been routine; Ameena, along with Henry's ayah and bearer, took the baby out for a walk.[8] But the destination of this particular trip as well as its lasting mark

---

8. A puja is a Hindu ceremonial worship that includes a range of specific practices, from brief rites within the home to more complex temple rituals. A tilak is a mark of auspiciousness—often a spot made with colored paste—that also indicates an acknowledgement of the sacredness of its wearer. In some Hindu traditions, guests to a puja are given tilaks as marks of honor and welcome. While they carry religious significance for Buddhists and Jains as well as Hindus, the ceremony and the spots themselves are not analogous to Christian baptism, as Sherwood fears. Women employed as wet nurses are referred to as both *dhayes* and amahs; ayahs were maids but, as in England, also served as nursemaids; bearers were servants employed to carry children who could not yet walk, or for long outings. (Baby carriages were not in wide use until the 1840s.)

on the baby's body are clearly *not* routine. Writing her memoir in the early 1850s, Sherwood emphasizes her own ignorance: Reasoning by way of analogy to the "drop of water laid on the brow by a clergyman of the Church of England" in baptism, she leaps to the conclusion that the spot is evidence that Henry has been somehow converted from Christianity to Hinduism ("Diary" 217). "Dreadfully terrified," Sherwood wanted her chaplain to rebaptize the child; she recalls that he has "some difficulty" convincing her that this is not necessary, that the caregiver's religion has not replaced the parents' (*Life* 298). Sherwood offers this moment as part of her religious narrative, an example of her lack of faith in the enduring superiority of Christianity; she explicitly codes her response as both ignorant and excessive. In representing but also minimizing the danger of this outing, *The Life of Mrs. Sherwood* depicts the religion and culture of the Indian staff as paraliptic threats. Ameena's influential alterity here leaves only temporary marks: a physical spot that can be washed off, an experience that Henry will not remember and that cannot change his religious identification. But at the same time, the fact that this happened during an otherwise ordinary excursion emphasizes the persistent danger it poses. Unlike the prospect of a child's death, which is felt proleptically, the child's socialization away from their family culture happens in the moment but just out of sight. It is the danger whose explicit erasure paraliptically speaks its constant supplemental presence.

The larger rhythm of *The Life of Mrs. Sherwood* is one in which moments like this that trigger the writer's sense of vulnerability are juxtaposed with tales of pleasant experiences of India and Indian culture. This reproduces the anxious temporal logic of both advice literature and serial fiction, in that Sherwood's memoir cultivates a reading experience in which we are prepared to be surprised. It also means that the segments of travelogue dramatize the ongoing context of domestic alterity that the text is otherwise at pains to contain. The story of Henry's offstage visit to a puja immediately follows a long account of the family's visit to Baber Ali Khan, the Nawab of Bengal, which Sherwood describes as "a most delightful and interesting expedition, a little bright spot in my life" (298). Her pleasure in the experience—the lavishly decorated boats, elaborate fireworks, and performances by dancers and jugglers—seems limited only by the concern that Henry might be disturbed by the loud noises; instead, she finds that he was "not the least annoyed" by them (298). This story of appreciation for Indian culture leads into the tale of danger averted ("It was shortly after the entertainment that Henry went to the puja [298]), which is effectively a transitional moment into her reflection on the decision to wean Henry at fourteen months—a decision that she blamed for his death and felt was a result of her own inadequate adaptation to India. Narratively, cultural appreciation leads metonymically to possible assimilation, resistance to which seems both relatively easy (washing away the tilak) and permanently debilitating (following English customs for weaning). While Sherwood's didactic frame for the puja story is her religious ignorance and the overreaction it caused, that very ignorance speaks through the difficulty of controlling—and even knowing the specifics of—the care being taken of her child. Ameena provides the milk that Sherwood herself cannot, literally replacing her; by taking him to a Hindu ceremony that leaves a lasting trace, Ameena—in Sherwood's text—threatens to replace the baby's mother morally and culturally, as well.

Advice literature reinforces and extends this possibility, unstably distinguishing between and conflating mothers and wet nurses in discussions of breastfeeding. Throughout the genre, it can be difficult to discern whether the advice on diet, controlling one's temper, taking regular exercise, and the like are aimed at nursing mothers or mothers supervising wet nurses. Margaret King Moore refers ambiguously and repeatedly to "a woman who is suckling," despite her insistence that there is no excuse for a mother not to breastfeed her own child (for example, 18). Similarly, Pye Henry Chavasse's nutritional advice is offered in response to the question, "What should be the diet of a wet-nurse or a mother who is suckling?" (*Advice to Mothers* 23), rendering them medically and rhetorically interchangeable. Biologically, breastmilk provides important nutrients and antibodies; before knowledge of sterilization or the full nutritional needs of infants, it was very difficult to raise a child "by hand"—that is, on some combination of "pap" and milk from an ungulate (cow, sheep, goat, or ass).[9] In the early nineteenth century, breastfeeding was both proclaimed a fundamental responsibility of motherhood and figured as a difficult task many women simply could not undertake. In my sample of advice books, breastfeeding appears as "the first duty of a mother," including the damning judgment that a "woman who cannot submit to a little trouble . . . for the benefit of her child, does not deserve to be called a mother," but also as something that can be carefully delegated to others (Moore 21). Of the eight sections in the chapter on "Nursing" in Thomas Bull's *Hints to Mothers* (1837), for example, five discuss challenges to maternal breastfeeding, one

---

9. As nutritional knowledge improved, more and more infants were raised "by hand" (like Pip in *Great Expectations*), more commonly referred to as "artificial feeding." Stevens et al. claim that due to bacterial buildup in bottles and other feeding devices, combined with lack of reliable milk storage or sterilization, "one third of all artificially fed infants" died before turning one. The first modern infant formula was that developed by Justus von Leibig in 1865 and was known as Leibig's formula; as the chemistry of human milk was better understood, essential nutrients were added (Stevens et al.; see also Valerie Fildes, *Breasts, Bottles, and Babies,* chapters 11–14). For an astute analysis of twentieth- and twenty-first-century debates, see Koerber.

focuses on "artificial feeding," and two offer advice for screening and managing a wet nurse—a focus that leaves little space for detailed guidance in how to nurse your own child. The circumstances that result in delegating "that nourishment which nature commands her to administer from her own" body are characterized as traumatic (Moore 11): "stern necessity," "ill-health," and only "if it be ascertained past all doubt that a mother cannot suckle her own child" (Bakewell 22; Bull, *Hints to Mothers* 171; Chavasse, *Advice to Mothers* 33). The two texts aimed at mothers in British India sympathetically invoke White women whose "mind[s] revolt . . . at the idea of a stranger taking upon herself such a responsible office" but insist that it is in the best interest of both mother and child: "A tropical climate undermines . . . an European constitution" (*Domestic Guide* 57; see also Goodeve 4–5 and discussion in Chaudhuri, "Motherhood" 529). Rhetorically, then, this genre figures motherhood *both* as feeding children with your own body *and* as controlling the body of another woman to do so.

Chavasse warns that "hirelings, let them be ever so well inclined, can never have the affection and unceasing assiduity of a parent, and therefore cannot perform the duties of lactation with equal advantage to the infant" (*Advice to Mothers* 32–33). In British India, however, this conviction persisted alongside the belief that the milk of an Indian woman was physically better for a White infant than that of their mother. *A Domestic Guide to Mothers in India* actively encourages readers to hire Indian wet nurses because "no infant thrives so well in India as those fed by these women (57). Sherwood recounts being advised by a White woman who oversees the care of a nursery full of healthy English children that "wet-nurses must be had for delicate children in India, even if the white mother [is] able to nurse her children for a time" (378). Sherwood expresses some concern for such nurses' own children and is told callously that the babies "commonly die." "The mothers never fret about them," the White nurse explains. "Whenever they nurse a white baby, they cease to care for their own" (378). This sense of an available pool of nurses relies on a racist and classist economy of value in which wealthy White babies are inherently more valuable and more loveable than Indian or poor ones, and the maternal feelings of wealthy White women are more intense and less alienable than those of their marginalized counterparts. Sherwood's description of her own experience appears to confirm this; in an episode omitted from the published *Life* she describes Ameena's baby being "given to the Grandmother without an apparent pang on the Mother's part" when she is hired ("Diary" 132). Later, Sherwood offers a detailed account of her own concern for the child of her daughter Lucy's *dhaye*, as well as the nurse's "placid" response to the baby's eventual death (*Life* 382, 386). These ghostly children persist paraliptically throughout discussions of wet nurses, the barely-mentionable infants whose existence is physically recalled by their mothers' lactating breasts.[10]

While colonial and class ideologies mandate lesser maternal feeling on the part of the poor Whites and people of color who tend wealthy White children, the implication that a baby's nurse could love it *like a mother* manifests the supplemental nature of paid childcare. In September 1807, a few months after Henry's death, the Sherwoods encounter Ameena, whom they had dismissed when Henry was weaned the previous February:

> Alas! it was the nurse of my departed child. She had been aware of our approach, and had sat waiting there to see her boy. The tears will flow when I think of these things, and the same reflections occur to my mind in this place as did when I first recorded this circumstance in my diary. There are moments of intense feeling in which all distinctions of nations, colours, and castes disappear, and in their place there only remains between two human beings one abiding sense of a common nature. When I saw the beloved nurse of my Henry brought into the boat, and unfeignedly weeping for her boy, I felt in truth that she was a human being like myself, and as dear to Him that made her as the most exalted saint that ever existed in the Christian world. (*Life* 317)

Ameena's "unfeigned[ ] weeping" here demonstrates her considerable emotional attachment to the boy, as well as the trauma of learning about her nursling's death so abruptly, but Sherwood subsumes the Indian woman's grief into her own experience of identification and recognition. "Distinctions of nations, colours, and castes disappear" (for Sherwood at least) in this moment of shared sadness for the loss of the precious White child, in the employee's mourning for the child she was hired to feed and tend—as though her emotions had been purchased along with her time, energy, and bodily fluid. Despite the putatively equalizing nature of this moment, which allows Sherwood to "feel" Ameena's humanity, it can only occur through the latter woman's apparent acknowledgement of the inherent (greater) value of the English child. But the identity between Sherwood's grief for Henry and Ameena's for that same child—also *"her* boy"—destabilizes the hierarchical difference between the two women . . . at least in their relations to the child. Later, Sherwood aestheticizes the interracial relationship between *dhaye* and child, while perhaps paradoxically reinscribing the paraliptic logic of the emotional bond

---

10. Polly Toodle's clandestine visit to her children is central to *Dombey and Son*'s plot, as I discuss below. George Moore dramatizes this from the perspective of the nurse in *Esther Waters* (1894). See also discussion in A. Roberts.

caregiving generates: Generalizing on the occasion of Lucy's becoming "reconciled" to her wet nurse, Sherwood notes that "it is touching to see the European babe hanging on the breast of the black woman, and testifying towards her all the tenderness which is due to its own mother" (*Life* 382).

Her children's *dhayes* thus stand synecdochally not only for the physical nourishment they provide but also the moral and emotional relationships enacted through care labor. Apart from Henry's trip to a puja, however, *The Life of Mrs. Sherwood* spends little time considering the possibility that White children could be morally or socially rather than physically harmed by familial supplementation, although several of her stories play out the fantasy of an English child "rescued" from cultural assimilation through the symbolically violent intervention of a White woman (see "Little Henry" and "Little Lucy"). Contemporary representations of governesses take up this concern. According to Kathryn Hughes, the volatility of the markets in the early nineteenth century both rendered an increased number of families wealthy, and therefore able to hire governesses, and at the same time meant that there were more governesses available for hire: Numerous families found themselves suddenly reduced from middle-class gentility to poverty by the very investments they had hoped would ensure their *upward* mobility (27–28). Young women—the daughters of such families—had very few acceptable ways to earn a living and found themselves needing to capitalize on the educations intended to outfit them for genteel marriages and lives of leisure (Hughes 27–28; see also Peterson, "Victorian Governess"). The task of a governess was to provide home-based education, typically for boys under the age of seven and for girls through their teen years; they were also expected to oversee much of the children's moral educations, and to provide older girls with lessons in "accomplishments" such as French, Italian, music, and drawing. Prior to the 1830s, such accomplishments were not associated with the middling classes but with the gentility; middle-class girls would, instead, have learned domestic skills from their housekeeping mothers. But as family wealth increased and more domestic work was delegated to servants, decreasing emphasis was placed on household management and such knowledge could even seem antithetical to a family's—or an individual young woman's—ambitions.[11] Governesses were thus hired not only as a sign of a family's wealth and to relieve the mother of even the least dirty domestic labor; they were also hired to replace maternal

---

11. Recall that in *Pride and Prejudice* Mrs. Bennett is insulted when Mr. Collins asks which of his cousins prepared the meal, and that in *Middlemarch* Rosamund Vincy's aspirational education has left her largely uninterested in and incapable of even the supervisory labor expected of a middle-class woman. For further discussion of this transformation, see Gorham 3–15; Nelson 77–86.

instruction that could not advance the family's upward mobility. They were hired—like wet nurses—to supplement maternal care.

Advice about and to governesses exhibits the same difficulty distinguishing paid from maternal care we saw with wet nurses. In a series of essays and pamphlets published in the 1840s about governesses, Anna Brownell Jameson and Mary Maurice take up the problem of distinguishing maternal from paid care directly and, in doing so, reinforce the rhetorical urgency of erasing the caregiver's individual life (history). "The Relative Social Position of Mothers and Governesses" (Jameson, 1846), *Mothers and Governesses,* and *Governess Life* (Maurice, 1847 and 1849) were published in support of the Governesses Benevolent Institution, which sought to ameliorate the appalling economic conditions of unemployed (including "retired") governesses, and to professionalize the career through classes, certification, and a registry of positions.[12] As in the discussions of wet nurses, the distinction between mothers and governesses is repeatedly drawn only to have it collapse: "The same education which would form the good mother, would form the good governess" (Jameson 264); "every young person ought to study, with the idea that she will in all probability have to teach what she is now acquiring. . . . For this reason, . . . every woman is, or ought to be, a teacher, or at least she should be able to teach" (Maurice, *Mothers* 24–25). Whether a teenage girl studies with a maternal or governessing future in mind, then, seems to make little difference to the actual course of study. The education is the same, and for the moment at least the responsibilities and orientation of the mother are not fully distinguishable from those of a hired teacher.

To stabilize this difference, advice literature turns to class in ways that are homologous to Sherwood's recourse to race, emphasizing the importance of an individual governess's performance of class identity. The education they both advocate for is aimed at "genteel" women, and both authors fear the possibility that it might be used as a path of upward mobility. "Fallen gentlewomen" and the "daughters of clergymen" are the most desirable candidates (*Advice to Governesses* 6; Maurice, *Mothers* 18). Maurice, for example, discourages "the daughters of small tradespeople and shop-keepers" from "qualify[ing] themselves for the office of governesses" as it will "unfit[ ] them for the duties they should fulfil in their own station" (*Mothers* 23). I've argued elsewhere that such members of the middle class, educated "at schools designed to produce governesses, are a spectre haunting" advice literature's depictions of governesses ("Instructive Sufficiency" 90). For Maurice, this class of teachers has

---

12. Mary Poovey provides a succinct history of the Governesses' Benevolent Institution (GBI) in *Uneven Developments* (232n2). See also Billings; Kaye; Peterson, "Victorian Governess."

contributed to a difficult economic situation. The oversupply of minimally qualified governesses helps her to explain the structurally bad working conditions of contingent labor: lack of respect, low pay, no job security, and so forth (*Mothers* 22). But both her and Jameson's emphasis on the dangers of hiring such teachers—who are, Jameson warns, like "machine[s]" (261)—speaks to the concerns that their class status amounts to an inalienable trait, a dangerously disruptive quality that will distort and even pervert the education they provide. Maurice suggests that families can "raise the position of governesses in society" if they hire "lady-like and elevated" individuals (*Mothers* 93).

The ideal governess is therefore figured not only as coming from the social class of (or just above) that of the family who hires her, but also as being distinctly malleable. In *Early Education; or, the Management of Children* (1820), Elizabeth Appleton recommends her readers to hire a relatively young governess, who will be more adaptable to the mother's pedagogical priorities: "Give her the theory" "with gentleness and persuasion," she explains; "she will practice upon your children with success" (4). The familial situation, in other words, mandates the erasure of any coherent or idiosyncratic self in a woman hired as governess. Another guide, in addressing governesses, advises that they analyze each new household carefully in order to "judge whether [one's] intended plans are compatible with the arrangements of the family" (Bureaud-Riofrey 58–59). Advice literature's emphasis on paid caregivers' essential adaptability effectively communicates that these hired teachers are—or must be—typical rather than unique; they are fungible hirelings rather than distinctive individuals.

Appleton emphasizes that governesses deliver instruction "under *superintendence* of [a] maternal and watchful eye" (1, emphasis added), and the anonymous author of the 1827 *Advice to Governesses* expresses the hope that maternal readers "will distribute ["this little work"] to those who have the superintendence of their children" (ix–x). Jameson cautions readers that it may be challenging for a governess to "be . . . regarded with watchful observation . . . her words weighed, her manners, her dress, her conduct in every minute particular cautiously, narrowly scrutinized" (36–37). Such oversight defines the relationship. The phrases "maternal management" and "management of children" were ubiquitous in late eighteenth- and early nineteenth-century advice literature, appearing frequently in the genre's titles and subtitles as well as dotting its description of its purview: *Observations on the Mortality and Physical Management of Children*; *Plain Observations on the Management of Children During the First Month*; *Maternal Management of Children in Health and Disease*; *Treatise on the Physiological and Moral Management of Infancy*; *Hints for the General Management of Children in India*; and so on.[13] It's worth lingering over the repetition. In *Keywords,* Raymond Williams identifies two etymological origins for *management*: *maneggiare*—which refers to animal training—and *ménager*—which refers to caring for the household (189–190). But while those meanings are both rooted in the world of the farm and agricultural estate, *management* and the related verb (*to manage*) and job title (*manager*) were increasingly applied to the realm of capitalist enterprise during this period. "As the term was extended to business," notes Williams, "there was still a clear distinction between owners and directors on the one hand and managers on the other" (190). Managers superintend but do not control processes; their responsibility for oversight does not extend to the authority to identify primary or new goals, values, possibilities, or purposes. At the same time, they are closely aligned with the institutions they serve, as management theorist Peter Drucker contends: "Management has to . . . think through the institution's mission, has to set its objectives, and has to organize resources for the results the institution has to contribute" (17, qtd. in Strickland 58–59). The maternal readers invoked by the genre are thus *middle* managers, supervising paid caregivers but subordinate to the patriarchal authority of the medical establishment.

In *Labor and Monopoly Capitalism*—an influential analysis of labor under industrial capitalism from the left—Harold Braverman emphasizes the spatial and temporal aspects of management. "Even an assemblage of independently practicing artisans," he concedes, "requires coordination, if one considers the need for the provision of a workplace and the ordering of processes within it" (47, qtd. in Strickland 10–11). That ordering—arranging across time and within space—is predicated upon control, an authority that comes from a hierarchical position within the organization. Writing about the managerial logic of writing program administration in the twentieth century, Donna Strickland argues that "management happens" "once organizations of any kind are organized hierarchically, with a class of experts structuring and overseeing the work of a group of nonexperts" (58). The peculiar position of managers is to—at least theoretically—have greater expertise than those they manage but less than those who manage them; they are responsible for the outcome but have little authority over the terms of the project for all that they must necessarily be aligned with its goals. Indeed, an essential component of management is to "shape . . . desires and . . . to create the felt sense of a shared project"—such as, in our context, the love of a particular child or an emotional investment in a family's future (Strickland 60). The ideal employee in management theory is

---

13. Respectively: Roberton; anonymous; Underwood and Hall; Bull, *Maternal Management*; Combe; Goodeve.

one who has so internalized the panoptic logic and mission of the workplace that their supervisor can trust them implicitly.

Advice literature emphasizes two particular features of the maternal management of nursery staff: first, the ability to see below the surface in order to judge character visually; and, second, a paraliptic attention that prevents malfeasance (or even undue influence) by regularly invoking its possibility. In selecting a governess or wet nurse, for example, it seems that a mother must be able to spot frauds: To hire a socially inferior governess who has acquired the necessary cultural capital through study rather than familial socialization is to undermine the very work one requires of her; to hire a wet nurse without milk is to threaten the very life one seeks to preserve.[14] Maurice cautions against expecting too much for too little: "the system of over expectation, will be met by one, of false profession, and deception" (*Mothers* 11). Jameson cautions against "unworthy pretenders" who seek teaching positions solely for economic reasons (12). Both reveal a conviction that the prospective governess's appearance is revelatory: She must be dressed neither too plainly nor too showily (Jameson 48–49; Maurice, *Governess Life* 22). The absence of "habits of refinement, neatness, and propriety" as they appear "in the person, the dress, [and] the arrangements" not only reveals "a disorderly mind" but is an "evil [that] necessarily extends to the children" (Maurice, *Governess Life* 21).

For wet nurses, the dangers are physical as well as social, the threat one of ill-health or even death rather than an inadequately intuitive gentility. In both cases, the exigency is that the economic transaction creates an incentive for the prospective employee to misrepresent the nature of the care for sale, a concern that speaks the impossibility of the caregivers leaving their own lives on the other side of the threshold. Andrew Combe cautions that a wet nurse's desire (or need) for continued employment may well be at odds with her charge's health if, for example, her milk starts to dry up. While under similar circumstances a nursing mother "takes the alarm at once, and seeks an immediate remedy," he contends, "an ill-chosen nurse . . . is often tempted to conceal her deficiency" not only because she lacks a mother's stake in the child's well-being but also because she is "afraid of losing her situation" (223); her employment, after all, is reliant on the bodily fluid she produces. Combe warns: "From the very concealment that is practiced, it becomes next to impossible that the food so provided can be either proper for the child, or given at the proper times" (224). (Recall the nutritional and hygiene challenges of bottle feeding at the time, compounded in such cases by secrecy.) The nurse's employment contract thus paradoxically motivates *bad* caretaking

---

14. For this as a more general phenomenon, see Stern.

decisions because it encourages her to put her own economic security ahead of the baby's health. "We cannot, therefore," Combe concludes, "attach too great importance to moral character in the first selection of a nurse . . . when deceit is once practiced, confidence can never be restored" (224). Reece recommends looking for a wet nurse who is "clean, healthy, sober, and temperate" (129), while Combe emphasizes someone who has "sound health, a robust constitution . . . cheerfulness and presence of mind, orderly, neat, and temperate habits, patient kindliness and good humour" (220). The bodily inspection of wet nurses, in particular, enacts a kind of rhetorical ownership of the poor White or Indian female body that is simultaneous with visual violation in its pornographic detail: The ideal is breasts that are "firm and well formed . . . convey[ing] to the touch a knotted, irregular, and hard feel" (Bull, *Hints* 172). The milk should be "thin, and of a bluish-white colour: sweet to the taste" and can be evaluated "by milking a little into a glass" (Bull, *Hints* 172; Chavasse, *Advice to Mothers* 34). Melisa Klimaszewski reads the requirement that a prospective nurse submit to such an invasive physical inspection as an effort on the part of "the higher classes . . . to reassert power over the working-class body that they perceive to be violating their family spaces in the most intimate way" (324). This physical availability compromises the poorer woman's integrity under the guise of maintaining it and, at the same time, establishes the mistress's actual power over her potential servant, asserting her dominance within the home at the very moment her physical maternity is replaced.

Mother and medical man are here allied, albeit temporarily, as experts. Their dominance over the caregiver is at least putatively premised on their greater knowledge: the features of healthy breasts, nipples, and milk; the ways clothing reveals "natural" gentility and adaptability rather than mechanized acquirements or a rigidly programmatic approach. But management involves not only careful screening but also ongoing supervision. Advice in managing either kind of caregiver therefore underscores the importance not only of clear instructions but also in visiting the classroom or nursery: "It is presumed that you visit your children's study daily . . . to encourage and observe," writes Jameson (31); Combe emphasizes this even further: "It is advisable that the mother should . . . watchfully superintend all [the nurse's] proceedings, and assure herself, by frequent and unexpected visits to the nursery, that everything is attended to with due regularity and in the right spirit" (226). Ironically, such visits deliberately disrupt the caregiver's efforts to create the desired regularity; they do so in order to make visible the extent to which the nursery or schoolroom is always open to view, always potentially under surveillance. Emerging at this time in the juridical realm to denote the "watch or guard over a person, etc., esp. over a suspected person, a prisoner, or the like" (OED), the concept of *surveillance* has also been closely associated with education and other modes of control from the outset, including the supervision of a large industrial workforce—or the poor children who will become that labor force. Jeremy Bentham's panopticon has been closely identified with these carceral, disciplinary logics, most famously by Michel Foucault's elaboration of it in *Discipline and Punish*. The panopticon was a circular structure that positioned prisoners in cells around a central hub occupied by the jailer. Premised on a one-way logic of visibility in which control was associated with the power to see without being seen in turn, Bentham argued that prisoners (or pupils) would soon internalize *the possibility of being perpetually observed* and use that spatialized anxiety to guide their actions (see Bentham, Letters I and XXI). Foucault extends this logic to time, exploring how the expectation of being observed intersects with the temporal patternings of daily life enforced by industrialized society's distribution of and ordering of time (149–156). Discipline for Foucault is thus both temporal and spatial: It relies on the sense of visibility within a hierarchy, or an architecture for life in which the body as it moves through time is always observed, monitored, judged, adjusted, patterned.

The core exigency that emerges from the cycles of uptake is that the caregiver's priorities and feelings are not always identical to those of her employer; whether wet nurse or governess, she is not always or necessarily a transparent vector for the mother's maternal care. Her love can compete for possession of the child, as when Ameena takes "her" boy Henry to a Hindu ceremony; her need for economic security can lead her to misrepresent the very commodity (breastmilk, gentility) that she sells. The judicious mother's knowledge may (but only may) help her in screening out undesirable applicants, but she also has the ongoing challenge of managing her staff—handling the distinct personalities, priorities, and cultures that live and work in her home to provide childcare. Reflecting decades later on her reaction to Henry's unauthorized trip to a Hindu ceremony, Sherwood criticizes herself, noting that "The woman [Ameena] should have been blamed, with Christian instruction, and the stain removed, and there the matter should have ended" (*Life* 298).

In this instance Sherwood does not suggest that her mismanagement ultimately threatened her child's life or soul, but later it appears to: Her decision to wean Henry at fourteen months was informed not only by inadequate medical advice but also by her difficulties managing the racial politics of her nursery staff. (Weaning, after all, means firing the wet nurse.) Ameena, "I suppose gave herself airs," Sherwood reflects, and the white woman at the head of our nursery establishment was anxious that she should be got rid of: her influence, the surgeon's, and every European also whom I consulted, gave their voices for this weaning. I was permitted to take that step which, humanly speaking, brought my baby to his grave in a few months afterwards. (*Life* 299)

The sense that good motherhood hinges on the successful management of staff pervades Sherwood's manuscript even more than the published *Life*. The manuscript reveals the extent to which Sherwood was overwhelmed by the complexities involved in managing a multiracial staff, particularly given her social and emotional isolation: "I made too much of a companion of the Baby's Nurse (Mrs. Parker)," she reflects critically, and as a result "her ascendancy in the family became too great. The Native servants would not obey her—& between them both I was often treated with scorn—. . . I was blamed by all parties. I became fretful & unhappy & at length quite a cypher in the family" ("Diary" 129–130).[15] Sherwood recurs to her difficulties with Mrs. Parker multiple times over the course of the manuscript. She considers that Henry's chronic illness may have been to blame: "Every anxious Mother who has had a sick infant must know how difficult it is to keep that infants [sic] nurse at a proper distance" ("Diary" 257). But she also believes that her isolation was a contributing factor: "It had not been with me as if I had had a Mother or Sister to speak to during the many long long heavy nights through which I watched my baby boy—with no one to speak to but Mrs. Parker. Who at least was white and spoke English" ("Diary" 257). Intimacy here upends the hierarchical relationship of employer and employee; Sherwood reflects ruefully that she "gave such sway to this white woman . . . that after a while she took the lead in every thing which should have belonged to my Province as Mistress of the family" ("Diary" 257–258).

Sherwood emphasizes how the collision of racial and class hierarchies in the colonial home, if not assiduously controlled and arranged—managed— renders the middle-class mother irrelevant and invisible (a mere "cypher").

---

15. Betty Parker was married to Luke Parker, introduced simply as "Mr. Sherwood's servant" (*Life* 235). She started serving Sherwood on the voyage to India; her children were raised alongside the Sherwood children, both biological and adopted, and she served as the head of Mrs. Sherwood's nursery staff. Chaudhuri notes that the Sherwoods had fifteen servants when living in Calcutta shortly after their arrival in India ("Servants" 550). She also emphasizes the extent to which White women's lack of linguistic knowledge limited their ability to communicate, as well as how their religious intolerance and racism impacted their understandings of and interactions with the Indians who worked for them ("Servants" 551–553).

Her analysis of her challenges with Betty Parker and the Indian staff suggests even more significant consequences. Parker's usurpation of Sherwood's authority creates broader disarray in part because the former's management is harsh and impatient: She has "by Nature a most violent temper" ("Diary" 257). Sherwood quotes a passage from her journal in which she resolves that she "must not suffer Betty to [go] in[to] passions in my presence & strike the servants & dictate to me what I must do" ("Diary" 257). In the affective truth Sherwood's narrative establishes, then, her subordination of her own domestic authority to Parker's—even though, in the moment, she could see the distinct problems with the latter's approach and values—not only leads to the mistreatment of her staff and the deterioration of her own mental health, but also makes her complicit in her child's death. (Recall that Henry was weaned in part because Parker was eager than Ameena should "be got rid of.") While Sherwood's inadequate supervision of where Ameena was taking the baby temporarily replaces his mother's religion with his nurse's, her abdication of nursery authority to Parker results in the infant losing the (supplemental) nourishment that apparently might have kept him alive. For all the Christian resignation Sherwood strives for, her account nonetheless insists that her managerial failures result in a household where both Indian and English servants can replace a child's mother, and where the consequences of this are likely to be both morally and physically devastating.

Sherwood cedes her supervisory role, apparently unable to exploit the affordances built into the mistress's control over the daily schedule and the space(s) of the home to ensure that the caregiver's supplemental presence does no more and no less than what's required. Although not facing the specific dangers of fraud or misrepresentation that advice literature enumerates, Sherwood's daily struggles with the fact of intimate strangers raising her children normalizes not only the axiomatically fictive nature of the nuclear family but also the paraliptic logic of supplementation itself. Ameena's and Parker's alterity renders Sherwood a blank cipher rather than a maternal manager, her invisibility not that of the panoptic overseer but of a nonentity. Toggling between Sherwood's writings and advice literature allows us to see the ways genres interact through uptake, generating cultural residues that come to adhere to particular figures until they are saturated with affect. Life writing's uptake affordances recreate the danger situation it depicts as typical rather than idiosyncratic, imbuing a particular experience with the authority of an affective and social fact while also substituting manageable threats (domestic mismanagement, religious ignorance) for the more disturbing possibility that motherhood is a generic caretaking role rather than an inalienable relationship. Childrearing advice literature's representation of paid childcare as a labor problem to be managed figures caregivers both as docile subjects whose bodies and minds are easily annexed to the middle-class family's social reproduction, on the one hand, and, on the other, as dangerously individual strangers whose possession of inalienable physiological and social maternal capital disrupts the integrity of that same family. These genres (re)circulate the relationship between paid childcare and middle-class mothers until it seems inescapably fraught, inevitably charged with sameness, difference, paralipsis, and supplementation. Governesses can be more influential and nurses more authoritative than mothers, Hinduism can replace Christianity, even in middle-class English homes.

Inevitably Heterogeneous

My title for this section comes, of course, from Charlotte Brontë's *Jane Eyre. An Autobiography* (1847), and the eponymous heroine's description of herself in relation to the Reed family (73). The nineteenth-century novel's generic interest in psychological interiority—its thematic and formal preoccupation with theories of mind—takes up and imaginatively extends the complexities of relying on intimate paid strangers to reproduce family. When advice literature or life writing admits that hired caregivers have perspectives of their own, the representation of them is limited and partial. This is true even in books addressing a caregiver audience rather than a managerial one. Such texts reproduce one rhetorical goal of advice to mothers, which is to subordinate the reader to the genre and to the outside authorities it represents. The consistent invocation of repression of self and suppression of desire, however sympathetically framed, fails to imaginatively evoke the complexity of, for example, a governess's interior life. Transposing these figures from challenging topic to characters in their own right, fiction enacts that paraliptic uptake affordance by situating paid caregivers in their own social contexts and creating motivations and desires for them that are not simply harnessed to the social reproduction of their employers. It also gives narrative shape and force to the more theoretical implications of these intimate strangers' presence in the middle-class home: that the middle-class family is not sufficient, that it can't reproduce without supplementation. In making such figures *characters,* fiction imbues them not only with their own cultural and familial backgrounds—further confirming the suspicions we've seen elsewhere in the genre ecology—but also with the ability to *judge.* The novelistic depictions of governesses, wet nurses, and other intimate employees to which I now turn dramatize the difficulty—indeed, the impossibility—of managing staff into complete docility, and how a different judgment is always at least potentially influential.

In this section I explore how different novel genres elaborated these aspects, raising the stakes by dramatizing the impossibility of erasing another's individual perspective and history, on the one hand, and of paying enough attention to control those alien desires, on the other. Fictional autobiography—represented here by Anne Brontë's *Agnes Grey* and Charlotte Brontë's *Jane Eyre*—and the multiplot novel—here, Charles Dickens's *Dombey and Son*—used the marginal yet essential figure of domestic and clerical employees to analyze the urgent possibility and anxious motivation for management itself. In the Brontës' governess novels paralipsis appears through the governess's moral and psychological judgment that enacts her inalienable difference. *Dombey and Son,* by contrast, dramatizes the lingering positive effects of caring relationships that transcend "question[s] of wages" as well as making a melodramatic case for caring supervision as capitalist management.

Judgement

In *Jane Eyre*'s second chapter, Jane is famously locked in the "red-room" as a punishment for challenging her cousin and aunt. Seething with a sense of injustice, she reflects on her relationship with the family:

> They were not bound to regard with affection a thing that could not sympathize with one amongst them; a heterogeneous thing, opposed to them in temperament, in capacity, in propensities; a useless thing, incapable of serving their interest, or adding to their pleasure; a noxious thing, cherishing the germs of indignation at their treatment, of contempt of their judgment. (73)

Much has been made of this self-characterization in discussion of the novel, and the way Brontë ties the character's psychological and emotional incompatibility with Mrs. Reed and her children to her situation in that family: The sentence begins with a lack of sympathy and outright "opposition in temperament," "capacity," and "propensities" before leaping metonymically to *uselessness* in relation to both interest and pleasure. Syntactically, Brontë creates an equivalence between Jane's difference (her heterogeneity), her uselessness, and her poisonousness to that family. I want to linger for a moment on the final clause, which takes us from inutility to toxic excess. Jane as familial supplement is irrelevant and excessive to the (emotionally whole) Reed family, but that very excess makes her poisonous—a poison that is specifically tied to that psychological difference, now refigured as the ability not only to react emotionally (with "indignation") but also to judge—to "feel contempt."

This capacity to evaluate critically is both one of Jane's central traits and one of the affordances of the fictional autobiography itself. The dual perspective of that form installs commentary and reflection at its heart: The character we see moving through the plot is explicitly shaped by the perspective of that character's future self. In *Jane Eyre* more than (for example) *David Copperfield* or *Great Expectations,* the commentary afforded by the genre is social as well as personal; while Dickens emphasizes the central characters' growth and psychological development—including important episodes of being taken in or misled by others—Brontë consistently focuses on Jane's capacity for evaluation and critical judgment. The red-room punishment results from her telling her cousin John that he is "wicked and cruel," "like a murderer" or "a slave-driver," and later she dispassionately judges her pupil Adele's capacity (67, 177). In reflecting on why she is willing to go to India as St. John's curate but not his wife, she reflects that it would leave her "heart and mind . . . free" and her "feelings" "unenslaved" (507). Positioned on the social margins, Jane consistently uses that position to critique.

This character trait is attached to Jane's familial and social position from the outset.[16] Her financial dependence on the Reed family is glossed in terms that echo contemporary characterizations of what M. Jeanne Peterson has helpfully labeled the governess's "status incongruence": "She was a lady, and therefore not a servant, but she was an employee, and therefore not of equal status with the wife and daughters of the house" ("Victorian Governess" 15). In Brontë's novel this heterogeneity allows the character, even as a child, to see and name what most others can or do not: John Reed's privileged cruelty, Georgina's deceit, the Reverend Brocklehurst's hypocrisy, and so on. Jane's capacity for judgment is explicitly attached to her position as a governess in the extended scene in which she observes Mr. Rochester and his guests, particularly Blanche Ingram. Positioned on the edge of the room ("behind the window-curtain") and attending at the behest of her employer and in her professional capacity, Jane's description of the scene and the other characters is interspersed with explicit commentary, and shifts uneasily between the past and present tense (254). After describing the ladies entering the room in the past tense, Brontë shifts to the present when coffee "is brought in" and remains there to describe the men who enter with it while Jane waits to see Mr. Rochester; after returning to the past tense to interpolate her reflections and opin-

---

16. Critical attention has focused on this from the novel's publication, starting with Elizabeth, Lady Eastlake's review of the novel alongside *Vanity Fair* in the *Quarterly Review.* See also Poovey, *Uneven Developments* 135–142; David 77–117.

ions, the narrative shifts again: Coffee "is" passed around, "conversation waxes brisk and merry," and Mr. Rochester himself "stands by the hearth" (251, 254). It is difficult to locate whether the evaluative, commenting mind is that of the young woman sitting in the room watching, the older woman reflecting and narrating, or (of course) both. If supervisory discipline operates through the visual register, Brontë's conflation of the governess's gaze with her ability to comment (and critique) is important. In this scene, Lady Ingram claims the ability for herself—"I am a judge of physiognomy, and in hers I see all the faults of her class"—but of course Jane has forestalled her by setting the scene and describing the other characters in detail as they enter the parlor she already occupied, partially hidden from view (255). The governess as fictional autobiographer, in other words, dramatizes the paid caregiver's ability to observe . . . and judge.

Anne Brontë's *Agnes Grey. A Novel* (1847) not only emphasizes the caregiver's capacity for independent judgment but also dramatizes a principled refusal to adapt. While *Jane Eyre* subordinates consideration of family and maternity to critical transformation of the marriage plot, criticizing the economics undergirding the logic of romantic marriage upon which capitalist patriarchy depends, *Agnes Grey* imaginatively fleshes out the psychology of the governess *while she is employed,* using the genre of fictional autobiography to explore more fully how middle-class familiality relied on the impossible erasure of caregivers' alterity. Brontë spends the first third of the novel on Agnes's work in a home with small children and emphasizes throughout the novel her critique of the childrearing, pedagogical, and ethical values evinced by her employers. By aligning readerly sympathy with the governess narrator rather than the managerial mothers, *Agnes Grey* illustrates at length that paid caregivers retain their own values, judging their employers and potentially influencing their charges in ways those employers can never fully control.

It must be said that by most measures Agnes does not seem to be a particularly effective governess, either in accomplishing the purposes for which she is hired or, in fact, making much of a lasting impression on her pupils at all. The younger daughter of a suddenly impoverished clergymen, Agnes goes out to teach against family advice because she craves independence and (naively) imagines that governessing will provide it. Her first situation, with the newly rich Bloomfields, sees her caring for young children; her second, with the gentry-class Murrays, sees her chaperoning teenage girls only slightly younger than herself. She is let go from both situations because, at least according to her employers, the children "ma[k]e so little improvement" under her tutelage (107). But her difficulty teaching the Bloomfield children and in "form[ing]" Matilda Murray stems at least in part from Agnes's rigid adherence to her own family's moral and behavioral codes, which she presents as being at odds with those of both families (206). Both in having Agnes imagine that she can teach through love (as her mother did her) rather than discipline, and in writing her as the heroine of a marriage plot in the second half of the novel, Brontë centers readers' attention on the persistence of Agnes's values, attitudes, judgments, and feelings—and how they shape her relationship to the families who employ her.

Agnes's judgements are scathing, immediate, and never-ending. Mary Ann Bloomfield is "careless and inattentive," "obstinate," "troublesome," and "provoking" (81, 88), while her brother Tom is not only "averse to every species of mental exertion" but "violent" and "annoying," (81, 84, 86). Agnes pulls no punches: She notes on her first meeting with Mrs. Bloomfield that her employer's company is "extremely irksome" (80), and describes Mr. Robson's drinking in detail, specifying that he is "not a *positive* drunkard" (103, emphasis added). In reflecting on her time in her second situation at Horton Lodge, Agnes reflects that she "was the only person in the house who steadily professed good principles, habitually spoke the truth, and generally endeavoured to make inclination bow to duty" (121). While we can sympathetically register the pedagogical difficulties of this untrained teacher, not to mention the various ways in which she is treated unkindly, the stance of the narrator throughout *Agnes Grey* is that of offended pride.[17]

I want to emphasize two things. First, more than *Jane Eyre*, *Agnes Grey* can be read as an uptake artifact of governess advice literature. In different ways, both the Bloomfields and the Murrays seem to do everything the advice literature warns against. The parents are either uninvolved (Mr. Murray), capricious (Mr. Bloomfield), or overly indulgent (Mrs. Bloomfield, Mrs. Murray). They give the governess no authority and place no confidence in her. They and their guests are rude, treating her (at best) as a nonentity. Wellwood House and Horton Lodge seem to have little by way of routine, and the parental visits to the schoolrooms—which, as we've seen, *are* advised—completely disrupt what little system Agnes attempts to put into place. But *Agnes Grey* is a negative uptake artifact of advice literature in another way, as well: Agnes's narrative commentary consistently emphasizes a moral code that she has brought with her from outside, and that she uses not only to condemn but to try to socialize her charges.

This may be most vividly evident in the frequently analyzed scene in which Agnes kills a nest of baby birds rather than allow Tom Bloomfield to torture them (104; see Shuttleworth, "Hanging" 39–41; Gardner). As I argue in

---

17. On Agnes as narrator, see Frawley; Hallemeier.

"Instructive Sufficiency," "this violence prevents Tom from engaging in behavior his father and uncle encouraged, and [is] in conscious defiance of the family's moral code," which is both anthropocentric and patriarchal (100). But while this scene dramatizes competing ethical stances, it is also strikingly a moment in which Agnes acts on her urges to punish Tom physically (either by boxing his ears or whipping him with a "birch rod" [84–85]). Unlike Agnes's ineffective pedagogy, which seems to make no immediate or lasting impact on her pupils, her act of dropping a "large flat stone" on Tom's "intended victims" violently enacts the disruptive power of a thinking stranger embedded within the familial whole (104). The fictional autobiography's extended representation of psychological interiority thus confirms advice literature's warnings: No paid caregiver is *simply* a hireling; their inclusion makes the family itself an inevitably (and dangerously) heterogeneous thing.

Fictional autobiography centers readers in the perspective of its narrator, giving us a phenomenological experience of that character and their role. By placing governesses in that position, *Jane Eyre* and *Agnes Grey* offer uptake enactments that challenge advice literature's impossible prescription that paid caregivers leave their lives, so to speak, at their employer's door. These novels' generic commitment to individualism develops that quality as an inalienable and sympathetic feature of women who are paid to provide childcare. The fictional governess's critical perspective is a dangerous possibility that cannot be easily filtered out at the threshold; it is an ongoing, competing narrative about (and at the heart of) the genre ecology of middle-class family. This draws out the anxious exigency of advice literature, developing the dangerous alterity of paid childcare as an affective and social truth that mandates constant supervision.

Influence and Impact

In returning now to Dickens and the multiplot novel, and specifically to *The Dealings with the Firm Dombey and Son, Wholesale, Retail and for Exportation* (1846–1848), I focus on the paraliptic nature of that genre. *Dombey and Son's* necessary shifts in perspective not only reinforce the anxious-making nature of the employee's capacity for independent judgment that fictional autobiography enacts and advice literature mobilizes, but also how that anxiety could motivate managerial attention. The novel is ultimately ambivalent about the desirability of familial and professional supervision controlling employees' impact. My analysis here focuses on the perhaps surprising structural similarities between Polly Toodle, the wet nurse whose loving care gives Paul and

Florence a maternal emotional touchstone, and James Carker "the Manager," who exploits Mr. Dombey's inattention to business and hubristic faith in his loyalty. In both cases, the multiplot novel's paraliptic shifts make visible the fictive nature of total supervision and the power of supplemental judgment and desire to disrupt—or at least change—a middle-class family. I therefore read *Dombey and Son* not only as taking up the spatialized anxiety we have seen in life writing, advice literature, and fictional autobiography, but also as an uptake enactment of the genre ecology's association of that emotion with managerial attention.

Both Polly Toodle's and James Carker's effects on their employer are narratively necessary, but while Polly's (maternal) influence is entirely beneficial and impossible to stop, the marital and financial "thunderbolt" of Carker's theft is directly credited to Mr. Dombey's careless overconfidence. *Dombey and Son* turns on questions of familial reproduction, the conflation not only of family and firm but also on what the reproductive future of "Dombey" is going to be; the novel thematizes and formalizes questions of domestic and professional management, drawing attention both to how supervision can never erase an individual's influence and to the catastrophic dangers and unexpected benefits of inadequate oversight. Focused on Mr. Dombey's megalomaniacal desire for a son who will carry on the mercantile business he inherited from his father, the novel as a whole is an object lesson in the impossibility of controlling human relationships and feelings.

Polly Toodle is hired to breastfeed and care for Paul Dombey after his mother dies in the novel's opening chapter. In this plot, the novel demonstrates that when you pay for childcare, you always get more than you bargain for. Melisa Klimaszewski's analysis in "Examining the Wet Nurse: Breasts, Power, and Penetration in Victorian England" helps us see the novel's uptake enactment of contemporary advice regarding the initial inspection of prospective wet nurses and their children, as well as the insistence on their separation during the period of employment; Dickens exaggerates this further through Mr. Dombey's insistence on renaming Polly during her tenure (28). *Dombey and Son* reinscribes the other genres' uneasy conflation of inalienable maternal care and alienable waged labor by refracting it through the patriarchal ego rather than that of the supplemented mother; Mr. Dombey feels "sore humiliation" that he should be "dependent . . . on a hired serving-woman who would be to the child, for all time, all that even *his* alliance could have made his own wife" (27, emphasis in original). His shame that a *hired* woman bears the same relation to his child as would have his wife reiterates the supplemental logic we have seen in advice literature's unstable distinction between maternal and paid care, and Sherwood's ambivalent celebration and distrust of her children's intimacy with their Indian caregivers. But in exaggerating the ego-centric logic of capitalist patriarchy through Mr. Dombey's megalomaniacal pride, Dickens also draws attention to that cultural formation's uneasy reliance on women's bodily and affective labor. Mr. Dombey hopes to mitigate that reliance by insisting that Polly and Paul's relationship will be "a question of wages, altogether," limiting its temporal range strictly to the term of her employment: "When you go away from here, you will have concluded what is a mere matter of bargain and sale, hiring and letting: and will stay away. The child will cease to remember you; and you will cease, if you please, to remember the child" (28–29). But memory, feeling, and proximity exceed capitalist control: The fact of previous connection extends the relationships temporally, so that Polly is not simply remembered but actively recalled to the Dombey family at irregular intervals—most significantly at Paul's deathbed and then during Mr. Dombey's bankruptcy and his own subsequent illness.

The hired caregiver thus provides care that exceeds expectations (or what is paid for), in terms of her lasting impact but also in terms of her presence in the home itself. Although Florence is one of Dickens's archetypally virtuous and virginal maternal daughters, Miss Tox nonetheless considers Polly's influence a factor in the daughter's loving return at the end of the novel: After recalling her early observation that "Dombey and Son . . . is a daughter . . . after all," Miss Tox emphasizes that "it's a credit to you, Polly, that you were always her friend when she was a little child. You were her friend long before I was, Polly . . . and you're a good creature" (912). Although the "credit" would seem to be Polly's early and astute investment in what turns out to be the real future of the family (firm), Miss Tox connects Polly's goodness to Florence's, and both to the economic and familial reproduction enacted in Florence's return—and, in particular, her return to her father as a mother herself, mother to a child "who taught me to come back" (911).

Klimaszewksi draws our attention to the scenes early in the novel where characters attempt to render such influence impossible, but managerial oversight in *Dombey and Son* can neither control the employee's influence nor prevent her independent judgment. In the familial plot centered on the Dombey children and their care, the novel dramatizes this in two ways. First, through Mrs. Chick and Miss Tox's routine visits to the nursery: They watch Polly breastfeed the infant as well as bathe him and put him to sleep (59). While a central component of the supervisory recommendations of advice literature, as we have seen, such visits soon take their toll on Polly, who is "in some danger of being superintended to death."[18] Despite this lavish oversight, however,

---

18. This reference to the toll Miss Tox's "constancy and zeal" take on Polly appears in the 1867 edition and is reproduced in the 1985 Penguin edition, which restores seventy passages

Polly develops significant emotional connections with both Paul and Florence, her instinctive nurturing maternity creating bonds that transcend the contractual transaction that nominally governs her work. Second, Dickens describes Mr. Dombey's observation of Polly at length, rendering these scenes in significantly scopic terms. Rather than himself going to the nursery, Mr. Dombey has Polly and baby Paul brought to him for extended periods in the morning and afternoon, situating them in a glass-enclosed room in which he can observe them without being seen. Klimaszewski's astute analysis emphasizes how these extended observations are demeaning for Polly; they are prolonged exercises in attempted panoptic control that requires that her breasts and body be available for visual penetration, given that the timing and length of these visits means that Mr. Dombey would have been watching Polly breast-feeding the baby. But Dickens subverts Mr. Dombey's desire for a visual hierarchy of control, as Klimaszewski explains: "Polly repeatedly gazes back at Mr. Dombey," and—unlike familial supplements in advice literature—"she has an articulated point of view" (338, 341). Although the novel is not especially invested in Polly Toodle's psychology, apart from figuring it as that of an idealized, nurturing mother, it nonetheless underscores the fact and possibility of the supplement having a perspective and imagination of her own. The heteroglossic world of the multiplot novel thus emphasizes precisely the agency and independence the other genres code as intransigent dangers, dangers that mandate perpetual anxious supervision.

This question of managerial oversight and employee autonomy are at the heart of the melodramatic plot of *Dombey and Son,* centered around the character of James Carker ("Mr. Carker the Manager"), who flatters and deceives his employer, taking advantage of his position as a "confidential agent" to bring the firm to the brink of bankruptcy and to elope with Mrs. Dombey (649). This narrative extends the domestic plot's interest in the asymptotic nature of supervisory control, and thematizes it explicitly as a problem of management. Indeed, by making Mr. Carker "the Manager," Dickens indicates that Mr. Dombey has already ceded his authority at the office as well as at home. If the novel's unifying focus is on the dangers of pride, then it is specifically on how pride leads to the loss of control, "the central concept of all management systems" (Braverman 47, qtd. in Strickland 11). *Dombey and Son* renders both familial and capitalist reproduction inherently vulnerable as a result of those structures' constitutive reliance on employees. Polly Toodle's love and James Carker's resentment are thus homologous; the supplements'

---

that Dickens excised from the serial at the proof stage "because of the space imposed by serial publication" (*Dombey and Son* 1985, 100; Fairclough 35). The 2002 Penguin edition, to which I primarily refer, uses the 1848 edition.

emotions transform this exaggeration of the capitalist patriarchal family and mark its urgent need as a middle-class mother's anxious oversight rather than her loving care.

Mr. Carker the Manager is introduced as standing "between Mr. Dombey and the common world," with Mr. Dombey's reliance on him figured by the layout of their offices and enacted through the delegation of tasks both small and large (194). At his employer's request, Mr. Carker "adjust[s] his eye-glasses for him, or find[s] him the right place in his catalogue, or hold[s] his stick" (426). He sharpens Edith Granger's pencils in a triangulated moment of courtship (428). After the Dombeys' marriage, he repeatedly speaks for the husband to the wife and vice versa, "appear[ing] to be a mediator between them" (707; see also 646–648, 709–711). This plotline—in which the employee acts as the employer's romantic supplement—emphasizes Mr. Dombey's defining overgeneralization of the managerial logic of work to domestic and erotic matters. Carker takes advantage of the space this opens up to steal: He diverts, entangles, and overextends the firm's funds and financial dealings; and he elopes with Edith Dombey (although he fails to realize that he has not redirected her emotions).

But while it can seem that *Dombey and Son* is therefore critiquing that overgeneralization—that conflation of firm and family—the novel's investment in exhibiting the dangers of pride shows how careless inattention is devastating in both realms. Mr. Dombey simply doesn't pay attention to the details. He doesn't coordinate and order the processes of either his home life or his workplace: In other words, he doesn't *worry* enough, despite his brooding obsession with his family's precarious future. In explaining how the firm of Dombey and Son could face the likelihood of ruin, Mr. Morfin tells Carker's siblings that "the distractions of death, courtship, marriage, and unhappiness, have left us with no head but your brother for this long, long time" (808). Emphasizing the ways in which the "distractions" of domestic and erotic affairs lead to the downfall of a global mercantile firm, Dickens thus emphasizes the extent to which successful management requires the right degree of anxiety. Riding together "characteristically enough," Mr. Dombey

> receives [Carker's] conversation with the sovereign air of a man who had a right to be talked to . . . In his dignity, [Mr. Dombey] rode with very long stirrups, and a very loose rein, and very rarely deigned to look down to see where his horse went. In consequence of which it happened that Mr. Dombey's horse, while going at a round trot, stumbled on some loose stones, threw him, rolled over him, and lashing out with his iron-shod feet, in his struggles to get up, kicked him. (651)

The man's arrogant carelessness is evident in his preparations (long stirrups) as well as his inattention in the moment (loose rein, not looking down). We are told that this is how he "characteristically" rides, suggesting that this failure to anticipate or project the possibility of danger is his habitual way of being (651). And while this attitude might appear part of Mr. Dombey's explicitly imperial and "sovereign" demeanor, it also indicates the complacency that leaves him open to domestic manipulation and exploitation, to simultaneously public and private shaming. Mr. Carker's (mis)management of the Dombey marriage and firm has relied on this complacent delegation of attention to the particulars. Like Miss Tox and Mrs. Chick, whose frequent visits to the nursery metaphorically threaten Polly's life, Mr. Dombey fails to supervise anything effectively. Ceding domestic authority in part, like Sherwood, through undue intimacy, Mr. Dombey's arrogant confidence that all eyes are upon him renders him incapable of the panoptic vision effective authority requires. Mr. Carker "abused his trust in many ways," explains Mr. Morfin; not simply focusing on his own gain at the expense of the firm, he has specifically complicated and extended Dombey and Son's dealings to create a worldwide "labyrinth of which only he has held the clue" (809). A professional man like James Carker promises to exchange his head for figures and attention to detail for a salary and position, not unlike the wet nurse's offer of breastmilk or the governess's promise of moral education and genteel accomplishments. But like the wet nurse without milk, the lower-middle-class governess, or the servant who assumes her employer's authority, Mr. Carker the Manager exploits his employer's willing inattention, "substituting estimates and generalities for facts" in a supplementation that seems not only to disrupt but to ultimately destroy capitalist reproduction (809).

The paradox—or perhaps the crux—of *Dombey and Son* is that Mr. Dombey's managerial failures are precisely what save the family (if not the firm). The early episode in which Polly defies his orders never to visit her family is the event that catalyzes the romance plot introducing Florence and Walter Gay; that plot gains its final momentum when Florence runs away from home "orphaned" when her father strikes her in his anger over Edith's flight (721). Indeed, the novel's final chapters underscore the mercantile success and matrimonial happiness that has resulted from the economic, social, and familial upheavals the novel has recounted: A nursemaid marries a gentleman; the instrument-maker's shop becomes profitable; and the epilogual tableau reproduces the Dombey family with a difference. While their last name may (silently) now be Gay, and small Paul and Florence are loved and healthy, their father makes his living in "wholesale, retail, and exportation"—just as their grandfather once did. The surprising parallel between Polly Toodle and

James Carker reinforces the extent to which their employer is dependent on their goodwill and good intentions; both exceed their charge, and neither ultimately knows their place. This is to the health of middle-class familiality on the one hand and to the temporary destruction of capitalist enterprise on the other. Dickens's critique of Mr. Dombey's conflation of the two can never quite overcome its logic—that familial-like capitalist reproduction requires a supplemented, contractual structure, one that not only invites but requires continued attention that looks into the future and around the corner.

●

In chapter 3, we saw how the demographic fact of high infant and child mortality rates at a time when children and childhood were increasingly sentimentalized was transformed generically both into reason for fear and into inevitable, blessed opportunity. Because of the association of children with temporality—and particularly futurity—in Western culture, their probable deaths are always already narrative, always at least implicitly stories that will be ended too soon. But that sense of prematurity itself participates in different narratives, intersecting with that of restoration to heaven and (re)union with Christ, on the one hand, and that of perhaps preventable tragedy and its consequent structures of blame. In mapping the dispersion of these narratives of child death, I traced the affective residue that emerges as the diffused and yet adhesive uptake capture—the loving, planful, anticipatory, paralyzed, fearful, and apprehending emotion that we apprehend as maternal anxiety. This chapter has argued that maternal anxiety is not simply a temporal emotion but also a spatial one, that the conflation of maternal care and concern rests on a paraliptic attention in which middle-class mothers are identified with caretaking activities that they personally neither deliver nor quite literally *see.* Just as the middle manager in professional enterprise supervises productive processes and the individual workers who enact them, the managerial mother supervises the processes that reproduce the values and practices of the middle-class family in the next generation, and the individual workers who enact that transmission. The logic of that supervision is both temporal—staging a process through time, anticipating and preventing things that might go wrong—and spatial—monitoring whether or not the workers are following orders when they are out of sight.

In both cases, the possibility of danger motivates and directs anxious maternal attention proleptically (into the future as it is shaped by the past) and paraliptically (to supplemental traces). At first, dangerous possibilities are rooted in specific conditions, but as the managerial situation recurs, it is unmoored from those circumstances and becomes an affective element of supervisory attention itself, the uptake capture that both responds to and helps (re)enact the situation. The triangular relationship between mother, paid caregiver, and child differs in crucial ways from similar structures in enterprise. The identity of the supervisor—an overseer on a factory floor, a clerical supervisor in a mercantile firm—is not attached to the day-to-day labor, to operating machines or writing in a clear and legible hand; his affective subjectivity is not predicated upon his intimacy with the work he watches over. But in the home and the nursery the role of "mother" remains attached to the daily routine of breastfeeding, naps, diapers, baths, walks, and meals. Maternal labor is embodied labor; maternal care is coded as both the essential expression of emotional connection and the activity that ignites and perpetuates it. It follows, then, that the wet nurses, nursemaids, and governesses who do their work too well are nearly as much of a problem as those who don't do it well enough. By supplementing the middle-class family in order to signify its class status, they also make it porous, opening it up to substances, influences, and judgements from class and racial Others. The managerial anxiety of middle-class maternal subjectivity is thus both catalyzed by and catalyzes the myriad genres—warnings, rumors, narratives, and so on—of the dangers posed by intimate strangers doing the work of childcare.

CHAPTER 5

Godfrey's Cordial and an Opium Pill

Empire, Family, and Maternal Attention

> There is one thing I wish to caution you against, and that is when
> children are cross and fretful, and will not sleep, ayas [sic] are in
> the habit of secretly giving them opium to make them repose,
> this is done very frequently, and is productive of very bad con-
> sequences: as long as they are undiscovered they continue the
> practice, till at last the child's constitution is undermined. I believe
> many children die from this cause; while the parents and doc-
> tor are alike incapable of assigning any satisfactory reason upon
> the subject, being ignorant of this fact. . . . These people do not
> like being disturbed, and they always give this if they can.
>
> —*A Domestic Guide to Mothers in India, Containing Particular Instructions
> on the Management of Themselves and Their Children,* By a Medical
> Practitioner of Several Years Experience in India (1836), p. 84

> Most of the patent medicines given to children contain the strongest
> and most heating aromatics in ardent spirits, or opium in different
> forms, and artfully concealed. Such are the active ingredients in syrup
> of meconium, or of poppies, Godfrey's Cordial, Dalby's Carminative,
> Daffy's Elixir, and similar preparations. . . . Nurses should never be
> permitted to have these dangerous and poisonous weapons in their
> possession; yet it is a fact of lamentably frequent occurrence, that
> such medicines may often be found concealed in their boxes, and in
> other places, ready to be given in large doses to a child, should the
> little sufferer's wakefulness or cries interfere with their night's rest.
>
> —J. T. Conquest, *Letters to a Mother, on the Management of Herself
> and Her Children in Health and Disease* (1850), pp. 346, 347–348

WARNINGS LIKE THESE—that paid caregivers were secretly giving babies opium or opiate-based patent medicines—appear through-out my sample of childrearing advice books. They occur both at predictable intervals (as in sections on nursery medicines) and without fore-shadowing (when discussing the appropriate diet for a nurse, for example). They operate rhetorically, then, much as convulsions do in Andrew Combe's *Physiology* or, for that matter, Daniel Quilp in Dickens's *The Old Curiosity Shop*. But unlike convulsions (and more like Quilp), opium is cultural rather than natural, saturated by classed and racialized associations. As gin had a century earlier, opium in the early nineteenth century metonymically signified the inadequacy of working-class sociality in Britain, especially the failure of poor women as mothers. In addition, opium was one of the most important global commodities; after the abolition of the slave trade in 1807, it became the British Empire's most important article of trade, literally underwriting its expansion and consolidation over the course of the next half-century. This symbolically dense substance carries with it histories of military aggression and both agricultural and economic exploitation. Opium is therefore always simultaneously a medicine, a poison, an Orientalized and habit-forming intoxicant, a working-class palliative, and the exploitative economic foundation of Britain's global dominance. In these warnings, the substance concretizes the alterity of paid childcare in British homes wherever they may be located. As they circulate through the genre ecology, opium warnings bind together the temporal anxiety of child death and the supervisory anxiety of paid childcare, mobilizing those narrative patterns and social hierarchies to generate a context in which managerial motherhood is premised upon the impossibility of adequate supervision. Ideal supervision is figured as the disembodied transcendence of a dead mother—or a global empire—whose reproductive force is structurally dependent on its anxious projection of danger.

My method in this chapter is partly inspired by the last two decades' rich work in thing theory and commodity culture.[1] I take opium literally, "following it"—in Elaine Freedgood's formulation—"beyond the covers of the text through a mode of research that proceeds according to the many dictates of a strong form of metonymic reading" (12). In order to understand what the substance is doing not only in the opium warnings that dot advice literature but also in narrativized episodes of infant dosing in life writing and fiction, we need to see the contexts adhering to it—material, symbolic, and economic. These sticky traces mean that opium catalyzes representations of motherhood as a protective stance, constantly on guard against a threat that will inevitably infiltrate the home and disrupt—or supplement—the family's social and physical reproduction; the drug's role in the violence of British economic

---

1. Sattaur provides a helpful overview of the development of thing theory. My approach in this chapter is particularly informed by Daly; Freedgood; and Fromer.

imperialism allows us to see how maternal supervision of the English middle-class home participates in the larger perspective of global capitalism, and is similarly premised on a sense of entitled fragility where vulnerability is trans-formed into colonial aggression. In the next section, I trace two metonymic chains: One illuminates opium's association with the illness and malnutrition that plagued the poorer classes under industrialization; the other traces its circulation as an Orientalized substance and global commodity for which Britain went to war. I then return to the genres I have examined throughout *Writing Maternity,* in order to identify opium's anxious reverberations for nineteenth-century motherhood, and to better understood the (re)productive contours of maternal anxiety.

Opium's Ideas

Opium is a narcotic derived from the latex of the white poppy (*Papaver somniferum*), and is thought to have been among the earliest cultivated intoxicants. The latex is harvested from the seedpods of the flower and then dried. Raw opium—a brown, gumlike substance—is then ground into powder or molded into solid pieces for sale. Morphine, the first opium alkaloid to be isolated and its chief active ingredient, was identified in 1804 and was in widespread medical use in Europe by the 1850s. Opiates relieve or suppress pain by acting on the brain and spinal cord to disrupt neural transmissions. (They mimic the effect of endorphins.) They also act as sedatives, inducing drowsiness and sleep; alleviate anxiety; and can cause a sense of euphoria or well-being. They slow respiration and heartbeat, suppress the cough reflex, and act on the gastrointestinal tract to relieve diarrhea and suppress the appetite. Addictive drugs, they produce physical dependence; chronic use requires increased dosage to produce the same effect, and contributes to physical and mental deterioration.

For centuries, its wide range of therapeutic applications meant that opium as a raw pill or in various diluted forms was a significant medicine. It seems to have been known to Homer as a drug that alleviates sorrow and eases pain, but under the Roman Empire doctors argued that it was unreliable—affecting individuals to different degrees of intensity—and that, in any case, it removed symptoms without treating the underlying cause of disease. In *De Materia Medica,* published in 80 CE, opium gets comparatively little space relative to other painkillers, and it seems to have largely fallen out of use in Europe during the Middle Ages. Paracelsus (c. 1493–1541) advocated for the utility of the drug, and it once again became a medical mainstay in the sixteenth century. Although Paracelsus coined the term, laudanum—a tincture of opium made with sweetened wine to mask the drug's bitterness—was not developed until the seventeenth century in England, by Thomas Sydenham. Medical use of laudanum and other opiates became increasingly common in Britain over the course of the eighteenth century: Population growth and concentration in urban centers, as well as the pollution generated by industrial processes, increased rates of a variety of ailments, including diarrhea and dysentery, coughs and colds, and cholera. Before the invention of modern painkillers—such as acetylsalicylic acid (aspirin) or paracetamol/acetaminophen (best known in the US as Tylenol)—Britons found opium an indispensable analgesic.[2]

"The Poor Child's Nurse"[3]

By the late eighteenth century in Britain and the British Empire, opium had become a standard medicine. Its therapeutic ubiquity may have made individual cases of dependence or addiction difficult to identify. This problem is enhanced by the fact that, as Barry Milligan notes, "the symptoms of dependence make their most pronounced appearance only during withdrawal . . . When withdrawal symptoms did appear between doses, the user often interpreted them as an independent sickness [or a recurrence of the original ailment] for which opium was ostensibly an appropriate treatment" (22–23). Both contemporary and historical accounts have tended to distinguish between opium use among the "literary" and working classes; while it was relatively acceptable for Thomas De Quincey to recount taking opium every Sunday as a stimulant to enhance his experience of the opera, or Samuel Taylor Coleridge to write poetry under its influence, its use as a working-class intoxicant cheaper than beer or gin—much less as a substitute for food—was something to be decried. Identification of regular opium use as a problem during this time was significantly limited to the working classes.[4] Until 1868, opium

---

2. Berridge remains the most comprehensive study of opium use in nineteenth-century Britain. On medicinal use (and abuse), see also Chepaitis; Foxcroft; Lomax; and Wohl 34–36. On the opium practices of the middle classes, particularly literary figures, see Hayter, *Opium*; Milligan. Dormandy is a helpful global history of the drug for a general audience.

3. This section's title is taken from the caption to a cartoon by William Newman that appeared in *Punch* in 1849. It shows an infant crying in the middle of an empty and messy room, not far from a small table on which stands a bottle of opium. See my discussion in "Infant Doping and Middle-Class Motherhood" 130–131.

4. Berridge discusses how opium use was interpreted differently depending on the class position of the user; see 49–72. That said, many relatively wealthy individuals struggled with

was entirely unregulated in Britain: There were no taxes on it, no licensing, and no standards for its composition. Opium itself and opiate-based patent medicines such as Godfrey's Cordial, Sydenham's Laudanum, Dalby's Carminative, Mrs. Winslow's Soothing Syrup, and so on were sold by druggists and apothecaries, prescribed by physicians and surgeons, and available at grocers and corner shops (see Berridge 28). There was no oversight of the strength or purity of a particular mixture, and no reason to assume that the same patent medicine would be made by the same recipe or to the same strength on different occasions. Two home recipes for Godfrey's Cordial illustrate this: The recipe in A. F. Crell and W. M. Wallace's *Family Chronicle of Health, Economy, and Good Living* (1824) calls for adding three fluid ounces of laudanum to a flavored sugar syrup made by adding six pounds of treacle to four pints of an infusion of sassafras, caraway, coriander, and anise (35–36); that in Joseph Worrall's *Domestic Receipt Book* (1832) makes roughly twice as much (one gallon of a less sweet syrup), but with roughly two-thirds the opiate (133–134).

By the 1850s, opium use among the poorer classes was understood as a significant social problem. This perception was fueled in part by the *Morning Chronicle*'s 1849–1851 series on the conditions of the laboring classes in England and Wales. This series, *Labour and the Poor in England and Wales*, opens with a letter by Angus Bethune Reach (1821–1856) that documents widespread opium use among the working poor in Manchester. Reach acknowledges in a cursory manner the extent to which unsanitary living conditions and the high cost of medical care made opium use a necessary component of urban life. He focuses primarily on women's employment in the factories as the root of the problem, and offers a sweeping indictment of working-class women's maternity. Quoting a "gentleman of whose perfect candour and good faith I have certain knowledge," he writes: "I believe that women frequently drug their children through pure ignorance of the effect of the practice, and because, having been brought up in mills, they know nothing about the first duties of mothers" (55). Reach's account repeatedly associates infant drugging with female employment and paid childcare (see also 47–49). In addition, he emphasizes with alarm the extent to which regular opiate use seemed to begin in infancy and continue throughout adult life. The series as a whole exhibits complicated and competing motivations. Often cited as an example of early public health work, as well as an early case of investigative journalism, the work of Reach and his colleagues exhibits a laudable interest in identifying how rapid industrialization and urbanization have compromised health and

---

their dependence on the drug—Coleridge is, of course, one of the most famous examples; see Caquet; Foxcroft; Lomax; Nicholls.

quality of life for broad swathes of the British population (Ginswick xi–xiii). At the same time, expectations about gender, family, and other forms of sociality shaped their apprehension and description of the evidence they gathered. These reports created the strong impression that married women of the laboring class typically worked outside the home after having children, and both implicitly and explicitly blamed this work for high rates of infant mortality and opium dependence.[5]

In Letter V (1 Nov. 1849) for example, Reach "return[s] to the dismal topic of infant mortality, the undue proportion of which arises from the neglect of mothers who are compelled to leave their young children at home while they labour in the mill": "The inevitable result of this system is the reckless and almost universal employment of narcotics. First, the child is drugged until it sleeps, and too often it is drugged until it dies" (5). Opium is thus both tool and sign of maternal neglect. In the same letter, Reach insists that there "are two exciting causes for the mass of infantine misery. First, but in a comparatively small degree, the unhealthy state of the houses; secondly and mainly, the neglect and all the concomitant evils consequent upon the mothers of children of tender age passing their days in the mill" (5). Such accounts did not simply criminalize working-class motherhood as mortally neglectful; they did so by positing a strange equivalence between working-class breastmilk and opium by describing the latter as the working woman's substitute for the former: Reach notes that infants are fed "loathsome syruppy poppy rather than their mother's milk" (5). Such stories were endemic in the nascent social science accounts of factory life. In her study of infant doping in Victorian Britain, Elia Vallone Chepaitis cites a pertinent story of a lace embroiderer in Nottingham recorded in the 1843 Parliamentary report on "Children's Employment." Too poor to pay for child care, Mary Colton found that she could simply keep her baby with her if she dosed it regularly with Godfrey's Cordial. Chepaitis explains that this was not uncommon among lace workers: "Infants were often sedated and left across their working mothers' laps, but the women could not interrupt their work to give them milk. It took less time to drug the infant, and promptly continue work" (20).[6]

---

5. Reach's coverage of opium use is discussed in Berridge 102 and passim; Chepaitis 36–40; Donovan and Rubery 27–28; and Wohl 34–36. On investigative journalism, see Donovan and Rubery; Waters.

6. Twentieth- and twenty-first-century historians have challenged this wholesale condemnation of the mothering of an entire class of women. "There is at least circumstantial evidence that much infant mortality in 19th-century England was due neither to carelessness, ignorance, or drunkenness, nor to infanticide. For the working-class populations . . . the deaths might more appropriately be attributed to the poverty and malnutrition that industrial capitalism entailed for their members" (Hansen 347; see also Wohl 34–35). Reynolds' work further cri-

Accounts of working-class opiate dependence blur the line between medicine and intoxicant: Although there are gestures toward the therapeutic role opium played, concern and condemnation are focused on questions of habitual reliance that apparently begins in the cradle. Opium, it seems, is intervening in "proper" familial ties, supplementing—and therefore substituting for—"proper" maternal care. Such frameworks recall those that emerged a century earlier, during the "gin craze" of the first half of the eighteenth century. An intoxicant without a history of medicinal use, gin arrived in Britain from the Netherlands in the late 1600s and was soon produced domestically. Because the beer trade had historically been subject to state regulation, gin was the cheaper intoxicant; gin shops proliferated in poor urban areas. This coincided with urbanization and specifically an increase in the numbers of women in the city, in part due to rising demand for domestic servants. While taverns and ale shops had been traditionally male spaces, gin shops were frequented by women as well as men. As a result, it seemed that more women and more poor people were drinking and getting drunk in public than had previously been the case—and this perception may well have been accurate. By 1736, Parliament was looking for ways to regulate the sale of gin. Stories circulated widely of child neglect and infanticide, which James Nicholls argues "bolstered the drive for prohibition by using the image of the drunken working-class or pauper mother to depict gin as both morally and economically ruinous" regardless of whether or not they were true (41). The diffuse sense that drinking was a (new) epidemic among poor and working-class women facilitated a focus on alcoholism's social effects that was often figured through images of child neglect and mistreatment, and justified state intervention on behalf of those children as a future national resource.

According to Nicholls, gin-drinking did not significantly diminish after 1751, but it ceased signifying the corruption of the urban poor as a class to the degree that it had earlier (48). By the 1830s, opium in many ways had to come to replace alcohol in doing this work. As Virginia Berridge argues in *Opium and the People*, the Victorians were more concerned with working-class opium use as a national problem than with the recreational use of it by middle-class writers and others; for members of the middle classes, whose self-medication often shaded into dependency, "opium was a simple part of life, neither exclusively medical nor entirely social" and was deemed a largely personal problem (Berridge 61). Opium *abuse* was apprehended as a working-class issue, specifically in terms of two issues: the extent to which members of the working

---

tiques this framework of blame; her findings challenge not only Victorian paradigms that associated women's waged work with infant mortality but also twentieth-century historiography.

classes relied on opium as a lifelong medical crutch, and the frequency of opium overdoses leading to death (Berridge 97). Its quality was unregulated, it was cheaper than alcohol, it suppressed the appetite, and it treated both pain and diarrhea—all of which contributed to a regular reliance on it by the poor.

"Iniquitous Traffic"[7]

As an ubiquitous drug whose medical, intoxicating, and poisonous functions swirled together to create a working-class Other against which the nurturing, domestic middle-class ideal could be imagined, opium carried with it the economic and sanitary precarity it treated by dulling pain and killing the appetite. As a global commodity that not only underwrote British imperial expansion in the nineteenth century but also catalyzed the first war fought explicitly in the name of free trade, it also carries the interdependent, exploitative logics of empire. Although the bulk of the opium sold in Britain in the eighteenth and nineteenth centuries came from Turkey, the drug was most closely associated with India in the British imagination until the second half of the century.[8] The triangular trade in which opium grown in British India was sold illegally in China in exchange for silk and tea was a financial cornerstone of the East India Company—and therefore the British Empire—starting in the 1770s. By 1800, opium was one of the Company's two most lucrative commodities. (The other was enslaved Africans.) The opium poppy had been cultivated in northeastern India on a small scale for centuries (Trocki 58); after the East India Company gained control of the area in 1757, they focused on that crop as a way to expand their economic and geographic control of the subcontinent and to raise profits. Granted a government monopoly, the Company mandated a focus on the opium crop and forcibly relocated farmers in order to create large plantations. It then became the basis of trade with China when the Company lost access to Spanish bullion during the American Revolution. (Spain supported the US.) Searching for a commodity so that it could continue to satisfy British demand for Chinese tea and silk, the East India Company engaged in a protracted and illegal smuggling operation, forcibly creating a Chinese market

7. This phrase comes from Viscount Sandon's speech in Parliament on 9 April 1840. See *Hansard*, vol. 53, c. 867.

8. By the end of the nineteenth century, opium carried dense associations with China and with crime, sensationalized in the opium "dens" of popular fiction, including *The Mystery of Edwin Drood* (Dickens, 1870), *The Picture of Dorian Gray* (Wilde, 1890), and "The Man with the Twisted Lip" (Conan Doyle, 1891). In the first half of the century, however, the drug was less stably criminalized and more generically Orientalized (see Milligan).

for opium despite the fact that it had been outlawed by the Qing government in the 1720s (S.-C. Chen 14). John F. Richards points out that in the 1830s and '40s, opium accounted for more than one-quarter of British India's export revenue, increasing to nearly a third in the 1850s (164). Carl A. Trocki has argued that "though difficult to prove beyond question, it seems likely that without opium, there would have been no empire" (qtd. in Derks 49). The slave trade largely underwrote imperial expansion in the seventeenth and eighteenth centuries; the opium trade did so in the nineteenth.

Starting in 1757, the Qing dynasty confined all European trade to the port of Canton (now Guangzhou) and established a limited area for the merchants to live and work just outside the walls of the city (S.-C. Chen 38–39). As Song-Chuan Chen explains, the Canton system not only limited trading contact, but also established a variety of rules to minimize European settlement and integration: traders could not bring European women to Canton, had to leave annually after the trading season was over, and couldn't learn the language (38). Stephen R. Platt vividly invokes the physical confinement this entailed for Western merchants, noting as well that this restriction symbolized "both the Qing dynasty's power to dictate international trade on its own terms and—to the British and other foreigners who suffered the same limiting conditions—the disdain the emperor felt for them" (9; see xvii–xxii). In 1839–1842, Britain undertook the first of two wars to force open the Chinese market. Contemporary and historiographic accounts of the First Opium War are divided about the role of the drug for which it is named, with many historians accepting the arguments of Lord Palmerston (the Foreign Secretary) and the ruling Whig party that the primary issues at stake were national pride and free trade. Until 1833, the East India Company had held a monopoly on British trade with China, and had carefully tended relationships with customs officials that ensured the smooth flow of Indian-grown opium into the country. When it renewed the Company's charter in 1833, Parliament abolished that monopoly (although the Company maintained its monopoly over the "cultivation and sale of opium in India" [Berridge 173]). This disrupted the smuggling operations that had been established over the previous decades, as multiple British agents began to compete in the area. Song-Chuan Chen argues that these merchants worked throughout the 1830s to convince Parliament that war with China was not only likely but inevitable (see 103–126). At the same time, there was increasingly intense debate at the Qing court about the dangers of opium and the importance of enforcing the ban on importation.

I want to highlight several events that precipitated the war, contributed to the framing of its debate in Parliament, and shaped how it was taken up by the British press in England. Charged with cracking down on illegal importation, in the spring of 1839 Commissioner Lin Zexu blockaded the foreign factories on the outskirts of Canton; he ordered the confiscation and then destruction of over 1,000 tons of opium.[9] During the subsequent diplomatic standoff (as Britain refused to pledge to give up all opium trade in China), a Chinese man was killed by a group of foreign sailors, and the British representative refused to turn them over to the Qing judiciary. In the fall, British ships effectively occupied Hong Kong and thereby blockaded Canton; shots were subsequently exchanged between British and Chinese warships. By the winter of 1840, Members in both Houses were posing questions in Parliament, and the matter was taken up in full in the spring. The debates in Parliament and in the British press tangled together questions of international law and national jurisdiction; the morality of trade in opium, particularly into a country where its import was banned; and British global sovereignty and property rights—as well as to what extent the Whig government's foreign policy had mistakenly brought Britain to the brink of war.[10]

In raising the question on 7 April 1840 in the House of Commons, Sir John Graham noted the "immense national [financial] interests" at stake in the opium trade, but defended China's right as a sovereign nation to regulate trade (*Hansard,* vol. 53, c. 669). In response, Thomas Babington Macaulay defended the government's position by emphasizing the impossibility of stopping the flow:

> Could the House believe that a mere order could put a stop to the trade in opium? Did they suppose that a traffic supported on the one hand by men actuated by the love of a drug, from the intoxicating qualities of which they found it impossible to restrain themselves; and on the other by persons actuated by the desire of gain, could be terminated by the publication of a piece of paper? (*Hansard,* vol. 53, cc. 714–715)

---

9. "Factories" in this context refers not to manufacturing plants, but to the offices, warehouses, and living quarters of the factors (or merchants) (Platt xx).

10. I've drawn this history chiefly from Platt; Lovell; Gelber; and Song-Chuan Chen, who offers a particularly efficient summary of historiographic debate; he identifies four understandings of Britain's motivations for the war: (1) a desire to "*open up* [an] insular and benighted China," primarily evident in scholarship from the early twentieth century; (2) a sense of national pride and honor, in response to the attacks on British citizens and property in Guangzhou; (3) expansion of trade, writ large; and (4) protection of the opium trade, in particular (6–7). Lovell provides a timeline that gives not only an efficient overview for the war and its precipitating events but also its position in the longer political histories of both countries (367–375). See also Dormandy 123–150; Derks; and Trocki.

Addiction and capitalist desire go hand-in-hand, equally inevitable, inexorably crossing borders and blurring boundaries.[11] Together—concentrated in the commodified substance—their market force renders government control irrelevant, the regulations of nations helpless in the face of human frailty and human greed. In Macaulay's speech, the border-crossing force of the intoxicating, medicinal commodity appears not only inevitable but ultimately desirable, as it is attached to British national pride and property rights. He marshals the destruction of British-owned opium by the Qing government and its expulsion of British citizens from Canton to justify military force to expand British sovereignty and markets. Analogies to the slave trade dot the Parliamentary discussion, shading references to the "iniquitous traffic in opium" fostered merely for "a love of gain, and by the misery of hundreds of thousands of human beings" with specific associations (Viscount Sandon, Sir S. Lushington, 9 April 1840, *Hansard*, vol. 53, c. 867). In the House of Lords' discussion, Earl Stanhope articulates the analogy directly, as part of an argument for giving up the opium trade despite the financial cost involved: "Their Lordships could not prevent slavery, but they had deemed it right to make an enormous sacrifice of money in order to have the satisfaction of knowing that slavery no longer existed in any part of the British kingdom" (12 May 1840, *Hansard*, vol. 54, c. 24). The moral argument against war was made as or more forcefully outside Parliament: The *Times* opened its editorial on the topic on 23 March 1840 by proclaiming that war with China was "nothing less than an attempt, by open violence, to force upon a foreign country the purchase of a deadly poison prohibited by its laws" (4).

As Julie Fromer writes of tea, opium was a "commodity cultivated in the Orient [that] crossed vast geographical distances to take its place" in English homes, "permeating the physical boundaries of nation and body and thus creating anxieties about cultural and physical pollution" (12). It is a particularly facile substance for this, since it "had a reputation for altering the consciousness of its user" (Milligan 30); narcotics, after all, work on both body and mind, their psychotropic effects limning that boundary—the boundary between nature and nurture, between inborn inheritance and the effects of daily socialization. Opium in the 1840s and '50s was not only a feature of daily domestic life—part of nearly every home medical cabinet—but also a matter of public debate questioning Britain's role as a moral and economic actor among nations that conflated the boundary-dissolving properties of the narcotic with its function as a global commodity. But while the substance

---

11. I follow Caquet in taking political discussion of the First Opium War to indicate an understanding of the drug's habit-forming properties (1028).

itself was foreign, its abuse was coded as part of the deficiencies of the British working class. Warnings that servants are dosing middle-class babies with opium mobilize these contexts to create a rhetorical situation of massively overdetermined danger. Classed and racialized fears of influence, infiltration, and transformation attach to physical fears for children's health. Opium stickily reinscribes what might be differences in childrearing practices as differences in values and identity: *They* are lazy, putting their own rest ahead of infants' health and life, while *we* attend to the children no matter how cranky or wakeful; *their* care kills, while *our* concern strengthens and restores. It also speaks to the very real conviction that care in the present moment shapes the future child. The danger of opium is not simply that it might kill children but that it—like a governess or a wet nurse—might fundamentally *change* them and thereby change the national future.

Opium Warnings

Of the 215 childrearing advice texts I have examined, 74 include some sort of warning that servants are likely to dose babies with opium or opiate-based patent medicines. My analysis here is drawn from the references in 31 unique titles. Advice literature's contribution to the genre ecology is through the affordances of the *warning*. Through this speech act, the diffuse sense of the narcotic as both necessary and dangerous, essential and unreliable, transforming persons, nations, and relationships, becomes explicit. Denotatively, warnings are "advice to beware a person or thing as being dangerous" (*OED*, "Warning," def. 3) and therefore catalyze an expectation of danger and an anxious rhetorical situation. Unlike admonitions, which focus on the solution, warnings focus on the problem, with attention and awareness—and hence anxiety—the available uptake captures and enactments. If we recall rhetorical genre theory's insight that genre "both constructs and responds to recurring situation[s]," then we can see that warnings do not simply mark a preexisting danger but also create it, generating an affective reality in which the future conditional threat can never be disproven or (fully) preempted (Devitt, "Generalizing" 580). As Brian Massumi argues, "Threat has an impending reality in the present. This actual reality is affective" (54). In the case of warnings that servants are secretly dosing babies with opium, the genre conflates the two issues I have explored thus far: Opium warnings attach the threat of child death to the paraliptic persistence of the caregiver's alterity, now signified by the drug. In iteratively staging a rhetorical situation in which paid care might be literally poisonous, the genre typifies the middle-class family's supplementation as rendering it always already vulnerable, its future and present both threatened by individuals located in its spatial and reproductive center.

The texts aver that the drug is part of the architecture of paid childcare; it is "often kept in the nursery," and, in fact, "few nurseries are without it" (Bull, *Maternal Management* 277; *New Family Receipt Book* 364; cf. Underwood and Davies 148). These descriptions of endemic opiate use are, for the most part, not neutral. Some authors simply note its extraordinary prevalence with mild surprise, while others express outright concern: As early as 1797, Michael Underwood describes dosing babies as a "destructive custom," and another text locates the problem in giving opium "without moderation" (72; *Philosophy* 104). Medical textbooks, including pharmacopoeia, offer complex considerations for determining the appropriate dose, and medical practitioners are themselves urged to use the drug sparingly and with care. In advice literature for a general audience, nearly half of the opium warnings I have coded (68 references in 31 texts) explicitly mention that a dose of opium "often prove[s] fatal," and one-third of those use this to explain larger demographic trends: "By errors of this kind [administering opium], I will venture to say, that one half the children who die annually in London lose their lives"; "It is probable many of the children said to be smothered in bed by their nurses lying upon them, are destroyed by secret doses of laudanum, given to produce sleep" (Beeton 1087; Buchan 35; Roberton 227n).

Formally, opium warnings nest inside other topics. Some appear clustered with information on other medicines—for example, when Thomas Bull proceeds from "Calomel" to "Opiates" in *Maternal Management*'s chapter on "The Use and Abuse of Certain Medicines." Here, the warning follows a basic statement of the drug's ubiquity:

> This class of medicine is often kept in the nursery, in the forms of laudanum, syrup of white poppies, Dalby's carminative, and Godfrey's cordial. The object with which they are generally given is to allay pain by producing sleep; they are therefore, *remedies of great convenience to the nurse*; and, I am sorry to be obliged to add, that, so exhibited, they are not *too often fatal to the little patient*. (110, emphasis in original)

As I noted at the beginning of this chapter, many appear more unexpectedly— in the midst of chapters on or discussions of teething, crying, sleep, or the employment of caregivers. In John Roberton's *Observations on the Mortality and Physical Management of Children* (1827), for example, a chapter on infant sleep moves from a description of ideal types of cradles ("the canopy [should] be large and lofty") to caution against "the bane of nurseries": "the administering laudanum and other preparations of opium to infants" (226). It seems that authors are led associatively to these discussions as they outline considerations for care under the ordinarily challenging circumstances of infancy. There is a metonymic logic to all of these interpolations—from cradles to sleep to narcotic; from teething to painkiller; from one medicine to another; the overall patterning is one in which the daily course of infant care is disrupted unexpectedly by a lethal threat that has been hovering alongside and out of view. As we've seen in previous chapters, this is a formal feature of advice literature, part of how it affords anxious uptake capture. In the case of opium warnings, however, the form enacts the specific anxieties attached to the drug: that it blurs boundaries and crosses borders; that it is transported and administered secretly; that it disrupts the normal course of events tragically and without warning; that its delivery is an act of racial and social aggression. The narrative telos of childhood death affords anxiety through suspenseful anticipation, while the paraliptic individuality of hired caregivers transmutes maternal care into managerial surveillance. The impossibility of anticipating the precise time or place a nurse will give the baby a deadly dose of opium collapses the temporal and spatial axes of maternal anxiety into one another.

Maternal readers are warned that "lazy," "ignorant," and "wily" servants cannot be trusted to resist the temptation of dosing infants (Bull, *Maternal Management* 111; Chavasse, *Advice to Mothers* 31; Barrett 67). This most frequently emerges around questions of sleep for both caregivers and children. As Thomas Bull points out, medical knowledge at the time prescribed opiates "to allay pain by producing sleep" (*Maternal Management* 279). Taken into the nursery, the means can replace the ends: Opium-based medicines are given to babies "for the purpose of procuring sleep in children" (Reece 68). It's worth lingering over the irony: The thing many parents most desire—a quiet, sleeping baby—is transformed into a sign of potentially deadly danger. (Even more than the issue of crying that I discussed in chapter 2, the indecipherability of a baby's sleep here generates anxiety.) Babies' nighttime rest in particular is closely related to that of those who care for them. Opium and opiate-based patent medicines are thus identified as the stealthy tool of those unwilling (or unable) to tolerate their own sleep being regularly disrupted: A dose of Godfrey's "leaves the nurse to her repose" (Rundell 364). It is given "on purpose to secure comfortable nights" and kept on hand "should the little sufferer's wakefulness or cries interfere with [the caregiver's] night's rest" (Roberton 227; Conquest 348). Opiates are, therefore, the tool of the caregiver who "does not choose to be disturbed in the night" (Hale 34). This can happen at almost any time, warns the author of *A Domestic Guide to Mothers in India* (1836): "There is one thing I wish to caution you against, and that is, when children are cross and fretful, and will not sleep, ayas [sic] are in the habit of secretly giving them opium to make them repose" (84). The servants accused of administering opium—Othered by class and in some contexts race—are consistently described in negative terms. While "ignorant" and "inexperienced," infant-dosing servants are also "unprincipled" and "selfish."[12] The paradigmatic selflessness of the ideology of nurturing motherhood comes into focus as the virtuous opposite of the self-interest of women whose caregiving can be bought and sold.

The conviction that dosing happens secretly, in the lacunae of maternal supervision and as a species of domestic fraud, is essential here. It is smuggled in illegally, "concealed in [nurses'] boxes" (Conquest 348), but unlike Britain's opium trade in China, this commerce damages *Britain's* future. As early as 1797, William Buchan warned that opiates "are every day administered by those who bear the character of good nurses," speaking the danger of fraud we saw in chapter 4 (34). But the sham is not simply that the baby's quiet is drug-induced, but that the narcotic is masking other neglect: These putatively "good nurses" "generally imagine that a dose of medicine will make up for all defects in food, air, exercise, and cleanliness," Buchan cautions (35). Another author is more specific, suggesting that after deliberately overfeeding a child, "the nurse displays her skills by exhibiting some cordial or soothing syrup" (Cameron 162). Opium thus masks both simple neglect and outright mistreatment. It can also substitute more directly, as when wet nurses "who have little milk . . . quiet the child when it wants the breast, by giving Dalby's carminative, or Godfrey's cordial" (Hopkins 211; see also Combe 223–224 and my discussion in chapter 4). A commodity itself, opium's danger lies in part in the fact that it can be endlessly converted into things that it is not: restful sleep, breastmilk, the appearance of doting care.

Many sources describe the symptoms of opiate dependence in children in some detail. These include low energy (languor and stupor); digestive problems, including constipation and loss of appetite; fever and convulsions; over time, a pallid and sallow appearance, as well as weight loss; and, ultimately, stunted growth and general physical debility. There's a good bit of repetition—even outright recirculation of phrases—in the description of symptoms. (This may derive from the culture of reprinting and copying I discussed in chapter 2, and might also derive from there being at any cultural moment a limited set of ways to describe the same physiological symptoms.) These descriptions

---

12. See Champney 90, Carpenter 366, and Barker 42–43 ("ignorant"); Barker 41 ("inexperienced"); Bull, *Maternal Management* 279 ("unprincipled"); and Beeton 1023–1024 ("selfish," "unprincipled").

also reinforce the class associations of the drug. "By their continued, habitual use," cautions Bull:

> . . . a low, irritative, febrile state is produced, gradually followed by loss of flesh, the countenance becoming pallid, sallow, and sunken, the eyes red and swollen, and the expression stupid and heavy, and the powers of the constitution at last becoming completely undermined. Such an object is to be seen daily among the poorer classes,—the miniature of a sickly aged person: death soon follows here. (*Maternal Management* 111)

Bull's language here closely echoes that of Marshall Hall's 1835 version of Michael Underwood's *Treatise,* not only in some of the physical descriptors ("pallid, sallow") but also in the associations with class and age: "The appearances which arise from the habit of giving opium are very peculiar. They may be seen in the dwindled, pallid, sallow, stupefied countenances of the infants of the poor, as you pass them in the street. The eye-lids are red and swollen; the whole face is the miniature of a sickly aged person" (Underwood and Hall 137–138). In both cases, the physical ("pale and sallow" in Bull) soon gives way to the psychological ("stupid and heavy"), reflecting opium's power as a narcotic to work on both body and mind. But the psychological difference of the opium-dosed child quickly blurs into dehumanizing class identification: Paleness, sallowness, and stupidity converge in this victim's resemblance to the "object . . . to be seen daily among the poorer classes." Opium dehumanizes middle-class children by making them resemble poor children; it replaces the chubby apple cheeks of normative bourgeois childhood with the prematurely aged pallor of their poor counterparts.

Opium warnings generate the vulnerability of White, middle-class children as an affective fact, figuring the British family, nation, and empire as inevitably threatened by the supplemental caregiving structures that enact class and racial identity. Smuggled into British homes—not unlike its smuggling into Chinese ones—the drug transforms the very bodies of middle-class children into those of their starving, abject Others. As we've seen, advice literature enacts this infiltrating danger rhetorically, typifying childrearing situations in order to cultivate the experience of threatening and even deadly surprise. The logic of the warning pervades and even shapes the genre alongside that of the prescription, repeatedly taking readers through the experience of being startled by a danger they forgot to anticipate. Opium is the most common surprise in this genre after that of an illness turned deadly, suggesting that at least part of the constitutive vulnerability of the bourgeois family is spatial and social permeability, its dependence on servants and global substances. Anxiety is the emotional experience of perpetual, shifting, future conditional threat as well as the affective vehicle for the watchful, supervisory, caring and careful attention that manages the household and (re)produces the future of family, nation, and empire.

Colonial Anxieties

Human attention cannot see all places or anticipate all things at once. In advice literature, maternal care is figured as the supervision that ought to protect children, monitoring not only babies' bodies and characters but also the bodies and (hidden) actions and motives of those paid to care for them. I return now to *The Life of Mrs. Sherwood* to examine more closely another episode in which Sherwood identifies her son Henry's death as both inevitable and evidence of the danger colonial living poses for British identity. In this episode, an uptake enactment of advice literature's warnings, I show how the autobiographical account reinforces the threat of infant dosing by recirculating it with the authority of (near) eyewitness.

As we've seen, Henry was born in December 1805 and died of whooping cough in the summer of 1807. Sherwood was devastated by her children's deaths. As I discussed in chapter 3, Sherwood's recounting of these losses strives to frame them and Henry's persistent illnesses in terms of her own spiritual growth; this narrative emphasizes both her grief and an eventual faith in the beneficence of God's plan. In her manuscript, she reflects gratefully that the "presence of tender & most lovely Infants" was God's protective gift to her during these early years in India: Her attention was so bound up in her children that she was not significantly tempted by Anglo-Indian social life ("Diary" 207–208). But Henry's illness in particular threw Sherwood into greater dependence on and intimacy with Betty Parker—an intimacy that distressed her in the moment and that she represents as both sign and cause of her mismanagement of her nursery staff. The spiritual narrative collides with colonial, racial, and class hierarchies, and therefore with narratives that offer competing explanations for the children's deaths and Sherwood's struggles. Because Henry was often ailing and his final illness prolonged, while Lucy's death from dysentery was sudden, these alternative possibilities are the most evident in the former narrative. *The Life of Mrs. Sherwood* enacts the situation of motherhood by attaching opium, paid caregivers, mortality, and maternal mismanagement to one another, dissolving their boundaries and rendering them all indicative of inadequate (maternal) attention and the consequent vulnerability of empire.

The anecdotal and picaresque logic of Sherwood's memoir affords surprise in these moments, phenomenologically enacting the experience she describes. "Sometime about or before this time I had a great shock," she begins one such episode:

> Being in my dressing-room next to the nursery, I heard my baby give a sharp cry. In a moment I was near him, and I felt certain that his nurse had crammed something into his mouth. I charged her with it, but both she and the ayah denied it. I was not satisfied. I watched my boy carefully; in a very little while he fell into a deep sleep. I still watched. I had fearful suspicions. The sleep became heavier and heavier. His extremities became cold. I sent for the medical man, and he soon discovered that my baby had been drugged with opium. I cannot say what means were used by the surgeon, but the baby lay like death for many hours. I think about twelve; he then revived gradually, but assuredly this was not the first time he had been so quieted. After this, of course, we could have no confidence in his nurse, and we changed her for a black woman to whom he had taken a fancy.
>
> It is my firm belief that half the European children who die in infancy in India, die from the habit which their nurses have of giving them opium. How many, many things were against my infant boy! It was ordained that he was not to remain long on earth; but I had not, when this happened, reconciled myself to the idea of parting from him. (299–300)

The contours of this anecdote narrativize those of the warnings. As uptake enactments of one another, life writing and advice literature respectively specify and project temporally the story they share, deepening the emotional intensity as the tale cycles through the genre ecology. As I noted earlier, the historical relationship of advice literature to Sherwood's experience and her written account of it is itself cyclical: *The Life of Mrs. Sherwood* both helps us understand events that medical men took up and circulated as likely danger situations and performs a kind of experiential narrativization that precisely confirms the truth of those projections. These uptake enactments iteratively reinforce not simply the facticity of the danger they circulate, but also the emotional residues that attach to it. Opium, hired nurses, and maternal attention become variously sticky with danger and anxiety.

Sherwood's account exhibits and intensifies the uptake capture—the emotional and dispositional stances the warning genre makes possible—by recounting the maternal experience and pulling readers into the rhythm of anxious attention in a sequence of short sentences while she sits by Henry's bedside waiting for the doctor to arrive. But this account also reveals the extent to which experienced scenes are understood through cultural scripts.

For one thing, there is no acknowledgement of the drug's medicinal value, no possibility that the nurse or ayah might have given Henry opium for a cough or other illness. This omission demonizes the caregiver and the alien substance she administers, as well as emphasizing the narrative telos of Henry's death. Furthermore, Sherwood does not herself witness the nurse giving Henry the opium, but in this account remembers having *felt* immediate certainty that this is what happened. The testimonies of both of the nameless servants are irrelevant and unreliable in her mind, compared with her own conviction and (later) the medical man's expert opinion. It may be, in fact, that opium warnings and rumors circulated extratextually, simultaneously confirming and giving shape to more diffuse fears of racial and religious difference. At the least, it seems clear that Sherwood's understanding of the events—either as they unfolded or upon recollection—was shaped not just by medical diagnosis but also by racialized expectations. We cannot tell. While Sherwood describes herself as "shocked," the incident confirms her prejudices as well as her already pronounced sense of physical and familial vulnerability. Her nurse's suspected behavior becomes yet another piece of evidence not only that her son's death was predestined ("many, many things were against my boy!") but also that infant mortality writ large can be blamed on specifically Indian malfeasance. Jostling with the advice literature's warnings in the genre ecology, this autobiographical account's depiction of fear in the face of a specific, imminent danger affords an anxious uptake capture by reinforcing the warning's authority as affective fact.

The Life of Mrs. Sherwood as published in 1854 emphasizes opium-dosing as a cultural and racial danger rather than an individual one: "It is my firm belief that half the European children who die in infancy in India, die from the habit which their nurses have of giving them opium." While both F. J. Harvey Darton's *The Life and Times of Mrs. Sherwood (Chiefly Autobiographical)* (1910) and Sherwood's manuscript blame individuals (Henry's wet nurse, Ameena, and a temporary nurse, respectively), Sophia Kelly's edits to her mother's memoir create a narrative in which the deadly alterity of colonial life adheres to the drug. This incident is part of a series of episodes in *The Life of Mrs. Sherwood* that I have lingered over throughout *Writing Maternity*, although I have taken up its pieces in relative isolation and without sustained attention to their narrative order. Here, I want to emphasize the cumulative effect of their sequence. After an extended (six-page) description of their visit to the Nawab of Bengal's celebration, Sherwood recounts Henry's return from a puja with a tilak on his forehead (292–298). This is immediately followed by two paragraphs reflecting on (and regretting) the decision to wean the little boy at fourteen months, including the implication that it was partially motivated by racialized nursery politics (298–299). *The Life of Mrs. Sherwood* then moves to the episode in which Henry is given opium, situating it chronologically roughly at the time of Henry's weaning (299–300). In Sherwood's manuscript, by contrast, the opium episode is recounted first, apparently occurring in the fall of 1806 rather than the following winter (207); the visit to the Nawab and the puja/tilak incident, followed immediately by the discussion of weaning, appear ten pages later, apparently in January 1807 (217–218). Kelly also makes the demographic generalization with which Sherwood concludes this tale specific to India: While Sherwood's manuscript reads "half the European children who die in infancy" it is "half the European children who die in infancy *in India*" in the published version (see Sherwood, "Diary" 209). In the published text, the cultural marking (tilak) and the ingesting of an Orientalized intoxicating and potentially toxic substance (opium) are both thus linked to the explicitly managerial issues that at least narratively kill the child. In the narrative logic this ordering creates, an Indian caregiver is fired for compromising the child's Whiteness, and then another Indian caregiver nearly kills him in retaliation.

India, its people, and its narcotic seem to encircle the White woman and her vulnerable child in *The Life of Mrs. Sherwood*. There is no way out but enhanced suspicion: The servant convicted of drugging the baby can be dismissed, but is (must be?) replaced by yet another "black woman." It's possible to read this as an allegory of colonial surveillance, in which White vulnerability mandates not exit but ever-escalating panoptic control. The spatial and temporal logics of anxiety collide in the colonial home—which, as Flora Annie Steel and Grace Gardiner emphasized at the end of the century "c[ould] no more be governed peacefully, without dignity and prestige, than an Indian Empire" (10). The maternal supervisor must not only anticipate possible future dangers but also monitor what is happening (literally) in the next room and during daily outings. The anxiety that motivates this managerial attention is thus a painful emotion—indeed, a paradigmatically neurotic or ugly one—and yet, in this instance, (re)productive. In Sherwood's writing, maternal anxiety has the same motive and logic as the imperial gaze, the objectifying, distancing, and yet fearful perspective of oppressive and yet intimate control.

Anxious Supervisions

Maternal management is thus a totalizing fantasy, its movement at least partially catalyzed by the dream that proleptic and paraliptic attention—to what's to come and what's happening out of sight—could obviate all danger and ensure social reproduction into the future. But that fantasy is a defensive one, predicated upon the illusion that preemptive action can nullify rather than perpetuate threat. In advice literature, we've seen the mobilization of opium warnings to rhetorically justify the anxious attention that stands as direct, nurturing maternal care in nineteenth-century middle-class (and therefore servant-keeping) British homes. In *The Life of Mrs. Sherwood,* we see how this attention is a performance of panoptic control, part of the violence of empire as it was enacted within British domestic spaces in the colonies. In turning now to Charlotte Mary Yonge's *The Daisy Chain; or, Aspirations, A Family Chronicle* (1856), I continue this emphasis, arguing that the novel invites us to understand the neurotic, fearful emotion of maternal anxiety as part of the authoritative, trustworthy, and omniscient parenting that is the productive— and virtuous—opposite of complacency.

Yonge's "family chronicles"—a title taken from *The Daisy Chain's* subtitle to name a subgenre of domestic realism—take up the logic of reproductive futurity with both precision and an imperial, totalizing drive. Sprawling novels whose plots turn on the futures of large families of orphaned children, *The Daisy Chain* (1856) and its sequel, *The Trial* (1864), *The Pillars of the House* (1873), *Magnum Bonum* (1879), and many others suggest that childrearing decisions have implications not only for individual lives and souls but for communities and the Empire as a whole in both the present and the future. In her Preface to *The Daisy Chain,* Yonge emphasizes the genre's embrace of the proleptic temporality of childrearing: A family chronicle is "a domestic record of home events, large and small, during those years of early life when the character is chiefly formed, and as an endeavour to trace the effects of those aspirations which are a part of every youthful nature" (vii). Catherine Sandbach-Dahlström, who identifies roughly eleven family chronicles in Yonge's oeuvre, emphasizes the extent to which these novels depict "an imaginary world that corresponds to contemporary visions of ideal family life" that is in both "social and religious terms . . . a confined world"; the familial "enclave," she contends, is both isolated from and threatened by "an unregenerate surrounding world" (60; see also Battiscombe and Laski 17–19). These novels, published between 1845 and 1889, center on the education and growth of large families of partially or completely orphaned siblings; as a result, they are at once elastic and limited in form and focus. Adapting the logic of the multiplot novel to tell the developmental story of a defined and beleaguered whole, Yonge's family chronicles take their form by braiding together several individual bildungsromans to depict family not simply as the basis of but *as* British society itself.[13] Valerie Sanders emphasizes the consequently episodic

---

13. Although Part I of *The Daisy Chain* was serialized in *The Monthly Packet* from 1853 to 1855, Yonge abandoned serial publication and published the novel as a whole in 1856 (Coleridge 184). The episodic nature of the narrative is more rooted in the braided bildungsroman form than in the affordances of serialization.

form of the family chronicles, although to my mind she discounts the ideological and formal coherence of Yonge's fiction.[14] My focus in this section is primarily on the narrative of one of the eleven May children—Flora May Rivers—whose confident, worldly, competent perfection is revealed to mask an absence of anxious self-reflection that, literally, jeopardizes the future of the family.

Yonge is the only Victorian novelist I have found to narrativize opium warnings, incorporating the dosing of an infant by its paid caregiver into the larger plot and thematic concerns of a novel. In other fiction of the period, references to opiate "soothing syrups" are used as a kind of shorthand to indicate the lethally misguided, careless, or even deliberately murderous childcare practices of the poor (think, for example, of Benjamin Disraeli's *Sybil* [1845]); Yonge takes up this association more fully in her later novel, *The Three Brides* [1876]). In *The Daisy Chain*, opium cathects this family chronicle's larger interest in disciplinary maternity onto its commitment to a missionary empire. This novel genre thus takes up the substance of advice literature's warning, which signified imperiled fragility in colonial life writing, making it trigger the anxious but disembodied care that for Yonge produces docile subjects globally.

The novel narrates the fortunes of the eleven children of the May family after their mother's death in a carriage accident that also cripples the eldest daughter. In following the family (the children range in age from six weeks to nineteen years at the opening of the novel) over the course of the next seven years, the novel explicitly focuses on the "aspirations" of several, testing and evaluating them through a matrix of self-interest and domestic-religious self-sacrifice. In particular, Yonge details the struggles of several of the older children: Flora, whose domestic and social skills make her dangerously worldly and self-satisfied; Norman, whose intellectual brilliance offers him a choice of highly visible careers as an MP, an Oxford don, or a poet; and Ethel, whose studious and undomestic bent is paired with a genuine religious faith.[15] The novel details Norman's and Ethel's progress from temptation to selfless service: Norman discards brilliant public careers at home for missionary work in New

---

14. Sanders is concerned to position herself as a "defender" of Yonge against claims that the author sacrifices novelistic interest to moral didacticism ("All-Sufficient"). I would gloss that opposition as the tension between individual development and societal—often parental—authority, and would contend that it is one of the animating exigencies of Yonge's fiction (see Schaffer, "Mysterious Magnum Bonum" and *Novel Craft* 92–95).

15. A significant portion of scholarly attention focuses on Ethel and the question of how—and how convincingly or cruelly—Yonge tames her ambition. See, for example, Sturrock; Schaub; Thorne-Murphy. Mia Chen centers her argument in "'And There Was No Helping It'" on Margaret, arguing that she challenges Victorian assumptions about the reproductive capacity of disabled female bodies.

Zealand; Ethel forsakes her classical studies for domestic responsibilities to her father and siblings, and charitable work in a nearby hamlet. Flora's story provides a negative object lesson, showing the temptations of worldly ambition, particularly when combined with a complacency that blocks genuine self-examination and -doubt. At the same time, the novel is structured around two church-building projects, one a foreign and the other a domestic mission, that unite family members in what Talia Schaffer describes as a maternally sanctioned "sacred trust" that rewrites both Melanesia ("as another version of England") and England ("in alienating, frighteningly racialized ways") (*Novel Craft* 93, 103).

In explicit contrast to Ethel, Flora is naturally adept at the domestic skills of a middle-class woman. Her remarkable aptitude for the work of managing a household first appears in the novel's major moment of tragedy: The carriage accident that kills the children's mother, cripples their sister, and injures their father—who is, significantly, the local GP. While Dr. May and the other siblings are bewildered with grief, Flora rises to the occasion, providing a modicum of order and comfort to the distraught household. She quickly moves into the role of household manager. Taking her mother's and eldest sister's places in many necessary logistical matters, Flora orders the meals and directs the servants; she teaches letters and numbers to many of her young siblings; and she later assumes the social duties that fall to the female head of the family. Aware of her own skill—and how indispensable she has quickly become—Flora receives no check to a lifelong tendency toward unreflective self-regard. Once she marries George Rivers, a family friend and member of the local gentry, Flora's ambitions grow proportionately. Despite her husband's lack of intellect, she pushes him into standing for the local Parliamentary seat and writes his campaign speech while still in bed after giving birth to Leonora, their first child. When they move to London at the beginning of the Season, she apparently weans the baby (who is then three months old), leaving her to the care of an inexperienced young nurse named Preston while she takes up the extensive social and charitable responsibilities of an MP's wife. (There is no suggestion that Preston is a wet nurse.) Preston gives the baby Godfrey's Cordial to quiet her cries of protest at being "set aside" (506), and Leonora becomes addicted to the opiate. She dies of opium withdrawal soon after Flora, belatedly concerned that she seems lethargic and unwell, resumes direct care of her. Both parents are devastated by the baby's death, but when George wishes to call the police to arrest Preston for murder, Flora insists that she is equally culpable: "If Preston killed her, I did!" (507). Leonora's death seems, then, to be a lesson in the dangers of the complacency that let Flora imagine that seeing her daughter at breakfast and late at night (after the baby was asleep) was sufficient maternal care; it exposes Flora's apparently perfect management for a sham. Rather than supervising every aspect of her busy life, she not only delegated what the novel considers her most important responsibilities to others, but also failed to supervise the execution of the delegated tasks.

As with the episode in *The Life of Mrs. Sherwood,* this moment is in part a straightforward uptake enactment of the advice literature's warnings: Without the mother's watchful care (and in part because her attention is directed elsewhere), the servant substitutes a narcotic for the nurture she has been hired to provide.[16] We can see this in the novel's several chancing references to how much Leonora sleeps, and that she is "pale," "dull," and "a perfect doll for quietness" in advance of the discovery (485, 502, 484). Yonge's longer description of Leonora's brief life and death extend this:

> Poor little Leonora had been very fretful and uneasy when Flora's many avocations had first caused her to be set aside, and Preston had had recourse to the remedy which, lulling her successfully, was applied with less moderation and judgement than would have been shown by a more experienced person, till gradually the poor child became dependent on it for every hour of rest. When her mother, at last, became aware of her unsatisfactory condition, and spent her time in watching her, the nurse being prevented from continuing her drug, she was, of course, so miserable without it, that Preston had ventured on proposing it, to which [Flora] had replied with such displeasure to prevent her from declaring how much she had previously given. (506)

In addition to echoing advice literature's description of the symptoms, Yonge draws the same class distinction as the other genres by drawing attention to Flora's "displeasure" upon hearing the mere name of the opiate: The drug marks a dividing line between middle- and working-class childrearing practices, as well as between those of even an insufficiently maternal mother and a hired nurse. Flora is thus exonerated from one type of complicity in Leonora's death; although her "many avocations" create a vacuum that apparently only the addictive substance could fill, Flora understands the dangers—or at least the undesirability—of the drug.

But in the passage above, opium actually substitutes for the mother's care. More directly, it seems that for Leonora—as for many working-class babies in the rhetorical imagination of the time—opium substitutes for the mother's

---

16. Tamara Wagner also reads this episode as an uptake enactment, calling it a "thinly fictionalised cautionary tale" (814). See also Banerjee 96; Lerner 148–154.

milk. By associating Leonora's fretfulness with the moment when Flora "caused her to be set aside" (as I interpret it, weaned), Yonge threatens to collapse the distinction between drug and mother. As was the case for the factory operatives Reach described in *The Morning Chronicle* and lace workers like Mary Colton, the opiate-based patent medicine appears as the deadly inversion of the breastmilk the children need to survive. These infants get *either* their mother's milk *or* Godfrey's Cordial—and, in the immediate and short term, it seems that the two substances do comparable work: Both quiet otherwise fussy babies. This of course ultimately breaks down, as we see with Leonora and can recall from Andrew Combe's warnings about wet nurses. In *The Daisy Chain,* Leonora's opium addiction is revealed by her physician-grandfather's diagnosis rather than her mother's abrupt reentry into the room. Flora summons her father, Dr. May, to London by expressing concern about the baby's "sleepiness' and "fretfulness," as well as a suspicious "look about the eyes" (503). After a brief physical examination, he exclaims, "This is the effect of opium!" (504). A few moments later, his condemnation of both parents and nurse is even more devastating: "What have you all been doing? . . . I tell you this child has been destroyed with opium!" (504). This outburst is characteristic of Dr. May, but it also reveals the scope of the surprise: Flora, the supremely competent domestic manager, has stumbled clumsily into the greatest "domestic affliction" imaginable. (Remarkably for a family of eleven children, this seems to be the first time the Mays have had an infant or young child die.) Generally "acknowledged" to be "superior in discretion and effectiveness," Flora routinely anticipates and smooths away small obstacles with invisible interventions—that is, she provides perfect and nearly invisible supervision (269). But here, she is shown to have failed at the middle-class mother's most fundamental responsibility: to ensure the health and longevity of her children. Leonora dies not because Flora herself wasn't *in* the nursery, but because she wasn't paying attention to what was going on there and didn't anticipate the dangers that could occur in her absence. Flora, the consummate manager, didn't adequately supervise her staff. Her maternal care was insufficiently concerned.

It's worth noting that until Leonora is obviously unwell, Flora never worries about anything; she shrugs off other characters' observations or subordinates their most obvious implication—that children are healthier in the country than in London—to her Parliamentary ambitions (see 485, 502). One of the character's most striking characteristics is her lack of self-doubt, the extent to which her managerial genius anticipates possible outcomes without enough emotional investment to fear danger. She is "never at a loss" and manages not only her "multifarious occupations" but also other people with a deft, manipulative tact that periodically worries her siblings (221, 308). The novel builds familial concern about Flora's complacent independence slowly; Margaret notes early on that "Flora could never need any interference," and Dr. May reflects sadly that "he was a little afraid of her cool prudence; she never seemed to be in any need of him" (164, 346). This complacency is an issue of religious faith for Yonge; her theology requires rigorous but balanced self-examination and scrutiny.

After Leonora's death, Flora confesses with fatalistic certainty that she will not see her daughter again in heaven. "I have never set my heart right," she tells her father; "I have seemed to myself, and to you, to be trying to do right, but it was all hollow, for the sake of praise and credit" (511). The narrator explains, "Her whole religious life had been mechanical, deceiving herself more than even others" (512), and while the narrative explicitly emphasizes the danger of ambition, the juxtaposition of Flora's plot with those of Norman, Ethel, and others draws attention as well to the threat posed by a lack of anxious self-examination and -awareness. While Norman's plot takes him through a near loss of faith when he engages in debates at Oxford, and Ethel's manifest domestic and temperamental "faults" are presented as requiring the self-conscious scrutiny that fosters genuine faith, Flora's many easy successes led her not only to be "greedy of credit and affection" but also to "think [her]self perfection" (583). Incapable of seeing into herself or confiding in others, Flora mistakenly assumes that what she cannot see or imagine does not exist. Like Mr. Dombey, she lacks the anxious scrutiny of self, others, past, and future that affords successful management and spiritual or emotional wholeness.

In contrast to the excessive intimacy Sherwood recalls with Betty Parker, Flora's relationship with Preston seems distant and impersonal: The nursemaid is so frightened of her employer's expression of displeasure at the mention of Godfrey's Cordial that she never admits she's given the baby the narcotic. Yonge generously makes Preston young and inexperienced, giving her an understandable and pitiable motive rather than a sinister one: She "had not known that the cordial was injurious, deeming it a panacea against fretfulness, precious to nurses, but against which ladies always had a prejudice, and therefore, to be kept secret" (506). The novel thus indicts Flora for surveillance that is judgmental as well as belated, but her rush to the sick baby's care exacerbates rather than exculpates her earlier crime. Flora's return to the nursery is the precipitating factor in the little girl's death. During the four or five months that Flora is busy with Parliamentary blue books, charity work, and various social engagements, Leonora is addicted to opium but stable; Dr. May's diagnosis is that she was "not . . . killed by any one dose, but had rather sunk from the want of stimulus, to which she had been accustomed" (506–507). The suggestion is thus that Flora's refusal to let Preston continue the opiate pushes Leonora's health over the edge. Through the narcotic, this episode collapses the opposition between maternal presence and child-death in the middle-class home. Flora's presence here is deadly.

The novel reinforces this implicit distrust of direct maternal care through its treatment of Flora after Leonora's death and the birth of another daughter, named Margaret after her grandmother and aunt. The baby is immediately given into the care of the nameless family nurse who had raised all the May siblings so capably, and Flora considers having her husband withdraw from Parliament so that they can leave the "London life" that is "temptation and plague" to her as well as a "risk . . . for the baby, now and hereafter" (588). Her sister Ethel counsels the grieving woman against such a step, and then their clergyman brother "show[s] her] that, for George's sake, [she] must bear with [her] present life . . . and that the glare, and weariness, and being spoken well of, must be taken as punishment for having sought after these things" (591). The childcare structure and location for Margaret are thus identical to the one that resulted in Leonora's death, although the specific nurse has changed, as well as the mother's apparent degree of complacency and consequent maternal-managerial attention. *The Daisy Chain* thus takes up and explains the individualizing logic of Sherwood's opium episode: The solution to the discovery that a servant has been drugging a baby is not to do without paid childcare, but to hire a new servant and watch them more closely.

Strangely for a novel in which the mother dies in chapter three, *The Daisy Chain* enacts a version of this anxiously supervisory maternal vision as ideal. The association of Mrs. May with Heaven, as with saintly patience and all other feminine virtues, is used throughout the novel as a protective but also stifling influence over her children. The novel thus provides an illustration of Carolyn Dever's argument that the Victorian ideal of the selfless, nurturing, angelic mother could *only* be imagined in the absence of physical (or at least narrative) mothers (see pp. xi and 7–8). Schaffer points out that Mrs. May is an "enforcer of social norms": She "demands self-suppressing behavior from her children in ways that surely would have invited rebellion had she lived longer" (*Novel Craft* 106). But Yonge idealizes Mrs. May—and, through her, maternity as a type—by converting her through death from a physical presence into a rhetorical effect that is underwritten by a religiously inflected nostalgia. One of the younger children mistakenly but tellingly refers to going to church as "going to mamma," conflating the mother's grave with the more orthodox place of worship (453). Similarly, Dr. May confidently reminds a son about to leave home as a sailor that his mother "may be nearer to you everywhere, though you are far from us" (262). Even before her death, Mrs. May's absence makes her presence all the more powerful. Her "gentle power" to quell "restlessness," "fidgeting," and "impertinence" (5) is framed by the knowledge that this is her first appearance downstairs since the youngest child's birth six weeks earlier. When we reflect that this is the eleventh child Mrs. May has had in nineteen years, it becomes clear that she is often not physically at the center of family activities and cannot herself be delivering daily care.

The emotional identification of the Mother with religious faith allows Yonge to use the dead Mrs. May as a kind of rhetorical principle of control. A flexible referent rather than an embodied character, their mother's desires become the language of appropriate choice among characters. What "mamma would say" blesses or condemns any potential project, authorizes or curtails habitual tendencies. An unfinished letter she leaves is crucial to this work. Written to her sister in New Zealand, the letter offers a "portrait gallery" of the children from youngest to oldest, emphasizing each one's strengths and weaknesses from their mother's perspective. Norman, the letter warns, "has never shown any tendency to conceit, but . . . has the love of being foremost, and pride in his superiority, caring for what he is compared with others, rather than what he is himself" (45). The mother fears that Flora "will find temptation in the being everywhere liked and sought after," but notes that Ethel's "manifest defects" in domestic matters "have occasioned a discipline that is the best thing for her character in the end. They are faults that show themselves, and which one can tell how to deal with" (45, 44). Yonge first presents this letter early in the novel, shortly after Mrs. May's death, and includes its full text for her readers; we read it alongside Norman and Ethel and after Flora (who notes that "it is a description of us all, and very much indeed we ought to learn from it" [43]). It thus simultaneously structures our interpretations of these characters and shapes their interpretations of themselves.[17]

The family chronicle bears out Mrs. May's early diagnoses; the novel at once obviates surprise and proves that mother does indeed know best. The letter provides substantive content for the characters' invocations of Mrs. May throughout the novel—with that letter as the origin, the references to "Mamma's" wishes or fears or standards carry meaning for readers that they otherwise would not. It operates in the novel as a kind of sacred text, providing personal insight that the characters take to be as deeply true as they do

17. It's noteworthy that in the letter Mrs, May finds herself unable to represent, much less criticize, Margaret—her eldest daughter and namesake who, once crippled, takes over her place as the moral center of the family. Although I concur with Mia Chen's reading of Margaret's socially reproductive role, it's clear that her supervision and judgment are not as wisely proleptic as her mother's. While Mrs. May's letter anticipates the problems Tom will have at school, for example, Margaret and her siblings mistakenly decide not to confide their younger brother's cheating at lessons to their father.

the Gospel. But of course the children only have access to Mrs. May's post-humous letter *because* she has died, and it therefore functions as a trace in the Derridean sense—in Spivak's formulation, "the mark of the absence of a presence, an always already absent present" (xvii). Mrs. May's letter carries the maternal word forward and transmutes maternal concern into a kind of sacred text. The version of Mrs. May that characters and readers abstract from the letter is, for example, what nominally guides Norman away from the intellectual ambition that the novel codes as (mere) worldly temptation and toward a path—missionary work—that he finds both challenging and unappealing except as a kind of sacrifice. Schaffer emphasizes the cruel strangeness of this within the emotional economy of the novel, even if Yonge's own commitment to missionary work offers one explanation. She points out that Norman and Ethel *both* "kill their intellectual selves," in Norman's case because his trajectory as a missionary leads him to "re-creat[e] [the] school life" he wishes to flee (*Novel Craft* 117, 107). Early on, Norman reveals that he's internalized his mother's written concern, deliriously reporting that in a dream she told him that "it was all ambition" (107); later, Ethel speculates that "the first grief, coming at his age, and in the manner it did, checked and subdued his spirits . . . But, perhaps, it is a good thing; dear mamma thought his talents would have been a greater temptation than they seem to be, subdued as he has been" (385). As Dever points out regarding Richardson's *Clarissa* (1748), the dead woman becomes "more powerful as an agent of discipline after her martyrdom than in life . . . To appropriate Foucault's terms, 'a power relation' sustained 'independent of the person who exercises it' consolidates the monitory function of disembodied female virtue" (22). Here, we see not only that Mrs. May's word can be more influential once it has been separated from her body but also that her death itself has helped produce that effect. The peculiarly present absence of the ideal mother, then, appears only possible through her tragic death.

It is both striking and important, to my mind, that Mrs. May's letter describes her children in terms of her own *worries* for them. Each of the portraits Mrs. May provides of her children lingers at least momentarily over some sort of concern, "anxiety" (twice), or "dread" (44–45). In addition to the descriptions of the older children, she fears—for example—that five-year-old Blanche is too fond of admiration, and that ten-year-old Tom has "not much perseverance or energy" (44). The ideal mother thus exhibits a searching vision that is reflective and (within the novel's narrative framework) clear-eyed. Flora's complacent maternity thus stands in stark contrast. Where Mrs. May observed, noted, and worried about embryonic problems in order to address them, Flora's lack of anxiety allowed the problem to escalate fatally. Talking with her aunt after little Margaret's birth, Flora reflects that "the credit

I gained [early on] made me think myself perfection, and I never did anything afterwards but seek my own honour" (582). It is not simply Flora's extra-
domestic work and attention that mark her as unmaternal; her unreflecting
self-satisfaction—her very *lack* of anxiety—makes it possible for her nurse's
classed practices to infiltrate her nursery and kill her child. By collapsing
future prospects into the present moment of children's lives, maternal anxiety
thus both relies on and expresses the logic of reproductive futurity on the level
of individual families as well as that of nations and empires.

The novel's identification of Mrs. May both with brick-and-mortar
churches and also with the disembodied surveillance of a missionary God
contributes to a spatial and emotional conflation of family, nation, and empire
that is an important component of the family chronicle's generic conceit. The
May family have almost no friends, although glancing references are made
to acquaintances and their place in the social network of Stoneborough. Dr.
May's practice is an important vector for connections that become emotionally and then literally familial. After he treats the orphaned Alan Ernescliffe,
he brings him back to the May house to convalesce with his younger brother,
paving the way for Alan's romance with Margaret May. (In *The Daisy Chain*'s
sequel *The Trial*, we learn that Alan's brother marries Blanche May.) Dr. May's
professional visit to the Rivers household results in another long-term connection, one that results in another two marriages: that of Flora and George,
as well as that of Norman and Meta. All the marriages in *The Daisy Chain*
are familiar—and familial—ones, confirming and cementing family ties rather
than threatening them (Schaffer, *Romance's Rival* 2–19). (Even Ethel's near-
suitor is a cousin, and one who shares her favorite brother's name.) The family's rare travels take them to spaces that are either ancestral (Oxford, where
generations of May men have gone to university), deadly (London), or colonial
(the majority Irish hamlet of Cocksmoor, and the Melanesian Loyalty Islands).
And while time in London and Oxford threatens to undermine the family's
spiritual and physical reproduction, the church-building projects that enact
their colonial work unify the siblings in shared and sacred projects. Schaffer's
reading of *The Daisy Chain* emphasizes the extent to which Yonge's depiction
of these domestic and foreign missions "rewrites" the locations and communities "to make [them] more contiguous with . . . British community" (*Novel
Craft* 109). Part of that is erasure: The likely Catholicism of Cocksmoor's Irish
community, like the indigenous religion of the Loyalty Islanders, is completely
erased, giving the Mays' Anglicanism the colonial fantasy of blank spiritual
and cultural slates on which to work. This fantasy operates by the same logic
as Dr. May's expansion of his family: The Ernescliffes are orphaned, with no
family but a distant cousin (invisible before dying and leaving them well-off);

the Rivers' connections are quickly and easily dismissed as emotionally and spiritually inadequate. The May family itself is an "incorporative apparatus," as Edward Said has described empire (168): It projects inferiority and erases the history of its Others in order to domesticate and adopt them.

In *The Daisy Chain*, mothers can know everything, and that surveillance brings both knowledge and control. Within the novel, this is offered as a comforting but also cruelly restraining vision that transforms motherly concern into a productive rather than neurotic emotion. Unlike Sherwood's experiential narrative, Yonge's fictional elaboration of an opium rumor draws attention to what a mother can do rather than what she cannot. The productively and protectively anxious mother is, for Yonge, not an impossibility but a rhetorical and religious ideal, nearly as effective as a textual effect as she might be in life. We can see in this how uptakes circulate and transform through the genre ecology: If advice literature affords a structural understanding, in which paid caregivers are always potential baby-killers, both life writing and domestic fiction generate individualized and narrativized versions of that story. The result that emerges does not fundamentally alter the rhetorical situation but cyclically recreates it, as each genre responds to and enacts it anew. Through this process, it becomes increasingly sticky with anxiety, layering uptake residue upon uptake residue until the maternal subject position is saturated by that emotion's attention throughout time and across space.

•

In considering the managerial nature of middle-class motherhood as it took form in the early nineteenth century, I want to emphasize the extent to which it was motivated and sustained by the anxious knowledge that caregivers were both not doing their jobs and doing them too well, by the impossibility of both delegating work and doing it yourself. Neither symbolically nor legally the heads of households, middle-class mothers managed staff in order to manage the care and education of their children. They did so while subject to class and gender ideology and also quite directly to serve the familial ambitions and identity of the patrilineal families into which they married. Good domestic management means knowing everything that is going on in the kitchen or the nursery without being in them. It relies on the doomed effort to imagine away servants' distinct racial, cultural, and personal histories, projecting onto them both a self-abnegating identification with the desires and futures of their employers and a stubborn alterity that is supervision's constant incitement.

Domestic fiction's dramatization of the literal dangers of complacent self-confidence suggests that maternal anxiety is a protective and productive emotion. Indeed, I would argue that it is, intimately tied to the future-oriented transmission of social identity between generations as well as to the expansion-oriented geographic ambitions of a global empire. Along both axes—the temporal and the spatial—we can see the ways in which maternal anxiety is essential to the maintenance of global capitalist patriarchy; we can see how its focus on the home and the Child as always being or likely to be threatened justifies the protective and aggressive actions of a militarist empire. Childrearing advice literature developed in the early nineteenth century because of a variety of historical and rhetorical felicity conditions; its central uptake affordances then resonated and were taken up in turn—captured in affective scripts, narrativized in enactments shaped by those feelings. In understanding that the sense of paralyzed overwhelm that seems a feature of middle-class motherhood is not new, it's my hope that we can focus on the material conditions it upholds, and identify ways to shift maternal attention away from its fearful, threatened sense of obstructed agency and toward the planful, anticipatory logics that can enact revolutionary change.

CODA

Genre as Advice

'VE ALWAYS LOVED Dickens's depiction of the newly married Bella Wilfer Rokesmith's "severe study" of *The Complete British Family Housewife* in *Our Mutual Friend* (1864–1865) (666). I love it not simply for the scene's comic excess but also because Bella's "constant necessity of referring [to it] for advice and support" is neither unthinking nor docile. Periodically, we're told, she "would suddenly exclaim aloud, 'Oh, you ridiculous old thing, what do you mean by that? You must have been drinking!' And having made this marginal note, would try the Housewife again, with all her dimples screwed into an expression of profound research" (666). The object of Dickens's satire is evidently the conflicting and difficult-to-follow directions of domestic guides like *Mrs. Beeton's Book of Household Management*—akin, no doubt, to what we've seen about convulsions, crying, sea-bathing, and breastfeeding. (To be fair, *Mrs. Beeton's* was more than 1000 pages long.) But my interest lies in Bella's cycle of study, rejection, and return—the fact that her insistence that the book's author "must have been drinking!" does little to diminish her apparent conviction that the tome has knowledge she needs. Uptake enactments, as I've shown throughout *Writing Maternity*, are not limited to following orders; any genre affords a range of possibility, a range that includes certain kinds of rejection or resistance as well as a variety of feelings. The specific response(s) generated at any given moment depend, in turn, on that moment's particular circumstances, which include the particular addressee's personal history, culture, and memory. But it seems to me that perhaps the *felt sense* of a genre—here, Bella's return to *The Complete British Family Housewife*—tells us something about how genre operates culturally, how it contributes to a structure of feeling, how its response to and (re)constitution of rhetorical situation sediments into cultural form. In other words, genre is not only a category of analysis or creation but also a category that helps to shape our apperception of the current and historical world.

Literary scholars have begun to draw on rhetorical genre theory in recent years.[1] There remains, however, a fundamental incommensurability to the two paradigms. One gloss to this is that in rhetorical theory genre is a category of invention and in literary theory it's a category of interpretation. This puts it crudely and therefore fails to do justice to either area, but usefully identifies the different centers of gravity. Even as thinking about form has become ever more nuanced, complicated, and in some strains phenomenological, genre for literary scholars remains (more or less) a category defined by formal, textual features. By contrast, rhetorical genre scholars often operate empirically, seeking through social science methods to understand how genre knowledge shapes action and imagined possibilities, and what specific genres actually *do*.[2]

It's telling that Tzvetan Todorov and M. M. Bakhtin are two scholars frequently cited in both traditions, since both theorists are interested in (1) the relationship of literary and non-literary genre and (2) how formal features *among other aspects* define genres. In one strain of his work, Todorov thinks about the transformations that generate complex (or "secondary" for Bakhtin) genres out of simple (or "primary") ones. In *Genres in Discourse* he thinks specifically about the speech acts that underlie genres: the speech act "inviting" in relation to the Luba genre of *the invitation*, for example; or the act of expressing belief in something that lies "outside the framework of natural explanation" in relation to the genre of *the fantastic* (21–22, 24).[3] For Todorov, the originary speech act enacts what we might consider the logical or rhetorical core of the genre, but the space between act and genre is the space that removes the latter from the realm of action. The Luba *invitation* is explicitly not *an act* of inviting, in Todorov's reading, for all that it is an "amplif[ied]" and "transform[ed]" version of it (21); a *fantastic* story is explicitly *not* the act

---

1. See for example Dimock, "Introduction"; Lecourt; Nelson and Gayk.

2. In literary study, see Dimock, "Introduction" and "Genre as World System"; Dubrow; Levine. In rhetorical studies, see Bazerman, especially *Shaping Written Knowledge*; Dryer, Special Issue: Rhetorical Genre Studies; the essays in Giltrow and Stein; Tardy et al. My work follows in the tradition of Frow (*Genre*; "'Reproducibles'") and Devitt (*Writing Genres*) in seeking to bring rhetorical genre theory to bear on literary questions.

3. Todorov identifies Congolese poet Clémentine Faïk Nzuji as his source for information about Luba cultural and literary practices (21n13).

of expressing belief. But at the same time a *fantastic* story is shaped by the extent to which it gives readers that experience, for this is the core of Todorov's definition: "The very heart of the fantastic," he explains famously, is that:

> In a world which is indeed our world, the one we know . . . there occurs an event which cannot be explained by the laws of this same familiar world. The person who experiences this event must opt for one of two possible solutions: either he is the victim of an illusion of the senses . . . and the laws of world . . . remain what they are; or else the event has indeed taken place . . . [and] this reality is controlled by laws unknown to us. . . . The fantastic occupies the space of this uncertainty. (*The Fantastic* 25)

In his definitional analysis of Jacques Cazotte's *Les Diables Amoureux,* Todorov points out that readers "hesitate" and "wonder" with the main character (*The Fantastic* 24). The fantastic cannot include dramatic irony, because if it did so then readers would not inhabit "the space of . . . uncertainty." This understanding of genre thus partakes of the same logic as Bakhtin's in *Speech Genres,* in emphasizing the relation to the audience as the elemental core.

To define a genre by its addressivity is to define it by the uptakes it seeks to secure, the exigency that animates it. This can seem limiting, suggesting that any specific iteration of a genre can be most interestingly analyzed in terms of intention. (Generations of literary criticism have, of course, challenged and complicated this.) But to say that a *genre* is defined by its relation to its audience is different from saying that a single text is. If we return to Bella we can perhaps see this more clearly. There is no doubt that *The Complete British Family Housewife* is seeking to inculcate a set of domestic practices, habits, and values in its readers and to identify those as features of gender, racial, and national identity. It is equally clear—from Dickens's satire, but also I hope from my analysis of childrearing advice literature in these pages—that that generic or textual *desire* is very different from *success.* In other words: Bella's fraught relationship with her particular advice book tells us something about Bella (that she frustrates easily; that she has a mind of her own; that she has a history of rebelling against advice) and something about the specific text in question (it may not be especially clear). It also tells us that the genre's defining relationship with its audience is that of establishing its authority over housewifery in general. We can see in such books the nascent field of domestic science. *The Complete British Family Housewife* has no more interpellated Bella than *Progressive Education* interpellated Elizabeth Gaskell; but Bella's cycle of frustration and return, like Gaskell's anxious rule-making, is conditioned by the typified rhetorical situation the genre as a whole projects.

I've thought for a long time that advice literature's originary speech act (à la Todorov) must be the prescription. *Advice* is more diffuse and elaborated, but still retains something of the prescription's focused rhetorical force. In the late eighteenth and nineteenth centuries, people routinely distinguished between "advice" and "counsel," with advice carrying a greater instructive and perhaps coercive authority. (*Counsel* involves a gentler assistance in thinking things through.) But if we think seriously about the prescription as a speech act, it opens up both interpretive and creative space for thinking about genre. A prescription, after all, has no perlocutionary force of its own. And while all speech acts are dependent on context—felicity conditions—for their effects in the world, the prescription specifically thematizes this: A prescription—whether written or oral, whether for a drug or a change in habits—does literally nothing if it is not taken up as ordered. It suggests—forcefully—but cannot compel. We might say more accurately that it generates possibilities that include not only the range from formal (perhaps reluctant or cranky) obedience to outright (perhaps angry or mocking) rejection, but also a nuanced set of interactions between feelings, beliefs, actions, and experiences.

I am deliberately echoing Raymond Williams's language about structures of feeling here, but I want to linger over the notion of advice rather than switching to that term (see *Marxism and Literature* 132). If we take seriously the logic of advice, we might have a way to think about genre that brings the sense of temporal and spatial movement of rhetorical genre to bear on literary texts. This, in turn, might give literary and cultural critics new possibilities for thinking about how systems, structures, and forms mediate between individual experience and memory, on the one hand, and cultural knowledge and memory, on the other. By thinking of genre as a species of advice, we have a way to identify in a text itself a set of considerations that are formal, addressive, and creative; that tie the reading experience to formal features of the text but resist any kind of definitive end to interpretation; that remind us that any uptake—whether creative or critical or a blend of the two; fanfic, translation, sampling, or literary criticism—depends on the individual's own layers of memory and experience as well as those that have sedimented onto the particular cultural form (or forms). Perhaps most of all, we have a category through which to think about continuity, change, and the possibilities for intervention not only in literary history but in the living, changing history that is always mediated by the genres through which we think, feel, imagine, and act.

WORKS CITED

Ackroyd, Marcus, et al. *Advancing with the Army: Medicine, the Professions, and Social Mobility in the British Isles, 1790–1850.* Oxford UP, 2006.

Advice to Governesses. John Hatcherd and Son, 1827.

Advice to the Young Mother in the Management of Herself and Infant. By a Member of the Royal College of Surgeons, Longman, Hurst, Rees, Orme, and Brown, 1821.

"Advise, *v.*" *Oxford English Dictionary,* OEO Third Edition, Dec. 2011, oed.com, Oxford UP, 2019.

Adorno, Theodor W. "An Address on Charles Dickens's *The Old Curiosity Shop.*" Translated by Michael Hollington, *Dickens Quarterly,* vol. 6, no. 3, 1989, pp. 95–101.

Ahmed, Sara. *The Cultural Politics of Emotion.* Edinburgh UP, 2004. Reprint, 2014.

Althusser, Louis. "Ideology and Ideological State Apparatuses (Notes Towards an Investigation)." *Lenin and Philosophy and Other Essays.* 1968. Translated by Ben Brewster, with an introduction by Fredric Jameson, Monthly Review P, 2001, pp. 85–126.

Applegarth, Risa. "Bodily Scripts, Unruly Workers, and Public Anxiety: Scripting Professional Embodiment in Interwar Vocational Guides." Reiff and Bawarshi, pp. 117–136.

———. *Rhetoric in American Anthropology: Gender, Genre, and Science.* U of Pittsburgh P, 2014.

Appleton, Elizabeth. *Early Education; or, the Management of Children Considered with a View to Their Future Character.* G. & W. B. Whittaker, 1820.

Archibald, Diana. *Domesticity, Imperialism, and Emigration in the Victorian Novel.* U of Missouri P, 2002.

Ariès, Philippe. *Centuries of Childhood: A Social History of Family Life.* Vintage, 1962.

Armstrong, Nancy. *Desire and Domestic Fiction: A Political History of the Novel.* Oxford UP, 1987.

Artemeva, Natasha. "Stories of Becoming: A Study of Novice Engineers Learning Genres of Their Profession." *Genre in a Changing World*, edited by Charles Bazerman, Adair Bonini, and Debora Figueiredo, Parlor P, 2009, pp. 158–178.

Attar, Dena. *Cookery and Household Books Published in Britain, 1800–1914*. Prospect Books, 1987.

Austin, J. L. *How To Do Things with Words*. Oxford UP, 1976.

Bachman, Maria K. "Who Cares? Novel Reading, Narrative Attachment Disorder, and the Case of *The Old Curiosity Shop*." *JNT: Journal of Narrative Theory*, vol. 37, no. 2, 2007, pp. 296–325.

Bailey, Joanne. *Parenting in England, 1760–1830*. Oxford UP, 2012.

Bakewell, Mrs. J. *The Mother's Practical Guide in the Early Training of Her Children: Containing Directions for Their Physical, Intellectual, and Moral Education*. Second edition. Hamilton, Adams, and Co., 1836.

Bakhtin, M. M. *Speech Genres and Other Late Essays*. Translated by Vern W. McGee, U of Texas P, 1986.

Banerjee, Jacqueline P. *Through the Northern Gate: Childhood and Growing Up in British Fiction, 1719–1901*. Peter Lang, 1996.

Barker, Thomas Herbert. *Practical Observations on the Diet of Infancy and Childhood*. Simkin, Marshall, and Co., 1850.

Barrett, Thomas. *Advice on the Management of Children in Early Infancy*. Whittaker and Co., 1851.

Battiscombe, Georgina, and Marghanita Laski, *A Chaplet for Charlotte Yonge*. Cresset P, 1965.

Bawarshi, Anis S. "Between Genres: Uptake, Memory, and US Public Discourse on Israel-Palestine." Reiff and Bawarshi, pp. 43–60.

———. *Genre and the Invention of the Writer*. Utah State UP, 2003.

Bawarshi, Anis S., and Mary Jo Reiff. *Genre: An Introduction to History, Theory, Research, and Pedagogy*. Parlor P, 2010.

Bazerman, Charles. *The Languages of Edison's Light*. MIT P, 1999.

———. *Shaping Written Knowledge: The Genre and Activity of the Experimental Article in Science*. U of Wisconsin P, 1988.

———. "Speech Acts, Genres, and Activity Systems: How Texts Organize Activity and People." *What Writing Does and How It Does It*, Lawrence Erlbaum, 2004, pp. 309–339.

Bebbington, D. W. *Evangelicalism in Modern Britain: A History from the 1730s to the 1980s*. Unwin Hyman, 1989.

Beeton, Isabella. *The Book of Household Management*. S. O. Beeton, 1861.

Benham, William, editor. *Catharine and Craufurd Tait, Wife and Son of Archibald Campbell, Archbishop of Canterbury: A Memoir*. 1879. Macmillan, 1890.

Bentham, Jeremy. *The Panopticon Writings*. Edited by Miran Božovič, Verso, 2011.

Berkenkotter, Carol, and Thomas N. Huckin. "Rethinking Genre from a Sociocognitive Perspective." *Written Communication*, vol. 10, no. 4, 1993, pp. 475–509.

Berlant, Lauren, and Kathleen Stewart. *The Hundreds*. Duke UP, 2019.

Berridge, Virginia. *Opium and the People: Opiate Use and Drug Control Policy in Nineteenth and Early Twentieth Century England*. Free Association Books, 1999.

Berry, Laura C. *The Child, the State, and the Victorian Novel*. U of Virginia P, 1999.

Bettany, George Thomas. "Andrew Combe." *Dictionary of National Biography, 1885–1900*, vol. 11, 1887, edited by Leslie Stephen, Smith, Elder, and Co., pp. 425–426.

Bhattacharya, Nandini. "Maternal Plots, Colonialist Fictions: Colonial Pedagogy in Mary Martha Sherwood's Children's Stories." *Nineteenth-Century Contexts*, vol. 23, 2001, pp. 381–415.

Billings, Malcolm. *The Story of Queen's College: 150 Years and a New Century,* James and James, 2000.

Bitzer, Lloyd F. "The Rhetorical Situation." *Rhetoric: Concepts, Definitions, Boundaries,* edited by William A. Covino and David A. Joliffe, Allyn & Bacon, 1995, pp. 300–310.

Bobotis, Andrea. "Rival Maternities: Maud Gonne, Queen Victoria, and the Reign of the Political Mother." *Victorian Studies,* vol. 49, no. 1, 2006, pp. 63–83.

Boone, Sarah. "Zombie Handbooks, Preserved Specimens: Victorian Sexual Advice and British Cultures of Reprinting." NAVSA/AVSA NYU/Purdue, NYU Florence, Italy, 17–20 May 2017.

Bowers, Toni. *The Politics of Motherhood: British Writing and Culture, 1680–1790.* Cambridge UP, 1996.

Branca, Patricia. *Silent Sisterhood: Middle-Class Women in the Victorian Home.* Croom Helm, 1975.

Brandt, Deborah. *The Rise of Writing: Redefining Mass Literacy.* Cambridge UP, 2015.

Brontë, Anne. *Agnes Grey.* Edited with an introduction and notes by Angeline Goreau, Penguin Books, 1988. (1847)

Brontë, Charlotte. *Jane Eyre.* Edited by Richard Nemesvari, Broadview P, 1999. (1847)

Brown, Michael. *Performing Medicine: Medical Culture and Identity in Provincial England, c. 1760–1850.* Palgrave Macmillan, 2011.

Buchan, William. *Domestic Medicine: Or, A Treatise on the Prevention and Cure of Diseases.* 15th edition. Strahan, Cadell, and Davies, 1797.

Buchanan, Linda. *Rhetorics of Motherhood.* Southern Illinois UP, 2013.

Bull, Thomas. *Hints to Mothers, for the Management of Health During the Period of Pregnancy and in the Lying-In Room.* Longman, Orme, Brown, Green, and Longman, 1837.

———. *Maternal Management of Children, in Health and Disease.* Longman, Orme, Brown, Green, and Longman, 1840.

Bureaud-Riofrey, Madame. *Private Education; or, Observations on Governesses.* Longman, Rees, Orme, Brown, Green, and Longman, 1836.

Burke, Kenneth. *A Rhetoric of Motives.* Prentice-Hall, 1950.

———. "Rhetoric—Old and New." *The Journal of General Education,* vol. 5, no. 3, 1951, pp. 202–209.

Cadogan, William. *An Essay Upon Nursing and the Management of Children, from Their Birth to Three Years of Age.* 1748. *Three Treatises on Child Rearing,* edited by Randolph Trumbach, Garland, 1985.

Cameron, D. A. *Plain Advice on the Care of the Teeth; with a Popular History of the Dentist's Art, and a Chapter to Mothers on the Management of Children During the Period of Teething.* Richard Griffin and Co., 1838.

Caquet, P. E. "Notions of Addiction at the Time of the First Opium War." *The Historical Journal,* vol. 58, no. 4, 2015, pp. 1009–1029.

Carpenter, William B. *Vegetable Physiology and Systematic Botany.* William S. Orr, 1849.

Champney, T. *Medical and Chirurgical Reform, proposed, from a review of the healing art throughout Europe, particularly Great Britain.* J. Johnson, J. Debrett, and Darton and Harvey, 1797.

Chaput, Catherine, et al., editors. *Entertaining Fear: Rhetoric and the Political Economy of Social Control.* Frontiers in Political Communication, vol. 18, Peter Lang, 2010.

Chase, Karen, and Michael H. Levenson. *The Spectacle of Intimacy: A Public Life for the Victorian Family.* Princeton UP, 2000.

Chaudhuri, Nupur. "Memsahibs and Motherhood in Nineteenth-Century Colonial India." *Victorian Studies*, vol. 31, no. 4, 1988, pp. 517–535.

———. "Memsahibs and Their Servants in Nineteenth-Century India." *Women's History Review*, vol. 3, no. 4, 1994, pp. 549–562.

Chavasse, Pye Henry. *Advice to Mothers on the Management of Their Offspring*. Longman and Co., 1839.

———. *The Young Wife's and Mother's Book. Advice to Mothers on the Management of Their Offspring. Advice to Young Wives on the Management of Themselves During the Periods of Pregnancy and Lactation*. Second edition. Longman and Co., 1842.

———. *Advice to a Mother on the Management of Her Offspring*. Fourth edition. Longman and Co., 1852.

Chen, Mia. "'And There Was No Helping It': Disability and Social Reproduction in Charlotte Yonge's *The Daisy Chain*." *Nineteenth-Century Gender Studies*, vol. 4, no. 2, 2008, http://www.ncgsjournal.com/issue42/chen.htm.

Chen, Song-Chuan. *Merchants of War and Peace: British Knowledge of China in the Making of the First Opium War*. Hong Kong UP, 2017.

Chepaitis, Elia Vallone. *The Opium of the Children: Domestic Opium and Infant Drugging in Early Victorian England*. PhD dissertation, U of Connecticut, 1985.

Clarke, Sir Arthur. *The Mother's Medical Assistant, Containing Instructions for the Prevention and Treatment of the Diseases of Infants and Children*. Henry Colburn and Co., 1820.

Cody, Lisa Forman. *Birthing the Nation: Sex, Science, and the Conception of Eighteenth-Century Britons*. Oxford UP, 2005.

Cohen, Monica F. *Professional Domesticity in the Victorian Novel: Women, Work, and Home*. Cambridge UP, 1998.

Coleridge, Christabel. *Charlotte Mary Yonge: Her Life and Letters*. Macmillan, 1903.

Colón, A. R., with P. A. Colón. *Nurturing Children: A History of Pediatrics*. Greenwood P, 1999.

Combe, Andrew. *A Treatise on the Physiological and Moral Management of Infancy*. Maclachlan, Stewart, and Co., 1840.

Combe, Andrew, and James Coxe. *A Treatise on the Physiological and Moral Management of Infancy*. Eighth edition, with an Appendix by James Coxe. Maclachlan and Stewart, 1854.

Conquest, J. T. *Letters to a Mother, on the Management of Herself and Her Children in Health and Disease*. Third edition. Longman and Co., 1850.

Corbett, Mary Jean. *Representing Femininity: Middle-Class Subjectivity in Victorian and Edwardian Women's Autobiographies*. Oxford UP, 1992.

Crell, A. F., and W. M. Wallace. *The Family Oracle of Health; Economy, Medicine, and Good Living; Adapted to All Ranks of Society, from the Palace to the Cottage*. Sixth edition. C. Smith, 1824.

Cullen, M. J. "The Making of the Civil Registration Act of 1836." *Journal of Ecclesiastical History*, vol. 25, no. 1, 1974, pp. 39–59.

Cunningham, Hugh. *The Invention of Childhood*. BBC Books, 2006.

Cutt, M. Nancy. *Mrs. Sherwood and Her Books for Children*. Oxford UP, 1974.

Daly, Suzanne. *The Empire Inside: Indian Commodities in Victorian Domestic Novels*. U of Michigan P, 2010.

Davenport, Romola, Jeremy Boulton, and Leonard Schwartz. "Urban Inoculation and the Decline of Smallpox Mortality in Eighteenth-Century Cities—A Reply to Razzell." *Economic History Review*, vol. 69, no. 1, 2016, pp. 188–214.

David, Deirdre. *Rule Britannia: Women, Empire, and Victorian Writing.* Cornell UP, 1995.

Davidoff, Leonore, and Catherine Hall. *Family Fortunes: Men and Women of the English Middle Class, 1780–1850.* U of Chicago P, 1991.

Davidoff, Leonore, et al. *The Family Story: Blood, Contract, and Intimacy, 1830–1960.* Women and Men in History, Longman, 1999.

Davies, Rebecca. *Written Maternal Authority and Eighteenth-Century Education in Britain: Educating by the Book.* Ashgate, 2014.

Davis, Angela. *Modern Motherhood: Woman and Family in England, 1945–2000.* Manchester UP, 2012.

"Deaths: Arranged in Chronological Order." *Gentleman's Magazine and Historical Review,* vol. 205, July 1858, pp. 89–95.

Demers, Patricia. "Mrs. Sherwood and Hesba Stretton: The Letter and the Spirit of Evangelical Writing of and for Children." *Romanticism and Children's Literature in Nineteenth-Century England,* edited by James Holt MacGavran, Jr., U of Georgia P, 1991, pp. 129–149.

Derks, Hans. *History of the Opium Problem: The Assault on the East, ca. 1600–1950.* Sinica Leidensia, vol. 105, 2012.

Derrida, Jacques. *Of Grammatology.* Translated by Gayatri Chakravorty Spivak, Johns Hopkins UP, 1976.

Dever, Carolyn. *Death and the Mother from Dickens to Freud: Victorian Fiction and the Anxiety of Origins.* Cambridge UP, 1998.

Devitt, Amy J. *Writing Genres.* Southern Illinois UP, 2004.

———. "Generalizing About Genre." *College Composition and Communication,* vol. 44, no. 4, Dec. 1993, pp. 573–586.

Dewees, William. *A Treatise on the Physical and Medical Treatment of Children.* Carey, Lea, and Carey, 1825.

Dickens, Charles. *Dombey and Son.* Edited by Andrew Sanders. Penguin Books, 2002. (1846–1848)

———. *The Old Curiosity Shop.* Edited by Norman Page, Penguin Books, 2000. (1840–1841)

———. *The British Academy/The Pilgrim Edition of the Letters of Charles Dickens, Vol. 2: 1840–1841.* Edited by Madeline House and Graham Storey, Oxford Scholarly Editions Online, 2016, doi: 10.1093/actrade/9780198114789.book.1.

Digby, Anne. *Making a Medical Living: Doctors and Patients in the English Market for Medicine, 1720–1911.* Cambridge UP, 1994.

———. *The Evolution of General Practice, 1850–1948.* Oxford UP, 1999.

Dimock, Wai Chee. "Introduction: Genres as Fields of Knowledge." *PMLA,* vol. 122, no. 5, 2007, special issue "Remapping Genre" edited by Dimock and Bruce Robbins, pp. 1377–1388.

———. "Genre as World System: Epic and Novel on Four Continents." *Narrative,* vol. 14, no. 1, 2006, pp. 85–101.

Disraeli, Benjamin. *Sybil: Or, The Two Nations.* Edited by Thom Braun. Penguin Books, 1985. (1845)

A Domestic Guide to Mothers in India, Containing Particular Instructions on the Management of Themselves and Their Children. By a Medical Practitioner of Several Years Experience in India. American Mission P, 1836.

Donnison, Jean. *Midwives and Medical Men: A History of the Struggle for the Control of Childbirth.* Historical Publications, 1988.

Donovan, Stephen, and Matthew Rubery. *Secret Commissions: An Anthology of Victorian Investigative Journalism.* Broadview P, 2012.

Dormandy, Thomas. *Opium: Reality's Dark Dream.* Yale UP, 2012.

Dow, Dawn Marie. *Mothering While Black: Boundaries and Burdens of Middle-Class Parenthood.* U of California P, 2019.

Dryer, Dylan B. "Disambiguating Uptake: Toward a Tactical Research Agenda on Citizens' Writing." Reiff and Bawarshi, pp. 60–80.

Dubrow, Heather. *Genre.* Methuen, 1982.

Eastlake, Elizabeth, Lady. "*Vanity Fair*—and *Jane Eyre.*" *London Quarterly Review,* American ed., Dec. 1848, pp. 82–99.

Edelman, Lee. *No Future: Queer Theory and the Death Drive.* Duke UP, 2004.

"Education. Art. 15 Advice to Young Mothers, on the Physical Education of Children. By a Grandmother." *Monthly Review,* vol. 105, Sept. 1824, pp. 99–102.

Ellis, Sarah Stickney. *The Mothers of England: Their Influence and Responsibility.* Fisher, Son & Co., 1843

Emmons, Kimberley. *Black Dogs and Blue Words: Depression and Gender in the Age of Self-Care.* Rutgers UP, 2010.

———. "Uptake and the Biomedical Subject." *Genre in a Changing World,* edited by Charles Bazerman, Adair Bonini, and Debora Figueiredo, Parlor P, 2009, pp. 134–157.

Enoch, Jessica. *Domestic Occupations: Spatial Rhetorics and Women's Work.* Studies in Rhetorics and Feminisms. Southern Illinois UP, 2019.

Fairclough, Peter. "A Note on the Text." *Dombey and Son,* by Charles Dickens, with an introduction by Raymond Williams, Penguin Books 1970, pp. 35–37.

Ferguson, Moira. "Fictional Constructions of Liberated Africans: Mary Butt Sherwood." *Romanticism and Colonialism: Writing and Empire, 1780–1830,* edited by Tim Fulford and Peter J. Kitson, Cambridge UP, 1998, pp. 148–163.

Fildes, Valerie A. *Breasts, Bottles, and Babies: A History of Infant Feeding.* Edinburgh UP, 1986.

———. *Wet Nursing: A History from Antiquity to the Present.* Basil Blackwell, 1988.

Fitzpatrick, Kathleen. *Anxiety of Obsolescence: The American Novel in the Age of Television.* Vanderbilt UP, 2006.

Fivush, Robyn. "Remembering and Reminiscing: How Individual Lives Are Constructed in Family Narratives." *Memory Studies,* vol. 1, 2008, pp. 45–54.

Foucault, Michel. *Discipline and Punish: The Birth of the Prison.* Translated by Alan Sheridan, Vintage, 1995.

Foxcroft, Louise. *The Making of Addiction: The "Use and Abuse" of Opium in Nineteenth-Century Britain.* Ashgate, 2007.

Francus, Marilyn. *Monstrous Motherhood: Eighteenth-Century Culture and the Ideology of Domesticity.* Johns Hopkins UP, 2013.

Frawley, Maria H. *Agnes Grey.* Twayne, 1996.

Freadman, Anne. "Anyone for Tennis?" *Genre and the New Rhetoric,* edited by Aviva Freedman and Peter Medway, Taylor and Francis, 1994, pp. 43–66.

———. "Uptake." *The Rhetoric and Ideology of Genre: Strategies for Stability and Change,* edited by Richard Coe, Lorelei Lingard, and Tatiana Teslenko, Hampton P, 2002, pp. 39–53.

Freedgood, Elaine. *The Ideas in Things: Fugitive Meaning in the Victorian Novel.* U of Chicago P, 2006.

Freud, Sigmund. *Inhibitions, Symptoms, and Anxiety*. The Standard Edition. Translated by Alix Strachey, revised and edited by James Strachey, with a biographical introduction by Peter Gay, W. W. Norton & Co., 1989. (1926).

———. *The Problem of Anxiety*. Translated by Henry Aldren Bunker, Martino Publishing, 2013. (1936).

Fromer, Julie. *A Necessary Luxury: Tea in Victorian England*. Ohio UP, 2008.

Frost, Ginger. *Victorian Childhoods*. Praeger, 2009.

Frow, John. *Genre*. Routledge, 2006.

———. "'Reproducibles, Rubrics, and Everything You Need': Genre Theory Today." *PMLA*, vol. 122, no. 5, pp. 1626–1634.

Galley, Chris, and Nicola Shelton. "Bridging the Gap: Determining Long-Term Changes in Infant Mortality in Pre-Registration England and Wales." *Population Studies*, vol. 55, no. 1, Mar. 2001, pp. 65–77.

Gardner, Marilyn Sheridan. "'The Good of My Life': Agnes Grey at Wellwood House." *New Approaches to the Literary Art of the Brontës*, edited by Julie Nash and Barbara A. Suess, Ashgate, 2001, pp. 45–62.

Garman, Emma. "A Liberated Woman: The Story of Margaret King." Longreads.com, 24 May 2016. https://longreads.com/2016/05/24/a-liberated-woman-the-story-of-margaret-king/.

Garrett, Peter K. *The Victorian Multiplot Novel: Studies in Dialogic Form*. Yale UP, 1980.

Gaskell, Elizabeth Cleghorn. *"My Diary": The Early Years of My Daughter Marianne*. Edited by Clement Shorter, Clement Shorter (privately printed), 1923.

———. *Mary Barton: A Tale of Manchester Life*. Edited by Stephen Gill, Penguin, 1985. (1848).

Gelber, Harry G. *Opium, Soldiers, and Evangelicals: England's 1840–42 War with China and Its Aftermath*. Palgrave Macmillan, 2004.

Giltrow, Janet, and Dieter Stein, editors. *Genres in the Internet: Innovation, Evolution, and Genre Theory*. John Benjamins, 2009.

Ginsberg, Michal Peled. "Sentimentality and Survival: The Double Narrative of *The Old Curiosity Shop*." *Dickens Quarterly*, vol. 27, no. 2, 2010, pp. 85–101.

Ginswick, Jules, editor. *Labour and the Poor in England and Wales, 1849–1851: The Letters to the Morning Chronicle from the Correspondents in the Manufacturing and Mining Districts, the Towns of Liverpool and Birmingham, and the Rural Districts. Volume I: Lancashire, Cheshire, Yorkshire*. Routledge, 1983.

Goldhill, Simon. "A Mother's Joy at Her Child's Death: Conversion, Cognitive Dissonance, and Grief." *Victorian Studies*, vol. 49, no. 4, 2017, pp. 636–657.

Goodeve, H. H. *Hints for the General Management of Children in India, in the Absence of Professional Advice*. Second edition. William Rushton, 1844.

Goodlad, Lauren M. E. "Seriality." *Victorian Literature and Culture*, vol. 46, no. 3/4, 2018, pp. 869–872.

Gordon, Charlotte. *Romantic Outlaws: The Extraordinary Lives of Mary Wollstonecraft and Mary Shelley*. Random House, 2016.

Gorham, Deborah. *The Victorian Girl and the Feminine Ideal*. 1982. Routledge Literary Editions: Women's History, Routledge, 2013.

Greenfield, Susan C., and Carol Barash, editors. *Inventing Maternity: Politics, Science, and Literature, 1650–1865*. UP of Kentucky, 1999.

Griffin, Emma. "The Emotions of Motherhood: Love, Culture, and Poverty in Victorian Britain." *The American Historical Review*, vol. 123, no. 1, Feb. 2018, Oxford Academic. doi: org/10.1093/ahr/123.1.60.

Grigg, John. *Advice to the Female Sex in General, Particular Those in a State of Pregnancy and Lying-In.* S. Hazard, 1789.

Gruner, Elisabeth Rose. "Plotting the Mother: Caroline Norton, Helen Huntingdon, and Isabel Vane." *Tulsa Studies in Women's Literature*, vol. 16, no. 2, 1997, pp. 303–325.

Hale, Sarah. *The New Household Receipt-Book: Containing Maxims, Directions, and Specifics.* T. Nelson and Sons, 1854.

Hallemeier, Katherine. "Anne Brontë's Shameful *Agnes Grey.*" *Victorian Literature and Culture*, vol. 41, no. 2, 2018, pp. 251–260.

Hallstein, D. Lynn O'Brien, editor. "Mothering Rhetorics." Special issue of *Women's Studies in Communication*, vol. 40, no. 1, 2017.

Hansard: The Official Report of All Parliamentary Debates. UK Parliament, http://hansard.parliament.uk.

Hansen, Elizabeth DeG. R. "'Overlaying in 19th-Century England: Infant Mortality or Infanticide?" *Human Ecology*, vol. 7, no. 4, Dec. 1979, pp. 333–352.

Hardyment, Christina. *Dream Babies: Child Care from Locke to Spock.* Jonathan Cape, 1983.

Harvey Darton, F. J., editor. *The Life and Times of Mrs. Sherwood (1775–1851) from the Diaries of Captain and Mrs. Sherwood.* Cambridge UP, 2011. (1910)

Hays, Sharon. *The Cultural Contradictions of Motherhood.* Yale UP, 1996.

Hayter, Alethea. *Opium and the Romantic Imagination: Addiction and Creativity in De Quincey, Coleridge, Baudelaire, and Others.* Crucible, 1988. (1971).

Hopkins, Joseph. *The Accoucheur's Vade Mecum.* Seventh edition. Highley and Sons, 1820.

Hughes, Kathryn. *The Victorian Governess.* Hambledon P, 1993.

Hughes, Linda K., and Michael Lund. *The Victorian Serial.* UP of Virginia, 1991.

Hughes, William Lee. "Impersonal Grief: Charles Dickens and Serial Forms of Affect." *differences: A Journal of Feminist Cultural Studies*, vol. 29, no. 3, 2018, pp. 86–106.

Hulbert, Ann. *Raising America: Experts, Parents, and a Century of Advice About Children.* Vintage, 2004.

Jalland, Patricia. *Death in the Victorian Family.* Oxford UP, 1996.

Jameson, Anna Brownell. "The Relative Social Position of Mothers and Governesses." *Memoirs and Essays Illustrative of Art, Literature, and Social Morals*, R. Bentley, 1846.

Jenner, Henry. *A Guide to Mothers and Nurses, in the Treatment and Management of Infants and Young Children.* Baldwin, Craddock, and Joy, 1826.

Johnson, Edgar. *Charles Dickens: His Tragedy and Triumph.* Viking, 1977.

Johnson, Samuel. *A Dictionary of the English Language: In Which the Words Are Deduced from Their Originals, Explained in Their Different Meanings, and Authorised by the Names of the Writers in Whose Works They Are Found.* Tho. Brown, R. Ross, and J. Symington, 1797.

Kaplan, Amy. "Manifest Domesticity." *American Literature*, vol. 70, no. 3, Sept. 1998, pp. 581–606.

Kaye, Elaine. *A History of Queen's College, 1848–1972.* Chatto and Windus, 1972.

Kennedy, James. *Instructions to Mothers and Nurses on the Management of Children in Health and Disease.* Richard Griffin and Co., 1825.

Kierkegaard, Søren. *The Concept of Anxiety: A Simple Psychologically Oriented Deliberation in View of the Dogmatic Problem of Hereditary Sin.* 1844. Translated by Alastair Hannay, Liveright, a Division of W. W. Norton and Co., 2015.

Kittredge, Katharine. "A Long-Forgotten Sorrow: The Mourning Journal of Melesina Trench." *Eighteenth-Century Fiction,* vol. 21, no. 1, Fall 2008, pp. 153–177.

Klass, Perri. Private Communication, 19 July 2019.

Klimaszewski, Melisa. "Examining the Wet Nurse: Breasts, Power, and Penetration in Victorian England." *Women's Studies,* vol. 35, 2006, pp. 323–346.

Koerber, Amy. *Breast or Bottle? Contemporary Controversies in Infant Feeding Policy and Practice.* U of South Carolina P, 2013.

Kollar, Rene. "Tait, Catharine (1819–1878)." *Oxford Dictionary of National Biography.* 23 September 2004, doi: 10.1093/ref:odnb/50739.

Kramer, Adam D. I., Jamie E. Guillory, and Jeffrey T. Hancock. "Experimental Evidence of Massive-Scale Emotional Contagion Through Social Networks," *PNAS,* vol. 111, no. 24, 17 June 2014, pp. 8788–8790.

Kurtyka, Faith. "Settling in to Genre: The Social Action of Emotion in Shaping Genres." *Composition Forum,* vol. 31, Spring 2015, http://compositionforum.com/issue/31/settling-in.php.

Laditan, Bunmi. Publication Announcement for *Confessions of a Domestic Failure. Facebook,* 1 May 2017, facebook.com/BunmiKLaditan/posts/1899244270322560:0.

Langland, Elizabeth. *Nobody's Angels: Middle-Class Women and Domestic Ideology in Victorian Culture.* Cornell UP, 1995.

Law, Cheryl. "Bakewell, Mrs. J. (FL. 1845–1864)." *C19: The Nineteenth Century Index,* ProQuest LLC., 2005–2018. http://gateway.proquest.com/openurl?url_ver=Z39.88-2004&res_dat=xri:c19index-us&rft_dat=xri:c19index:DNCJ:76.

Lay, Mary M. *The Rhetoric of Midwifery: Gender, Knowledge, and Power.* Rutgers UP, 2000.

Leclerq, Émile-Carolus. *The Physician's Verdict.* 1857. Wellcome Library no. 45025i, http://wellcomelibrary.org/item/b1202837x#?c=0&m=0&s=0&cv=0.

Lecourt, Sebastian. "'Idylls of the Buddh': Buddhist Modernism and Victorian Poetics in Colonial Ceylon." *PMLA,* vol. 131, no. 3, 2016, pp. 668–685.

LeDoux, Joseph. *Anxious: Using the Brain to Understand and Treat Fear and Anxiety.* Penguin, 2015.

Lerner, Laurence. *Angels and Absences: Child Deaths in the Nineteenth Century.* Vanderbilt UP, 1997.

Levine, Caroline. *Forms: Whole, Rhythm, Hierarchy, Network.* Princeton UP, 2015.

Lomax, Elizabeth. "The Uses and Abuses of Opiates in Nineteenth-Century England." *Bulletin of the History of Medicine,* vol. 42, no. 2, 1973, pp. 167–176.

Loudon, Irvine. *Medical Care and the General Practitioner, 1750–1850.* Clarendon P, 1986.

Lovell, Julie. *The Opium War: Drugs, Dreams, and the Making of China.* Overlook P, 2014.

MacPike, Loralee. "The Old Cupiosity Shape: Changing Views of Little Nell, Part I." *Dickens Studies Newsletter,* vol. 12, no. 2, 1981, pp. 33–38.

———. "The Old Cupiosity Shape: Changing Views of Little Nell, Part II." *Dickens Studies Newsletter,* vol. 12, no. 3, 1981, pp. 70–76.

Malhotra, Ashok. "The English 'Self' Under Siege: A Comparison of a Memsahib's Private Journals and Her Novel *The History of George Desmond.*" *Nineteenth-Century Literature,* vol. 72, no. 1, 2017, pp. 1–34.

Marland, Hilary. *Dangerous Motherhood: Insanity and Childbirth in Victorian Britain.* Palgrave Macmillan, 2004.

Mascarenhas, Kiran. "Little Henry's Burdens: Colonization, Civilization, Christianity, and the Child." *Victorian Literature and Culture,* vol. 42, no. 3, 2014, pp. 425–438.

Massumi, Brian. "The Future Birth of the Affective Fact: The Political Ontology of Threat." *The Affect Theory Reader,* edited by Gregory Seigworth and Melissa Gregg, Duke UP, 2010, pp. 52–70.

Mathison, Ymitri. "Converting the Idolatrous Heathens: British Missionaries in the South Sea Islands and India in Children's Fiction." *Mother Tongue Theologies: Poets, Novelists, Non-Western Christianity,* edited by Darren Middleton, Pickwick, 2009, pp. 140–156.

Matus, Jill L. *Unstable Bodies: Victorian Representations of Sexuality and Maternity.* Manchester UP, 1995.

[Maurice, Mary.] *Governess Life: Its Trials, Duties, and Encouragements.* John W. Parker, 1849.

——. *Mothers and Governesses.* John W. Parker, 1847.

McBride, Theresa. "'As the Twig Is Bent': The Victorian Nanny." *The Victorian Family: Structure and Stresses,* Croom Helm, 1978, pp. 44–58.

McCuskey, Brian. "The Kitchen Police: Servant Surveillance and Middle-Class Transgression." *Victorian Literature and Culture,* vol. 28, no. 2, 2000, pp. 359–375.

——. "Not at Home: Servants, Scholars, and the Uncanny." *PMLA,* vol. 121, no. 2, 2006, pp. 421–436.

McDonagh, Josephine. *Child Murder and British Culture, 1720–1900.* Cambridge UP, 2003.

McKeon, Michael. *The Secret History of Domesticity: Public, Private, and the Division of Knowledge.* John Hopkins UP, 2005.

McKnight, Natalie. *Suffering Mothers in Mid-Victorian Novels.* St. Martin's P, 1997.

Mechling, Jay. "Advice to Historians on Advice to Mothers." *Journal of Social History,* vol. 9, no. 1, 1975, pp. 44–63.

Menke, Richard. *Telegraphic Realism: Victorian Fiction and Other Information Systems.* Stanford UP, 2007.

Middup, Linda Claridge. "'Dear! How Tiresome It Must Be to Be So Religious . . . and Where's the Use of It?' Religious Identity and the Empowerment of Femininity in Mary Martha Sherwood's *The Fairchild Family* (1818) and *The Rose: A Fairy Tale* (1821)." *Nineteenth-Century Gender Studies,* vol. 9, no. 3, 2013, http://www.ncgsjournal.com/issue93/middup.htm.

Miller, Carolyn R. "Genre as Social Action." *Quarterly Journal of Speech,* vol. 70, 1984, pp. 151–167.

Miller, Susan. *Trust in Texts: A Different History of Rhetoric.* Southern Illinois UP, 2008.

Milligan, Barry. *Pleasures and Pains: Opium and the Orient in Nineteenth-Century British Culture.* UP of Virginia, 1995.

[Moore, Margaret King.] *Advice to Young Mothers on the Physical Education of Children. By a Grandmother.* Longman, Hurst, Rees, Orme, and Brown, 1823.

Morrison, Kevin A. "'Dr. Locock and his Quack': Professionalizing Medicine, Textualizing Identity in the 1840s." Penner and Sparks, pp. 9–27.

Munich, Adrienne. *Queen Victoria's Secrets.* Columbia UP, 1996.

Murphy, Lamar Riley. *Enter the Physician: The Transformation of Domestic Medicine, 1760–1860.* U of Alabama P, 1991.

Necker de Saussure, Albertine Adrienne. *L'Éducation Progressive, ou Étude du Cours de la Vie,* vol. 1. A. Sautelet & Co., 1828.

——. *Progressive Education; or, Considerations on the Course of Life,* vol. 1. Translated from the French, Longman, Orme, Brown, Green, and Longmans, 1839.

Nelson, Claudia. *Family Ties in Victorian England*. Praeger, 2007.

Nelson, Ingrid, and Shannon Gayk. "Introduction: Genre as Form-of-Life." *Exemplaria: Medieval, Early Modern, Theory*, vol. 27, no. 1–2, 2015, pp. 3–17.

The New Family Receipt Book, Containing One Thousand Truly Valuable Receipts in Various Branches of Domestic Economy. John Murray, 1824.

N. [Newman, William.] "The Poor Child's Nurse." *Punch; or a London Charivari*, vol. 17, no. 35, 1849, p. 193.

Ngai, Sianne. *Ugly Feelings*. Harvard UP, 2005.

Nicholls, James. *The Politics of Alcohol: A History of the Drink Question in England*. Manchester UP, 2009.

Nichols, Jr., Buford L., et al., editors. *History of Pediatrics, 1850–1950*. Raven P, 1991.

Nowacek, Rebecca S. *Agents of Integration: Understanding Transfer as a Rhetorical Act*. Southern Illinois UP, 2011.

Nussbaum, Felicity. *Torrid Zones: Maternity, Sexuality, and Empire in Eighteenth-Century English Narratives*. Johns Hopkins UP, 1995.

"Obituary: Pye Henry Chavasse, F. R. C. S., Birmingham." *British Medical Journal*, vol. 2, no. 2, 22 Sept. 1879, p. 521.

Oliphant, Margaret. "Charles Dickens." *Blackwood's Edinburgh Magazine*, vol. 77, no. 474, Apr. 1855, pp. 451–466.

Ongstad, Sigmund. "The Definition of Genre and the Didactics of Genre." Rethinking Genre Colloquium. Ottawa, Ont. 3–5 April 1992.

"Our Library Table." *The Athenaeum*, vol. 664, 18 July 1840, pp. 570–571.

Owens, Kim Hensley. *Writing Childbirth: Women's Rhetorical Agency in Labor and Online*. Southern Illinois UP, 2015.

Parker, Andrew. *The Theorist's Mother*. Duke UP, 2012.

Penner, Louise, and Tabitha Sparks, editors. *Victorian Medicine and Popular Culture*. Pickering and Chatto, 2015.

Perry, Ruth. "Colonizing the Breast: Sexuality and Maternity in Eighteenth-Century England." *Journal of the History of Sexuality*, vol. 2, no. 2, 1991, pp. 204–234.

———. *Novel Relations: The Transformation of Kinship in English Literature and Culture, 1748–1818*. Cambridge UP, 2004.

Peterson, M. Jeanne. *The Medical Profession in Mid-Victorian London*. U of California P, 1978.

———. "The Victorian Governess: Status Incongruence in Family and Society." *Victorian Studies*, vol. 14, no. 1, Sept. 1970, pp. 7–26.

The Philosophy of Medicine: or, Medical Extracts on the Nature of Health and Disease. By *A Friend to Improvements*, C. Whittingham, 1799.

"Physical Exercise of Children." *Chambers's Edinburgh Journal*, vol. 7, no. 297, 7 Oct. 1837, pp. 294–295.

Plain Observations on the Management of Children During the First Month, Addressed Particularly to Mothers. Underwood, 1828.

Platt, Stephen R. *Imperial Twilight: The Opium War and the End of China's Last Golden Age*. Knopf, 2018.

Pollock, Linda A. *Forgotten Children: Parent-Child Relations from 1500 to 1900*. Cambridge UP, 1983.

Poovey, Mary. *Making a Social Body: British Cultural Formation, 1830–1864.* U of Chicago P, 1995.

———. *Uneven Developments: The Ideological Work of Gender in Mid-Victorian England.* U of Chicago P, 1988.

Porter, Dorothy, and Roy Porter. *The Patient's Progress: Doctors and Doctoring in Eighteenth-Century England.* Stanford UP, 1989.

Porter, Roy. "Reforming the Patient in an Age of Reform: Thomas Beddoes and Medical Practice." *British Medicine in an Age of Reform,* edited by Roger Kenneth French and Andrew Wear, Routledge, 1991, pp. 9–45.

Price, Leah. *How to Do Things with Books in Victorian Britain.* Princeton UP, 2012.

Propen, Amy, and Mary Lay Schuster. "Understanding Genre Through the Lens of Advocacy: The Rhetorical Work of the Victim Impact Statement." *Written Communication,* vol. 27, no. 1, 2010, pp. 3–35.

Quaranto, Nick. "How to Be a Parent in 2017." *Twitter,* 22 July 2017, 2:34 p.m., twitter.com/qrush/status/889090262630322176.

[Reach, Angus Bethune.] "Labour and the Poor: The Manufacturing Districts. Manchester. Letter V." *The Morning Chronicle* 1 Nov. 1849, p. 5. Gale Digital Collections. Gale Document Number BC3207338699.

Reece, Richard. *The Domestic Medical Guide; in Two Parts.* Longman, Hurst, Rees, and Orme, 1805.

Regaignon, Dara Rossman. "Intimacy's Empire: Children, Servants, and Missionaries in Mary Martha Sherwood's 'Little Henry and his Bearer.'" *Children's Literature Association Quarterly,* vol. 26, no. 2, 2001, pp. 84–95.

———. "Infant Doping and Middle-Class Motherhood: Opium Warnings and Charlotte Yonge's *The Daisy Chain.*" Rosenman and Klaver, pp. 125–144.

———. "Instructive Sufficiency: Re-Reading the Governess Through *Agnes Grey.*" *Victorian Literature and Culture,* vol. 29, no. 1, 2001, pp. 85–108.

Reiff, Mary Jo. "Geographies of Public Genres: Navigating Rhetorical and Material Relations of the Public Petition." Reiff and Bawarshi, pp. 100–117.

Reiff, Mary Jo, and Anis S. Bawarshi, editors. *Genre and the Performance of Publics.* Utah State UP, 2016.

Review of *Advice to a Mother on the Management of Her Offspring* by Pye Henry Chavasse. *Dublin Quarterly Journal of Science,* vol. 29, 1860, pp. 473–475.

Review of *Advice to Mothers on the Management of Their Offspring* and *Advice to Wives on the Management of Themselves During the Periods of Pregnancy, Labour, and Suckling* by Pye Henry Chavasse. *Provincial Medical and Surgical Journal,* vol. 8, no. 2, 1844, pp. 24–25.

Review of *Advice to Young Mothers on the Physical Education of Children. The Lady's Monthly Museum,* vol. 17, Mar. 1823, pp. 161–162.

Review of *Hints to Mothers, for the Management of Health, during the period of Pregnancy and in the Lying-in Room; with an Exposure of Popular Errors in connexion with those Subjects,* by Thomas Bull. *British and Foreign Medical Review,* vol. 5, 1838, p. 215.

Review of *Hints to Mothers, for the Management of Health, during the period of Pregnancy and in the Lying-in Room; with an Exposure of Popular Errors in connexion with those Subjects,* by Thomas Bull. *The Monthly Review,* vol. 1, no. 1, 1838, pp. 142–143.

Review of *The Mother's Practical Guide in the Early Training of Her Children,* by Mrs. Bakewell, Second Edition. *The Metropolitan Magazine,* vol. 41, no. 163, Nov. 1844, pp. 407–408.

Reynolds, Melanie. *Infant Mortality and Working-Class Child Care, 1850–1899*. Palgrave Macmillan, 2016.

Richards, John F. "The Opium Industry in British India." *The Indian Economic and Social History Review*, vol. 39, nos. 2 & 3, 2002, pp. 149–180.

Robbins, Bruce. *The Servant's Hand: English Fiction from Below*. Columbia UP, 1986.

Roberton, John. *Observations on the Mortality and Physical Management of Children*. Longman, Rees, Orme, Brown, and Green, 1827.

Roberts, Ann. "Mothers and Babies: The Wetnurse and Her Employer in Mid-Nineteenth-Century Britain." *Women's Studies*, vol. 3, no. 3, 1976, pp. 279–293.

Roberts, M. J. D. "The Politics of Professionalization: MPs, Medical Men, and the 1858 Medical Act." *Medical History*, vol. 53, no. 1, 2009, pp. 37–56.

Rosenberg, Charles E. "Medical Text and Social Context: Explaining Buchan's *Domestic Medicine*." *Explaining Epidemics*, Cambridge UP, 2010, pp. 32–56.

Rosenman, Ellen Bayuk, and Claudia C. Klaver. *Other Mothers: Beyond the Maternal Ideal*. Ohio State UP, 2008.

Royde Smith, Naomi. *The State of Mind of Mrs. Sherwood*. Macmillan, 1946.

Ruddick, Sara. *Maternal Thinking: Toward a Politics of Peace*. Beacon P, 1989.

[Rundell, M. E.] *The New Family Receipt Book, Containing One Thousand Truly Valuable Receipts in Various Branches of Domestic Economy*. John Murray, 1824.

Russell, David. "Rethinking Genre in School and Society: An Activity Theory Analysis." *Written Communication*, vol. 14, no. 4, 1997, pp. 504–554.

Said, Edward. *Culture and Imperialism*. Vintage, 1994.

Saint-Amour, Paul K. *Tense Future: Modernism, Total War, Encyclopedic Form*. Oxford UP, 2015.

Salecl, Renata. *On Anxiety*. Routledge, 2004.

Sandbach-Dahström, Catherine. *Be Good, Sweet Maid: Charlotte Yonge's Domestic Fiction: A Study in Dogmatic Purpose and Fictional Form*. PhD dissertation, U of Stockholm, 1984.

Sanders, Valerie. "'All-Sufficient to One Another?' Charlotte Yonge and the Family Chronicle." *Popular Victorian Women Writers*, edited by Kay Boardman and Shirley Jones, Manchester UP, 2004, pp. 90–111.

———. "Life Writing." *The History of British Women's Writing, 1830–1880*, edited by Lucy Hartley, Palgrave Macmillan, SpringerLink, 2018, pp. 212–228, doi: 10.1057/978-1-137-58465-6.

Sattaur, Jennifer. "Thinking Objectively: An Overview of 'Thing Theory' in Victorian Studies." *Victorian Literature and Culture*, vol. 40, 2012, pp. 347–357.

Schaffer, Talia. "The Mysterious Magnum Bonum: Fighting to Read Charlotte Yonge." *Nineteenth-Century Literature*, vol. 55, no. 2, 2000, pp. 244–275.

———. *Novel Craft: Victorian Domestic Handicraft and Nineteenth-Century Fiction*. Oxford UP, 2011.

———. *Romance's Rival: Familiar Marriage in Victorian Fiction*. Oxford UP, 2016.

Schaub, Melissa. "'Worthy Ambition': Religion and Domesticity in *The Daisy Chain*." *Studies in the Novel*, vol. 39, no. 1, 2007, pp. 65–83.

Schivelbusch, Wolfgang. *The Railway Journey: The Industrialization of Time and Space in the Nineteenth Century*. U of California P, 1986.

Seigel, Marika. *The Rhetoric of Pregnancy*. U of Chicago P, 2014.

Sheldon, Rebekah. *The Child to Come: Life After the Human Catastrophe*. U of Minnesota P, 2016.

Sherwood, Mary Martha. Diary of Mrs. Sherwood, 1804–1808. Sherwood Family Papers (1437), box 2, folio 1. UCLA Special Collections.

——. *The Life of Mrs. Sherwood, Chiefly Autobiographical, With Extracts From Mr. Sherwood's Journal During His Imprisonment in France and Residence in India.* Edited by Sophia Kelly, Darton and Co., 1854.

——. "Little Henry and his Bearer." *The Works of Mrs. Sherwood, Being the Only Uniform Edition Published in the United States,* vol. 3, Harper and Bros., 1836, pp. 6–35.

——. "Little Lucy and her *Dhaye.*" *The Works of Mrs. Sherwood, Being the Only Uniform Edition Published in the United States,* vol. 3, Harper and Bros., 1836, pp. 37–75.

Shuttleworth, Sally. "Demonic Mothers: Ideologies of Bourgeois Motherhood in the Mid-Victorian Era." *Rewriting the Victorians: Theory, History, and the Politics of Gender,* Routledge, 1992, pp. 31–51.

——. "Hanging, Crushing, and Shooting: Animals, Violence, and Child-Rearing in Brontë Fiction." *The Brontës and the Idea of the Human,* edited by Alexandra Lewis, Cambridge UP, pp. 27–47.

Small, Helen. "The Bounded Life: Adorno, Dickens, and Metaphysics." *Victorian Literature and Culture,* vol. 32, no. 2, Sept. 2004, pp. 547–563.

Smith, Hugh. *Letters to Married Women; on Nursing and the Management of Children.* G. Kearsly, 1767.

Sparks, Tabitha. *The Doctor in the Victorian Novel: Family Practices.* Ashgate, 2009.

Spinuzzi, Clay. *Tracing Genres Through Organizations: A Sociocultural Approach to Information Design.* MIT P, 2003.

Spinuzzi, Clay, and Mark Zachry. "Genre Ecologies: An Open-System Approach to Understanding and Constructing Documentation." *ACM Journal of Computer Documentation,* vol. 24, no. 3, 2000, pp. 169–191.

Spivak, Gayatri Chakravorty. "Translator's Preface." *Of Grammatology* by Jacques Derrida, pp. ix–lxxxvii.

Steedman, Carolyn. *Labours Lost: Domestic Service and the Making of Modern England.* Cambridge UP, 2009.

——. *Strange Dislocations: Childhood and the Idea of Human Interiority, 1780–1930.* Harvard UP, 1995.

Steel, Flora Annie, and Grace Gardiner. *The Complete Indian Housekeeper and Cook.* Edinburgh P, 1893.

Stern, Rebecca. *Home Economics: Domestic Fraud in Victorian England.* Ohio State UP, 2008.

Stevens, Emily E., Thelma E. Patrick, and Rita Pickler. "A History of Infant Feeding." *Journal of Perinatal Education,* vol. 18, no. 2, 2009, pp. 32–39.

Stewart, Kathleen. *Ordinary Affects.* Duke UP, 2007.

Stitt, Jocelyn Fenton, and Pegeen Reichert Powell, editors. *Mothers Who Deliver: Feminist Interventions in Public and Interpersonal Discourse.* State U of New York P, 2010.

Stoler, Ann Laura. *Race and the Education of Desire: Foucault's History of Sexuality and the Colonial Order of Things.* Duke UP, 1995.

Stone, Lawrence. *The Family, Sex, and Marriage in England, 1500–1800.* Harper & Row, 1977.

Strickland, Donna. *The Managerial Unconscious in the History of Composition Studies.* Southern Illinois UP, 2011.

Sturrock, June. *"Heaven and Home": Charlotte M. Yonge's Domestic Fiction and the Victorian Debate Over Women.* U of Victoria P, 1995.

"Surveillance, *n.*" *Oxford English Dictionary,* OEO Third Edition, Dec. 2011, oed.com, Oxford UP, 2019.

Tadmor, Naomi. *Family and Friends in Eighteenth-Century England: Household, Kinship, and Patronage.* Cambridge UP, 2001.

Tait, Catharine. "Mrs Tait's Narrative." Benham, *Catharine and Craufurd Tait,* pp. 254–393.

Tange, Andrea Kaston. *Architectural Identities: Domesticity, Literature, and the Victorian Middle Classes.* U of Toronto P, 2010.

Tardy, Christine M., Bruna Sommer-Farias, and Jeroen Gevers. "Teaching and Researching Genre Knowledge: Toward an Enhanced Theoretical Framework." *Written Communication,* 22 May 2020, doi: 10.1177/0741088320916554.

Thaden, Barbara Z. *The Maternal Voice in Victorian Fiction: Rewriting the Patriarchal Family.* Routledge, 1997.

Thorne-Murphy, Leslee. "The Charity Bazaar and Women's Professionalization in Charlotte Mary Yonge's *The Daisy Chain.*" *Studies in English Literature, 1500–1900,* vol. 47, no. 4, 2007, pp. 881–899.

Todd, Janet. *Rebel Daughters: Ireland in Conflict 1798.* Viking, 2003.

Todorov, Tzvetan. *The Fantastic: A Structural Approach to a Literary Genre.* Translated by Richard Howard, P of Case Western Reserve U, 1973. Hathi Trust Digital Library. https://hdl.handle.net/2027/mdp.39015046373455

———. *Genres in Discourse.* Translated by Catherine Porter, Cambridge UP, 1990.

Tomalin, Claire. *Charles Dickens: A Life.* Penguin, 2011.

Tomkins, Alannah. *Medical Misadventure in an Age of Professionalization, 1780–1890.* Manchester UP, 2018.

Tomkins, Silvan S. *Shame and Its Sisters: A Silvan Tomkins Reader.* Edited by Eve Kosofsky Sedgwick and Adam Frank, Duke UP, 1995.

Tompkins, Kyla Wazana. *Racial Indigestion: Eating Bodies in the 19th Century.* New York UP, 2012.

Tosh, John. *A Man's Place: Masculinity and the Middle-Class Home in Victorian England.* Yale UP, 1999.

Trocki, Carl A. *Opium, Empire, and the Global Political Economy: A Study of the Asian Opium Trade, 1750–1950.* Routledge, 1999.

Turner, Mark W. "Periodical Time in the Nineteenth Century." *Media History,* vol. 8, no. 2, 2002, pp. 183–196.

Underwood, Michael. *Dr. Underwood's Treatise on the Diseases of Children; with Directions for the Management of Infants.* Tenth edition, with additions, by Henry Davies. John Churchill, 1846.

Underwood, Michael, and Marshall Hall. *A Treatise on the Diseases of Children; with Directions for the Management of Infants.* Ninth edition, revised, with notes, by Marshall Hall. John Churchill, 1835.

Underwood, Michael, and Samuel Merriman. *A Treatise on the Diseases of Children; with Directions for the Management of Infants from the Birth.* Eighth edition, revised, with notes and observations, by Samuel Merriman. Callow and Wilson, 1827.

Unicef. "Levels and Trends in Child Mortality: Report 2018." https://data.unicef.org/wp-content/uploads/2018/10/Child-Mortality-Report-2018.pdf.

Vallone, Lynne. "'A Humble Spirit Under Correction': Tracts, Hymns, and the Ideology of Evangelical Fiction for Children, 1780–1820." *The Lion and the Unicorn,* vol. 15, 1991, pp. 72–95.

Vandeburgh, C. P. *The Mother's Medical Guardian.* Edwards and Knibb, 1820.

Wagner, Tamara Silvia. "The Sensational Victorian Nursery: Mrs. Henry Wood's Parenting Advice." *Victorian Literature and Culture*, vol. 45, no. 4, 2017, pp. 801–819.

"Warning, *n.*" *Oxford English Dictionary*, OEO Third Edition, Dec. 2011, oed.com, Oxford UP, 2019.

Waters, Catherine. *Special Correspondence and the Newspaper Press in Victorian Print Culture, 1850–1886.* Palgrave Macmillan, 2019.

Weltman, Sharon Aronofsky. "'Be no more housewives, but Queens': Queen Victoria and Ruskin's Domestic Mythology." *Remaking Queen Victoria*, edited by Margaret Homans and Adrienne Munich, Cambridge UP, 1997, pp. 105–122.

Williams, Raymond. *Keywords: A Vocabulary of Culture and Society.* Revised edition. Oxford UP, 1983.

———. *Marxism and Literature.* Oxford UP, 1977.

Wilson, Adrian. *The Making of Man-Midwifery: Childbirth in England, 1660–1770.* University College London P, 1995.

Winsor, Dorothy A. "Genre and Activity Systems: The Role of Documentation in Maintaining and Changing Engineering Activity Systems." *Written Communication*, vol. 16, no. 2, 1999, pp. 200–224.

Winter, Sarah. *The Pleasures of Memory: Learning to Read with Charles Dickens.* Fordham UP, 2011.

Wohl, Anthony S. *Endangered Lives: Public Health in Victorian Britain.* Harvard UP, 1983.

Woods, Robert. *Children Remembered: Responses to Untimely Death in the Past.* Liverpool UP, 2006.

———. *The Demography of England and Wales.* Cambridge UP, 2000.

Woodward, Kathleen. *Statistical Panic: Cultural Politics and Poetics of the Emotions.* Duke UP, 2009.

Worrall, Joseph. *The Domestic Receipt Book, in Two Parts, Containing 866 Authenticated Recipes, Chiefly on Domestic Economy.* Second edition. J. Hartley, 1832.

Worth, Aaron. *Imperial Media: Colonial Networks and Information Technologies in the British Literary Imagination, 1857–1918.* Ohio State UP, 2014.

Wrigley, E. A., R. S. Davies, J. E. Oeppen, and R. S. Schofield. *English Population History from Family Reconstitution, 1580–1837.* Cambridge UP, 1997.

Yonge, Charlotte M. *The Daisy Chain; or, Aspirations, A Family Chronicle.* 1856. Macmillan, 1890.

———. *The Three Brides.* Macmillan, 1876.

———. *The Trial: More Links in the Daisy Chain.* Macmillan, 1864.

INDEX

CPSIA information can be obtained
at www.ICGtesting.com
Printed in the USA
BVHW042336240822
645446BV00001B/1